THE Prayer Tree

ANNIE JONES

ALABASTER
BOOKS

This is a work of fiction. The characters, incidents, and dialogues are products of the author's imagination and are not to be construed as real. Any resemblance to actual events or persons, living or dead, is entirely coincidental.

THE PRAYER TREE
published by Alabaster Books
a division of Multnomah Publishers, Inc.
© 1998 by Annie Jones

International Standard Book Number: 1–57673–239–8

Cover illustration by Heidi Oberheide
Cover design by Brenda McGee

All Scripture quotations, unless otherwise indicated, are taken from *The Holy Bible*, New International Version © 1973, 1978, 1984 by International Bible Society. Used by permission of Zondervan Publishing House.
All rights reserved.

Alabaster is a trademark of Multnomah Publishers, Inc.

For information:
Multnomah Publishers, Inc.
Post Office Box 1720
Sisters, Oregon 97759

98 99 00 01 02 03 04 05 — 10 9 8 7 6 5 4 3 2 1

For the women of my family, by blood and by choice:
Oleeva, Marge, Laura Lou, Cynthia, Susan, Nancy,
Edana, Jody, Alana, Patje, Debbie, Lynne, Sherry,
both Tammys, Mary I., Carrie, Brianna, Maven, Emily,
Kelly, Maggie, Elaine, Keller,
Natalie, Sarah, and Brittany.
For all those who have gone on before us and those to come.
And especially for my mom.

And for the women who have helped me bring
this book to fruition:
Karen S. and Karen B.
Jennifer B., Beth, Deanna, and Janella
With special thanks to Smoky Mountain Romance Writers

I really never would have even tried this
without your support, y'all!

The Prayer Tree

In the spring of 1942, the women of New Bethany, Tennessee, planted apple trees. In a field north of town, these women gathered around the trees on a given day each month to pray for "the boys" away at war. Long after the war, the tradition had endured.

Year after year, now decade upon decade, the women of the town had come each spring to plant new trees. The quiet grove of their creation stands testament to the faith, hope, and strength of their mothers and their mothers' mothers. Through the branches of the pines and maples, cherry trees and weeping willows planted each new year, the wind whispers a promise: What we have done will not be forgotten. To love, nurture, and hope—to be a woman, a wife, a mother, a sister, a friend abides with us always.

Each spring for over fifty years new prayer groups have formed with women participating for myriad reasons including faith, community duty, and social function. No matter why they came, they all went away feeling better about themselves, their community, their faith, and most of all about that special bond that forms when women strive together, laugh together, bicker together, and become friends.

However, time and the pressure of the world in which we live have taken their toll on the custom of the prayer tree. In the past years, the number of women volunteering to give one year to pray for the common good of their neighbors and one another has dwindled. This year, in the tiny southern town of New Bethany, when the women go to the grove, singing, hand in hand to show their solidarity and hope, there will only be one prayer tree.

Prologue

Late nights like these, the answers evaded Naomi. Not the big answers to life's awesome questions: *Who am I? Why am I here? What happens when we die?*

For her, those answers came—not easily, but clear and unwavering these days. She was Naomi Beauchamp, who years ago had followed her young and foolish heart to Maine from the small town of New Bethany, Tennessee. She had been a wife abandoned by her cruel husband, left alone to raise a child. And now...now she was a mother of a son who no longer thought he needed a mother and the daughter of a mother whom she had never stopped needing. She'd learned to take care of herself and knew to the depths of her soul that no man bought his own salvation. She learned daily that God was good—and, at times, people were not. Life had taught her plenty of lessons—some fun, most hard—in bringing her to her thirty-ninth year. But she'd made it through, and when she moved on from this life she had no fear of what lay beyond. Until that time, the questions nagged at her.

What now? What else? When, Lord? When? They thrummed through her like a distant drumming, calling, warning her away then calling her again, the vibration of them almost palpable.

Tonight, they felt unendurable.

She threw back the thick overlay of her bedcovers. Despite the coolness of imminent spring in Maine, a light film of sweat clung to the back of her neck, beaded on her upper lip, and matted her short, curly hair to her temples. The numbers on the clock glowed an eerie green in the darkness of her solitary bedroom: quarter past three. She stood beside her slippers, the ones with the fleece lining meant to guard her toes from the stinging cold of the pocked linoleum floor. Out the window, the moonlight poured over her yard. *What now? What else? When, Lord? When?* The answers did not come.

Snow, blue white in the night, still lay in drifts against the pottery shed where she had intended to begin work today. For years she'd made her living that way, creating folksy ceramic wares, chowder pots and chowder mugs and plaques that proclaimed "Chowder's On!" for the tourists that flooded into town each summer.

She hated chowder pots. She hated what her life had become. But she didn't know what else to do. She tried to breathe, but the air in her gas-heated home seemed suddenly thick as…as…as chowder. She gritted her teeth. Her sensible blue chenille robe snagged as she tried to tug it down off the brass hook behind her door.

Fine. She'd go without it.

In several thundering footsteps she was out the back door and in her yard, barefoot, her flannel gown thrashing about her ankles. *What now? What else? When, Lord? When?* The questions drove her on, down the narrow walkway and to the tiny shed. The door resisted, its latch mottled with rust from a winter of disuse. She clenched her jaw and grunted, giving it all her strength.

The metal rasped then gave with a screech that cut through the night like some night owls from her childhood memories. Her knuckles scraped roughened wood, it tore away at her skin and left thin lines of red on her fingers, but she didn't care. She flicked on the light. The door banged shut once, bounced open, and then fell closed in one final slam. Naomi pressed her back against it, her gaze darting here and there, taking in her familiar surroundings piecemeal.

Everything was just as she'd left it when she closed up last fall, though perhaps a bit more grimy and grim looking in the starkness of the single bulb flickering against the frosty night. What did she think she'd find out here? she wondered, her heart hammering as if it would burst. "What now?" she murmured, the traces of her Tennessee accent still softening the hard edge of her voice.

Something in her life was about to change. It had to. She knew it had to. She could not go on like this, feeling so alone with no close friends and no family nearby, now that her son was away at college. She could not go on hiding behind the safety of habit and predictability, never challenged, never called to meet life on God's terms and not her own.

And she could not, not for the life of her, make another sturdy little chowder mug and sell it to a total stranger. She reached over to the nearest shelf and picked up a gray-and-blue mug—a flat bowl, really, with a broad, ribbed handle. It weighed heavy in her hand, just as her discontent weighed upon her heart.

"What now, Lord?" She called to the cobweb-covered rafters.

Let go.

She gripped the mug more tightly.

"What else?" she called again, her voice raw.

Let it go.

She clenched her fingers around the mug handle until her skin burned.

Let it go.

She felt the words as steady and deep as the rhythm of those unanswered questions that would not let her sleep.

"When, Lord?"

Now.

The mug slid from her fingers.

Maybe the cold was to blame, or maybe the mug had a flaw, a weakness that gave way the instant it hit the wooden floor. Whatever the cause, the effect of the mug shattering into a handful of jagged, chunky pieces was positively freeing.

She felt a small smile tug at her lips. She hadn't smiled in…she couldn't remember the last time. Now, suddenly, she felt like a kid again, bobbing up for that first painful, invigorating gulp of air after plunging off the high dive into the deep unknown. Something *was* about to change in her life, and the Lord was paving the way for it. It sang through her being and in her bones and in the sweet, giddy satisfaction of breaking that mug.

"What now?" She said again, this time, actually talking to herself. Her gaze fell on a big, squatty bowl topped by a stout-handled lid with a notch in it just right for the kind of wooden ladles they sold all over town. She curled her toes against the icy floor. She swallowed hard, then made her lunge, calling out "Chowder's on!"

Wham! The piece went down and it, too, broke.

She couldn't hold back a sharp hiccup of a laugh from low in her chest. She'd had no idea it would feel that wonderful to do something so destructive. Or was it destructive? Perhaps the proper word was cathartic.

Perhaps the Lord had been waiting to answer her questions, to help her to move on to whatever lay ahead, until she let go of this life. Perhaps the sense of unknown longing in her aching and restless spirit was God's way of preparing her to do just that. Or perhaps the isolation here had finally gotten to her and, as her precious little Southern mama would say, she had finally gone round the bend.

The invocation of Mama's take on things made Naomi straighten up and take account. The cold air stung her lungs, coming out in a moist cloud from her open lips. The reasonable thing to do would be to go back inside, warm herself over the floor vent, then crawl back into bed and try to get some much needed rest. Tomorrow she could clean up the fragments and forget this ever happened. Tomorrow she could start on the pots and mugs for the coming year's tourist season, just as she had planned to do today.

She shuffled forward, reached out, and let a thick speckle-glazed mug fill her palm. Or tomorrow she could find herself headed in a whole new direction.

Crash. The piece fractured against the boards just inches from her toes. She hurled down another mug, a smile twitching on her lips. Another piece plunged. Then another. Until finally, all the odd and unwanted remnants of last year's stock lay in crumbled heaps on the floor.

It did not give her the answers to her questions, but seemed to have opened her to the possibilities of what those answers could bring. With that she felt content, and she went back into her house, curled up in her bed, and fell into a deep, dreamless sleep.

The electronic chirp of the phone jarred her awake before the morning's sunlight could stream in and do the job. The sound shot through her like lightning finding its mark. Her pulse raced. Bad news.

Good news seldom came at odd hours. Her thoughts went

to her elderly mother, then to her son.

"Please, God, let them be safe. Oh, please," she pleaded, her muffled words rich and full in their throaty Southern intonation. Look on the bright side, she told herself, half buying the time to let herself wake up fully and half stalling in hopes the ringing would stop. Maybe, she supposed, a neighbor had seen the light on in her shed last night and heard the commotion. Maybe this was only the sheriff calling to see if she had been murdered or had merely gone insane. The levity of that prospect lightened her mood.

The phone chirped again.

I can do this, she told herself, recalling last night's readiness to face whatever the Lord had in store for her. She grabbed up the phone with confidence. "Hello?"

"Nomi, honey."

"Mama?" She sat bolt upright.

"Nomi, honey, you have to come home."

"Mama, are you all right?" She used both hands to hold the receiver.

"Me? Oh, baby girl, I'm fine. Great honk, did you think I'd call you myself to tell you I'd gone on to be with Jesus?"

"No, Mama, I—"

"Then hush up and listen." There was a pause on the other end, a stirring silence Naomi told herself was meant for effect, though she felt it was nothing of the sort. Finally, Mama spoke again. "You have to come home, Nomi. They've ruined it. It took 'em more than fifty years, but they've finally done it. Run it straight into the ground. You have to come."

"Ruined what, Mama?" Naomi pulled her knees up to her chin and hugged her legs. Her fear had faded, replaced now by a feeling Naomi couldn't quite define. "Mama, what are you talking about?"

"I was in on it, you know. Right from the start I was one of the first ones."

"Mama, talk sense. In on what?"

"The trees, Naomi. You've heard me tell the story umpteen thousand times before. It was '42, your daddy had already shipped out. We planted 'em in the grove and prayed, and now they're going to..." Again that ponderous silence. Then coughing, then Mama spoke, only it was as if she was mumbling to herself. "You've got to come back. Even if it is all over, you gotta come back and take your turn. Come back and give the Lord, New Bethany, and me just the one year."

"A year?"

"It's a lot to ask, I know, but I don't put many demands on you. And it's not just for me, it's for all of us."

What was for all of them? A year? For New Bethany and the Lord and Mama? Naomi felt five years old and baffled as a lost child. What did this mean? Could she really just pick up and go? Uncertainty tinged with a vague excitement stirred within her....

What now? What else? When? The questions whispered through her mind, and a calm settled over Naomi. She did not have the answers, but she knew what she must do to find them. "Okay, Mama, calm down. I'll close up things here and come home."

"For the whole year?"

Naomi swallowed hard. She had to do this, and the Lord would be with her. She took a deep breath. "I'll come home for as long as it takes, Mama. For as long as it takes."

One

It was hot for mid-May. Not summer hot. Not that turn-the-tar-road-to-black-goo hot of July or that dog-tired, draining heat of endless late August, but a damp and clinging, almost oppressive hot. Air so thick you couldn't stir it with a stick, the old folks would say. Humid more than hot.

Rose Holcolmb—born Rose Tancy Mason right here in New Bethany, Tennessee, fifty-six years ago come fall—hadn't seen a spring like this since her now grown girls were babies.

"Bad omen," she murmured, dabbing a linen handkerchief at the beads of sweat under her collar. Not that Rose believed in omens. Portents, neither.

No, Rose's faith lay firmly rooted elsewhere. A Sunday school teacher for twenty-odd years—some more odd than others—at the Antioch Baptist Church before it burned down and on most of the committees at the new church until that unfortunate falling out with the new minister, Rose trusted wholly in her redemption bought by the blood of Christ.

Still, today she muttered under her breath again, "It's not a good sign, not a good sign at all. I can't quite put my finger on it, but something about all of this is just not right."

She raised one arm to rest atop her four-year-old tan Caddie and squinted out at the mishmash of trees in the tranquil grove before her. "Tell me again why we are doing this."

"Because it *has* to be done." Gayle Shorter Barrett, her tone as crisp as her outfit despite the dank conditions, strode around the snub nose of her jewel-toned Town and Country minivan. "You know as well as I do, Rose, that the incoming prayer circles are expected to come out to the grove to decide what kind of tree they will plant to represent their coming year of service. We should have done it before now, even a few days ago would have looked more…deferential to the nature of the circles. As it is we'll barely have time to—"

"Circle," Rose drawled, her gaze dead-on Gayle's pinched expression.

"What?"

"Circle. Just one this year."

Gayle blinked.

"You said *circles*. Prayer *circles*." Rose felt obliged to explain. "But this year it's just us. Just the one circle."

Gayle blinked again, her lips pale and tight beneath understated matte lip color. Rose got the distinct impression that the younger woman wished she'd keep her mouth shut, as if saying the truth aloud would somehow make it…well, less true.

A breeze whipped up around them, but the effect was more that of a door swung open from a sauna than of anything cooling.

Gayle patted at her hair, though not a strand of chestnut brown or pale-as-lemon streaks had blown out of place. To Rose's best recollection, nothing in Gayle's life ever seemed out of place.

Rose was old enough to know that Gayle's seeming perfection was a bad sign. And Gayle was old enough to handle the reality of what they were doing here today, of what their contribution to the legacy of the prayer circles really meant—even if she chose to avoid harsh realities in her everyday life.

"Truth be told, Gayle, there aren't even enough signed up for a single circle this year. Just the three names on the list—"

"Oh, they say that every year, Rose." She flicked away the

dismal outlook with a dismissive wave. "Not enough volunteers. They only had four small circles last year—one of those formed only a week before the tree dedication service."

"Well, it's less than twenty-four hours until the service now, Gayle, and it's just you and me and—"

"Someone always comes forward at the last minute. You know that."

Rose stared at Gayle a moment and sighed. Southern women, she thought, more with sadness than with contempt, had raised the art of denial to a level no one, except another Southern woman, could fully appreciate. Many considered steel-willed a self-delusion, or at least the appearance of it, a coping skill as essential as a clever mind, a strong body and, of course, impeccable manners.

Rose, however, had never cultivated the denial skill, and so she planted her hands on the waistband of her khaki, sharp-pleated trousers and cocked her head just so at her companion. "Did I ever tell you about the time Cissy Jewell and I were standing on a corner downtown when a very young, very...let's say *perky* bottle-blonde drove by in a red convertible?"

Gayle hesitated, her eyes narrowed and wary, but only for a moment. Clearly her suspicion that she was about to get a lesson had succumbed to her curiosity over the juicy bit of thirty-year-old gossip. "No. What happened?"

"Ol' Cissy tugs at the knot in her headscarf with one white gloved hand and sniffs, 'Where on earth did a woman like that get a hold of such an expensive car?' Well, my jaw dropped about to the sidewalk and I said to her, 'You have got to be kidding'—oh, are you old enough to recall when Odel Jewell owned the largest car dealership in the tri-county area?"

Gayle nodded, her smile duly contained. "Go on."

Rose smirked. "So then I just out and out said to Cissy, 'Are you the *only* person in town that doesn't know your husband is having an affair with that woman?'"

"You didn't!"

"As I live and breathe." She held up her right hand.

"And what did Cissy say?"

"She looked me right in the eye and said, 'Yes, Rose Mason, I *am* the only person in town who does not know about my husband's mistress. But I don't see how I'm going to be able to continue not knowing if people like you don't start cooperating with me.'"

Gayle laughed. "Yes, that sounds like Cissy. But I don't see how that applies here, Rose."

"It applies, sugar, because I'm every bit the same woman I was thirty years ago—in fact, more so. And I am not going to stand here today, much less try to pretend for an entire year, that we are not just the only prayer circle in New Bethany, but we are most probably the *last* prayer circle this town will ever see."

"Don't say that."

Rose saw the whispered words form on Gayle's lips more than heard them above the sound of another car approaching.

"Lucy's here," Rose said. "Let's get this over with." She stepped toward the place where Lucy Jewell parked her station wagon, which had the magnetic logo of her home day care still stuck to the side. Rose lifted her arm to wave, but Gayle caught it on the upswing and dug her fingers into the soft flesh like a frightened child grasping at her mother's skirt hem.

"You don't really believe that, do you? That this will be the last tree planted?"

Rose knew the younger woman well enough to understand what she was really asking. "You don't want an opinion, Gayle, you want comfort." *If only I could give it to her, God. If only I could...*She put her hand over the younger woman's much smoother one. "You want me to say it will be okay. That *everything* will work out."

Gayle stiffened.

Rose watched the reaction in silence. Best not to delve into whatever lay bubbling beneath the clamped-down emotional stew pot that was Gayle Shorter Barrett. But she would not lie to the woman, either, even to assuage her anxiety.

"You're asking me to stand as a hedge against time." Rose heard the quiver in her own voice, aware it came from the depths of her shaky emotions. "You want me to tell you that this small-town custom, this way of life we've always known and even taken for granted, is worthwhile, worth saving. That it will not fade away after we've made our contribution."

"I wish you could do just that, Rose." Gayle glanced down.

Rose figured she not only hit the nail on the head, but she drove it through the drywall. She was equally certain Gayle wasn't just thinking about a prayer circle or a fifty-year-old tradition. But this was not the time to pursue it.

Gayle held Rose's gaze, ignoring the powerful urge to turn away, for doing that would only reveal the ugliness of her weakness and uncertainty.

"Things will work out, one way or another." Rose finally said, giving Gayle's arm a squeeze. "Now here comes Lucy. Let's get this thing done. Oh, and don't tell her that story about me and her mother, you hear?"

"Why not?" Gayle gave as close to a refined snort as could be accomplished. "Lucy knows what a rat her father was."

"Does she? Really?"

Gayle fixed her gaze on plump, blonde-headed Lucy, who was whacking her way out of her parking space right in the middle of the only patch of tall weeds around. "Of course she knows about her daddy. Why else would she always hook up with low-down, good-for-nothing men just like him?"

"I'm sorry I'm late. I'm sorry." Lucy picked her way through the weeds to join them, apologizing with every step. "Ray was supposed to take over the after-school pickup for me, but he got detained by his work and so I—" She stopped to clear her throat, holding her hand in a tight fist over her cinched mouth. "Oh, my, I must have roused up some dust."

Gayle gave Rose a knowing look. Even Lucy, schooled at her mother's knee in martyrdom to callow men, couldn't hold together the pretense that her boyfriend of the last three years had not just let her down—as he always let her down.

Lucy coughed, fanned her face, then blew a long, noiseless whistle through her lips.

The fanning put Gayle in mind of a woman much older than Lucy's thirty years. The near silent air from Lucy's rounded lips made Gayle think of the factory siren that used to sound out over town that the day's work was done. For today. And it was clear, Lucy was done making excuses for no-account Ray. For today.

Lucy clomped on up beside Rose and Gayle. She heaved a sigh, then slumped her shoulders forward. Her shapeless canvas satchel of a purse, something that put Gayle in mind of a combination mailman's pouch/diaper bag/gunny sack—only not as attractive—slid from Lucy's rounded shoulder to the soft ground with a definite thud. "Anyway, I'm here now." Lucy held her arms out to her sides, offering herself, it seemed, for their use or their chastisement.

Gayle's heart ached for Lucy, it really did. Miss Mary Lucille, as many of her day-care charges called her, played surrogate mom to a goodly share of the town's toddlers, but everyone knew that what she wanted more than anything else on God's earth was a child of her own.

"Where do we begin?" Lucy folded her arms.

"First things first." Rose shaded her eyes and scanned the grove of trees. Her kerchief, caught between her thumb and forefinger, flipped back over her knuckles and wrist.

There is a monogram on that fine linen kerchief, you can be sure, Gayle thought. For all of Rose's talk of the ending of the old ways, and for all of her sporty, tailored wardrobe that looked straight out of Katharine Hepburn's closet, Rose was also a woman of the old ways. As big a talker as the older woman could be, Gayle strongly suspected that terms like "breeding will tell" and the nasty-intentioned, backhanded "Isn't that *sweet?*" still crossed Rose's mind if not her lips.

"And the first thing we need to do is find the last trees planted. Four all the same…poplars, I believe," Rose said.

"Poplars. What were those women thinking?" Gayle muttered.

"The tulip poplar is the state tree," Lucy said, as if that justified anything.

"The state tree?" Gayle rolled her eyes. "That makes it even less original than I'd thought. Whoever was in charge of that mess last year should be made to apologize to everyone who ever came into this intent on doing a good job of it."

Lucy gaped at her.

Gayle forced a winning smile and said her piece on the subject as tactfully as she could manage. "Well, think of it, won't you? Four prayer groups all taking the easy way out and planting the same tree to represent each group?"

"Maybe they were just being practical." Lucy flicked back

her straight-as-a-stick, chin-length hair.

"Nuh-uh. No, ma'am." Gayle shook her head. "Practical is when you strike a bargain with the nurseryman to get four trees for the price of three. But to just up and order three of the same tree, and something as uninteresting as poplars to boot—"

"Maybe they *liked* poplars."

"This isn't so much about kinds of trees, Lucy," Rose chimed in. "It's about—"

Gayle cut her off. "Fact is, I don't care if a poplar tree once fell across a creek and saved all of their granddaddies from drowning in one fell swoop." She knew she was raging but she didn't care. Last year's handling of the prayer circles was one of the main reasons she'd finally succumbed and signed up to participate this year. "*This* prayer group will not repeat the insensitivity of last year's groups. To have given the selection such little thought, and then to just settle on identical trees— well, it was just—" Gayle crinkled up her nose and lowered her voice—"common."

Rose laughed aloud, but Lucy's lips rounded in a comprehending O as she nodded.

Lucy, too, was a woman of the old ways. Struggle as they all might against the stereotype, against being pigeonholed as Southern belles or women of the "new" South—or whatever the politically correct term might be, they were all the products of their upbringing, of life in New Bethany.

Rose as much as herself and as much as poor Miss Mary Lucille.

Lucy checked her watch. "I hope this won't take long. A new single mother has moved into town, and she's coming by to interview for a job. She has a toddler and the rumor is she's never been married."

Gayle couldn't tell if it was shock or pride in Lucy's voice.

Perhaps it was envy. This single mother had the one thing Lucy truly wanted: a child. And she apparently had gotten it by bypassing the one other thing Lucy could not seem to lay her hands on: a husband.

Oh, Lucy could find a man. She'd dated more than one on a semiserious basis over the last decade. But not a one of those relationships had the makings of a marriage. Despite her intense longing, or perhaps because of it, Lucy could not seem to attract the love, honor, and obey type of man, the kind who made as good a father as he did a friend—the kind like Gayle's husband of eighteen years, Ted.

Gayle shifted her gaze. The gentle flutter of the small spring leaves and blossoms on the trees before her turned to a blur of green, white, and pink-cast confetti through the sudden wash of tears bathing her eyes. The stifling air caught in her constricting lungs. Just the thought of Ted, of all he'd been and done for her, of his faithfulness and wicked sense of humor couched in subtle Southern charm, of his unwavering love for her made Gayle wince with unrelenting guilt.

She did not deserve this man, nor the children he had given her, nor her beautiful home, nor the friends and family who doted on her. She did not even deserve the privilege of serving in this prayer circle, of participating in something so good and sacred. She knew that. And every morning she woke before sunup and lay awake wondering if this was the day everyone else discovered it, too.

"Y'all don't think I should hold it against her, do you?" Lucy chewed at her lower lip.

Gayle forced a hard swallow, feeling exposed.

"Of course not, Mary Lucille. It's not our place to cast judgments on others."

Rose's kind words helped ease the pressure in Gayle's chest.

"Unless, of course, we're absolutely sure she did whatever heinous thing she's accused of." Rose gave Lucy a friendly squeeze around the shoulders, her expression gleeful. "Then it's skewer her up and roast her over the fiery tongues of town gossip, I say."

Lucy actually gasped.

"I'm only kidding, Lucy," Rose said softly. "You check this woman's references, interview her, and make your decision based on her ability to do the job. That's the best thing you can do."

"And the best thing we can do is to get on with this." Gayle tipped her head toward the far edge of the grove. "I've spotted those poplars."

"Then let's head over there and see how they're faring. That may give us some good ideas about the kind of trees we want to put next to them. Right, Gayle?" Rose pointed the way, then glanced back at Gayle. "You comin' or are you going to hang back to wait for any late joiners?"

"There aren't going to be any late joiners, Rose, and you know it." Gayle sniffled and tipped her head back determined not a single teardrop would slip onto her lashes. Deserving or not, this job, this circle, needed her and she could not let them down. "Let's get on with this."

TWO

I say we go with a weeping willow. It's attractive yet resilient, and—"

"Just listen to how terrible that sounds, Rose!" Gayle's face froze in a sweetly civil expression that reminded Lucy of her own mother's determined attempts to cover her true feelings in almost any given situation.

Lucy had never noticed the similarities between Gayle and her mother before. But then, Lucy mostly knew Gayle through shared charities, when Gayle was running fund-raisers with various social clubs and Lucy was pitching in on behalf of the many children who would reap the rewards.

"Really, Rose, *really* listen to that." Gayle, her tone low and thick, managed to carry the act off much better than Lucy's mother ever had. She possessed a composure that kept her from sounding shrewish over always being the one to bring focus and common sense to a group. Gayle almost purred out her thoughts. "A *weeping* willow? Is *that* the image you want to send down through the generations?"

"Good night nurse! It's a *tree*. A tree, not our monument to a venerable leader in the Great War of Northern Aggression." Rose was obviously quite amused with her thundering imitation of old Southern indignation and pride. She gave Gayle a smirk. Then she put her back to the four straggling poplars at the edge of the meandering orchard filled with every kind of tree the rich Tennessee soil would support. "I happen to think a willow makes a perfectly lovely statement and would represent our circle beautifully."

Gayle snorted, not a delicate debutante scoffing type snort, either, but something that sounded like it should come from behind the broken screen door on the tackiest place in the trailer park. It startled Lucy, but had no effect whatsoever on Rose, who pressed on with her rationalization.

"The willow is and has always been the symbol of grace and dignity, strength and singularity. A willow," Rose went on, using her hands in a graceful gesture, "does not break, but bends in the wind. It's a survivor and therefore it's the tree I recommend we plant."

"Nuh-uh. No siree, no." Gayle slashed her hand out, then turned up one finger to wag in Rose's direction as she spoke. "You want a tree to make a living testament to grace and dignity and *survival*, Rose, you have got to go with the unchanging evergreen."

"The—" Rose blinked. Not a natural, soothing blink but steady, deliberate, sometimes keeping her eyes shut for a few seconds, then following with a blink, blink, blink pattern.

Gayle did not seem affected by Rose's unspoken communication. She just stood there, her skinny little arms folded neat as a bow over her chest, her tanned and flawlessly made-up face void of expression.

The afternoon heat rose around the three of them like silent, toxic vapor.

Rose patted the side of her neck, then waved her hand, her hankie flying like anything but a flag of surrender. "Look over my shoulder, Gayle."

Though the command was not directed at her, Lucy did just that thing.

"I wonder," Rose said, her tone sweet as honey and sharp as pepper at the same time. "Can you possibly count *all* the pines and cedars and evergreens dotting these few acres?"

Gayle pursed her lips.

"How 'bout you just count the ones you can see from where we are standing."

Lucy didn't actually try to count the trees, but she did take note of the many fat and full or tall and spiky evergreens poking up above and out from behind the other varieties, which was more than Gayle even pretended to do.

Gayle wiped away the thin veil of sweat on her forehead with the back of her hand, disguising the necessary evil of public grooming as a fluffing of her sprayed-to-an-armor-finish bangs. "What's your point, Rose?"

"My point is that evergreens have been done and done to death, sugar. Now, willows—"

Lucy puffed out her cheeks and blew a cooling breath up onto her own wilting bangs. That sound and the deep growling of her stomach shut out Rose's droning about willows and ways of life and who knew what all.

"—with their lithe branches swaying in the wind they, like a thousand arms reaching out for—"

Lucy tugged at her collar, then peeled free the sweat-heavy cotton jersey pasted to the gentle roll of her midsection. She gave her full skirt a shake to air the damp fabric a bit, her attention captured by the way it moved in her hands.

She owned five dresses exactly like this one in assorted colors. When she'd hauled them home from the mall in one gigantic shopping bag, she told her mama that she'd bought them because they were practical and comfortable. They did not hold wrinkles and just about anything that her babies—her name for the children in her care—could get into came right out. The upshot of everything from finger paints to stomach flu had washed out of these dresses with just a little soap powder and elbow grease. That's what she'd told her mother.

"Rose, dear, you are investing far too much symbolism into this." Gayle's voice rose enough to intrude on Lucy's thoughts, but only for a second.

Lucy caressed the pale blue pleats falling over her rounded hips. She had bought this dress in every color available, in fact, because Ray told her the style had a slenderizing effect. "Honey, your behind don't look so much like two hogs sharing the same gunny sack in that getup," is what he'd said.

"*I'm* investing too much in this? You're the one, Gayle, sugar, who suggested that what we're doing here, now, will have long-ranging effects." Rose's tone had a dangerous, lazy quality that none of them would underestimate.

Gayle's mollifying tone was proof of that. "Rose, I know how much this matters to you. To us all. I'm just trying to understand how you can choose anything but an evergreen. A willow starts out a sad little whip of a sapling, then grows far too tall to fit in. While an evergreen will be as lovely now when we plant it as it will be in the future. Now and the future, that's what we have to consider."

"Wrong. Wrong. Wrong." Given her tone, Rose might as well have yawned and muttered blah, blah, blah.

Lucy pretended to look interested in Rose and Gayle's conversation, but she let her thoughts drift to Ray. She pictured his sad eyes, his lazy smile.…With a sigh, she fanned her heat-flushed face. Rough around the edges as Ray was, a girl like her was lucky to have a man like him, and Lucy knew it.

Of course, so did Ray, which made fully trusting him a very difficult thing indeed—

"So, what do you think, Lucy?"

Rose's direct question startled her. She dropped her skirt then smoothed it down, cleared her throat, wet her lips, began to speak then stopped. Her brow scrunched down at the bridge of her nose and she focused on the two women waiting for some kind of response. "Excuse me?" she finally murmured. "That is, I'm sorry but I wasn't…what do I think about what?"

"About the tree, Lucy," Gayle snapped. "Good gravy, honey, can't you concentrate just this once, just for a little bit?"

"I *was* concentrating."

"But on *what?*" Gayle asked.

Lucy thought her "my lips are sealed" look was straight from Scarlett O'Hara until she let her gaze fall to the ground for just a moment and her hesitation did her in.

"Mary Lucille, that man isn't worth the time of day, much less all the time you spend worrying over him," Gayle said softly, the cultivated tones of her accent soothing as cool water flowing over scorched skin.

"I wasn't—"

Rose cocked her head to the right, her foot tapping the soft whispering grass. She might as well have said, "Don't you lie to me, young lady," in her best Sunday school teacher voice.

Lucy fanned the clinging hair away from her cheek, dismissing the subject all together. "Now, what was it about the tree you wanted to know?"

"Evergreen or willow," Gayle deadpanned.

Lucy gulped. *Land's sake, willow or evergreen?* She didn't have the slightest idea—or opinion—which was better. Fact in point, she didn't care. She had no investment in the real nature of the task at hand or the tradition it represented.

She intended to join in the prayers, of course. And, she supposed, her prayers would have as much merit as anybody's—though nothing in her life had led her to believe that God heard or considered even her most earnest petitions.

She believed in God and loved the Lord as best she could

with her understanding of him, and she acknowledged the good will and spiritual benefit of prayer on one's well-being. But that's not why she joined the prayer group. She'd only signed up this year because she'd learned that Rose had volunteered to host the meetings at her house. And Rose lived directly across the street from Ray.

"Well, I…I'm hardly qualified. I don't know anything about—" *I just wanted an excuse to spy on Ray one night a month*, she wanted to scream. "Please don't give me the responsibility of choosing. Not me."

"Well, *somebody* has to do it and—"

"Forget it, Gayle." Rose threw up her hands, then looked from Gayle to Lucy and back, an odd, almost resigned expression on her face. "This isn't working, ladies," she announced.

"What?" Lucy blinked, confused.

"This." Rose held out her hands. "This whole situation. We can't even decide on a tree. How are we ever to agree in prayer on behalf of others when we can't even agree on what kind of tree to plant?"

"Well, if one of us would concede." Gayle glared at Rose. "Or one of us would just *pick a side*." She aimed her ire at Lucy. "Then we wouldn't have a problem."

"Wouldn't we?" Rose put her hands to her hips.

Gayle turned her face toward Rose again but could not look her in the eyes.

Lucy ducked her head.

"Face it, ladies, a prayer circle should not be about picking sides or total concession to one person's view."

"What are you saying, Rose?" Gayle did meet her gaze now.

"I'm stating the obvious, Gayle. This isn't working."

~ ~ ~ ~ ~

Rose looked from Gayle's pinched, harried expression to Lucy's lackadaisical, distant stare and made a quick conclusion. They were all drowning—all three of them—not in humidity but in a hopeless situation. Well, she, for one, was not going to go down easily.

Rose had lived a lifetime in this community. Her mother had planted a tree for a circle the same year Rose's daddy served in Korea. Her mother-in-law had served the year Rose's late husband, Curry, had been wounded in Viet Nam. All Rose's life she had watched the tradition and the trees flourish.

For years she'd admired the custom. When she became a young mother herself, she decided the circles had become outdated and far too socially oriented. She would often ridicule them. And when they turned, in her eyes, to a bunch of gossiping vultures looking for other's misfortunes to make themselves feel better, she'd come to despise the prayer circles and their awful trees.

At that point, she'd prided herself on the fact that she'd never once joined them or even been tempted to do so. Until, of course, this year. This year, she joined because she *had* to….and she would serve with all her heart and soul. Her conscience demanded no less. She would not allow this group to flounder or fail. She just couldn't.

"This *has* to work." Gayle sounded near desperate.

Rose inclined her head. "But as it is it *isn't* working, and we all know that. Three people are not enough to form a workable prayer circle."

"Then we'll just be a prayer triangle," Gayle suggested through clenched teeth.

"And what if one of us is forced to drop out halfway through and then someone else simply has a conflict that means she can't make one of the prayer sessions? What will we have then?"

No one answered.

"I'll tell you what we'll have," Rose said. "Nothing. It's obvious three people are just not going to be enough."

"Well, what exactly do you propose we do about it, Rose?" Gayle jerked her chin up. "We all signed up to do this, accepting the responsibility to do no less than what hundreds of our friends and family members have taken on over the last fifty years."

"Don't you lecture me about what this group means and where it came from, Gayle Barrett. I can point to the tree my mama planted in my daddy's honor. I've seen the intent of the groups go from a spiritual bond to various issue-oriented support groups to social gatherings to…other things."

She stopped abruptly and drew a deep breath, trying to ignore the way her lips were twitching tight against her teeth.

"I know where these groups have been and I know where they are going." Rose fixed Gayle with a knowing glare. "But I also know that if any of that, the past or the future, the very nature of what they have always hoped to accomplish, means *anything,* there is only one thing for us to do now to save this one circle."

"What?" Lucy asked with a touch more awe than merited.

Rose turned to Gayle, who studied her in silence.

For the first time since they'd arrived, Rose retreated in attitude enough to glance down at the handkerchief crumpled in her hand. She half-wondered if the awful foreboding she'd felt as she got out of her car was for this, not at all about a sign of unnaturally hot weather. Rose fought against the wave of discouragement in her heart and the roiling in the pit of her stomach.

She wanted these women to *know* what they had to do, or at least to have the capacity to figure it out on their own. She wanted them to take as much initiative in this matter as they had in signing up for the group and even in coming here today. She did not want to have to tell them outright what they must do—because heaven help them all if *she* was left to be the spiritual leader of the group.

Even her heartfelt promise, the vow that finally brought her to this circle, could not demand this of her. A leader had to know where she was going. And Rose was lost. Hopelessly, aimlessly, scared straight-to-her-soul lost.

"What is it we have to do, Rose? Tell us how we can save the circle?"

Rose flinched at the pleading "lead us" tone in Lucy's voice. She bit her lip and looked to Gayle, willing her to make the connection, to remember why they had really come together, beyond duty and guilt and whatever else may have compelled them.

"Think about it," Rose said softly. *Show them, Father, please show them. Because I can't...I just can't.* "It's often the avenue of last resort, though it really should be our very first instinct. It's why we've come together, Mary Lucille."

"To pray."

"What?" Lucy asked after Gayle's hushed response.

"Pray, Lucy." Gayle let out a long sigh, then extended her hand to the bewildered looking woman. "That's what we pledged to do, and that's what we *have* to do if we have any hope of keeping this circle alive."

Lucy moved her arm outward, only really reaching her pinkie finger toward Gayle. Their hands touched more than clasped.

Gayle looked to Rose again, her hand came open, then out.

33

Rose balled up her hankie. She had the distinct feeling that completing this circle was a bigger step than any of them knew. She lifted her head a moment to listen to the wind in the trees, wishing they would sing out the message of God to show her that this was the right way.

"Rose?" Gayle inched her open hand closer.

Lucy edged her splayed fingers in Rose's direction.

"Let's pray," Gayle urged.

Rose held her breath, looked from one face to the next. The trees rustled in the background, but Rose heard no booming voice telling her what to do. Still, in her heart, she knew. She exhaled and grabbed first at Gayle's hand, then at Lucy's.

They all bowed their heads, Rose shut her eyes so tight they practically stung.

"Dear Lord," Gayle began and then stalled.

Rose opened her eyes just a bit but did not raise her head. She heard and saw Lucy's scuffed tennis shoes shifting from left to right then back again in the grass. She wondered if Gayle had paused to give her or Lucy the chance to chime in. Neither of them did.

"Dear Lord," Gayle began again, "here are your servants, Rose and Lucy and Gayle. Just three of us, Lord, this year for the prayer circle. Just three."

When she paused again, the quiet had a presence all its own. All background noise seemed swallowed up in it. The wind, the buzz of cars driving by on the highway…all became a blur, indistinguishable as separate sounds.

"We've promised to pray and to uphold and to believe with hope for anyone in our community who might need it through the coming year. We can't accomplish this task on our own, Lord, not even if there were three thousand of us. We need you and your grace. And we need another person. Please, send us at least one more person to complete this circle. Or else we may not be able to do this at all."

"In the name of Jesus they said—" Rose murmured.

"Amen," Lucy and Gayle replied in unison.

They stood in silence a moment longer, then Lucy's hands slipped away. Rose started to withdraw her hand from Gayle's, but before she did, she felt a firm squeeze. A message of unity? Of comfort? Or was Gayle trying to prolong contact, to draw from her a strength that Rose knew she did not possess?

She did not find her answer in Gayle's eyes as the woman quickly shaded them and glanced back at the poplars. "This was all well and good, ladies, and I will trust with you that the Lord shall provide. But that doesn't solve our immediate problem."

"Problem?" Lucy plucked the clinging fabric of her dress from her sides.

"About which tree to plant, Lucy," Gayle said as though talking to a child.

"Aren't we going to wait until we get another member?"

Well, Lucy surely seemed to have the faith of a child, Rose conceded.

Gayle shook her head. "We don't have time for that, Lucy. The service is tomorrow. We have to choose a tree now and get our order to the nursery before it closes." Gayle checked her elegant gold wristwatch and clucked her tongue. "Which brings us right back to the question we asked you before. Which do you vote we plant? Willow or evergreen?"

"I say apple."

Despite the softness of the female voice from behind them, all three women started. Their heads turned slowly, as if they weren't sure if they'd really heard anything at all.

The source of the suggestion, a slender woman in a fitted, sleeveless white T-shirt and wild print gypsy-style skirt flaring around her sandaled feet, moved closer.

Gayle let out a yelp of alarmed recognition. "As I live and breathe! Is that you, Naomi?"

"Indeed it is." The dark-haired woman broke into a smile and marched right up to where they stood, flipping the sunglasses caught between her fingers up against her wrist with every step. "Isn't this a nice surprise? It's so good to see you, Gayle."

"I'd say the same to you, Naomi," Gayle said in that just-too-precious-to-ponder tone of Southern women setting up for the kill. She lowered her chin and her long, black lashes. "Only I'd be lying if I did."

Gayle gave the woman a thorough, narrow-eyed once-over, then folded her arms over her chest like a warrior's shield, ready for battle. "After all these years, imagine you coming back to New Bethany and lighting right here—in this grove, of all places."

"Yes…imagine," the newcomer replied, her eyes sparking mischief.

"Tell me, Naomi—" Gayle clenched her teeth—"what brings you here?"

"Well, Gayle, I wouldn't want to appear presumptuous, but after hearing about your little membership dilemma, I'd have to say that I'm the answer to your prayer."

hree

"Sign her up, Lucy." The oldest woman in the group said with the authority of Sherman issuing orders on the outskirts of Atlanta.

Naomi restrained a grin. She didn't want to seem to be having fun at her old friend's expense, but Gayle's reaction was priceless.

"Rose, you can't be serious." Gayle's face went pale beneath her polished tan.

Apparently Rose was, for the pretty, round-faced young woman with a haircut that made her look like a Campbell's soup kid rummaged through her shapeless, trendy canvas bag. "Oh, dear, I have that paper in here somewhere," she said. When she yanked free a tattered paper folded in quarters with a ballpoint pen clipped to it, she exclaimed, "I've found it."

She thrust the pen and paper at Naomi, who accepted them with a graceful poise that she did not feel.

"You can*not* be serious, Naomi." Gayle flicked one hand at the page Naomi was flattening out and getting ready to sign. "You haven't even set foot in New Bethany for almost ten years and now you just show up here from out of nowhere—"

"Maine."

Gayle blinked. "What?"

"I've been in Maine, Gayle." She clicked the pen hard once with her thumb.

"Oh, well, pardon me," Gayle fluttered her lashes, a look of almost abject boredom on her face. "*North* of nowhere—"

Naomi chuckled at the jab.

"Wherever you've been off to, the point is that after all these years you've suddenly shown up here saying you've come as an answer to our prayers?" The delicate precision with which Gayle folded her arms made Naomi think of her grandmother folding away her thin, white angora sweater for the summer. "Excuse me if I question your motives."

The paper crackled like the fuse lit on a firecracker as Naomi scrawled her name beneath those of the other women. "Question them all you want if it makes you happy, Gayle."

Gayle opened her mouth, probably to do just that, but Naomi beat her to the draw.

"Send out engraved invitations for an afternoon tea to discuss that very thing, why don't you? Gather together all the pedicured and pedigreed Junior Leaguers and Daughters of the Confederacy that you can muster. Oh, and don't forget to include any ex-sorority sisters that might be in town. I'm sure they'd all provide timely insight into my motives. Plus they'd leave you with the most precious potluck dinner recipes and perhaps some resourceful tips for keeping your big ol' bouffant hairdo from wilting in this unseasonable weather."

Naomi heard the older of the two women huff out a cynical laugh. The younger woman started to giggle, caught herself, and ended up making a peculiar gurgling sound deep in her throat.

Only the artificial sunniness of her slathered-on Southern accent protected Naomi from the frostbite in Gayle's glare as the woman asked, "Are you quite through?"

"Why, yes, I believe I am." Naomi stole one quick glance over the other signatures above hers to see if she recognized the family names of either of the two strangers there. She didn't, but looking at the pair of women, it didn't take a master detective to guess which was Rose and which was Mary Lucille.

"Here you go, Ms. Mary Lucille," she said, charm oozing from her every pore.

The young woman accepted the paper, her mouth agape. She sought out Naomi's signature with almost the same level of subtlety the salesclerks used to show when they followed Naomi's every movement through New Bethany's only truly "nice" store, fearing her kind would steal them blind. Mary Lucille all but underscored the scribbling with her finger as she mouthed it twice, her brow compressed.

"Bow-shawm. Bow-*shawm?*" She articulated Naomi's surname in that way many Southerners have of wrapping their tongues around a French pronunciation as though it were a delicacy dripping in rich, buttery sauce. The young woman fixed her features in a pouting kind of puzzlement that only lacked a feathered fan to set it off as the mark of old Southern mannerism. "Now, I don't recall any—" Her face brightened. "Oh, of course, Bow-Shawm! Of the Bluegrass Mills Beauchamps?"

"No, it's Bee-chum, dear," Naomi corrected, drawing her shoulders up. "Of the white trash Beauchamps."

Rose let loose a hearty laugh at that.

"Oh, Naomi, really." Gayle scoffed.

Naomi's lips lifted on just one side. "Really."

"Now you see why including this woman in a serious endeavor such as a prayer group is totally improbable?" Gayle looked to the others for support.

"Why, Gayle?" Naomi cocked her hip. "Because a Beauchamp is far too common to serve on one of New Bethany's last remaining sacred cows—oh, excuse me, I meant, sanctioned circles?"

"Sure you did," Gayle muttered. "And that—that attitude of yours is just what *I* mean. It isn't a matter of whether you are *common* or not."

Though you are, of course, Gayle said with a look the words that her upbringing—and perhaps, just perhaps, a teensy bit of suppressed friendship and the memory of how close they had once been—forbade her to say aloud.

"Nuh-uh, this is a matter of how committed you are. The very notion that you could just show up here at the very last minute like this—"

"Isn't that exactly what you prayed for?" Naomi asked so softly that her voice almost seemed a part of the breeze ruffling the trees in the grove.

Gayle paused, took only a heartbeat to regroup, and then charged on. "And making all manner of wisecracks about sacred cows and debutantes, potluck suppers and…and…"

Naomi, Rose, and Mary Lucille leaned in, drawn by Gayle's uncharacteristic hesitation.

Gayle rolled her eyes and whispered, "White trash," looking for all the world just like the old folks used to do when they said *colored* long after it had become an unacceptable racial reference.

Naomi stifled an out and out grin.

"Why, it's just too tacky to consider, Naomi. Rose? Lucy? You understand that, don't you?" Gayle acknowledged the ladies in a way that declared she was not really asking for an opinion but voicing one on behalf of them all. "If Naomi joined this prayer group, she'd soon turn everything we tried to do into one big old belly laugh for herself, just like she did those other things I just mentioned."

Naomi's hand shot up. "Hold it right there, Gayle. Now, that is not true."

"Oh?" Gayle adjusted her posture, and her gold jewelry flashed in the sunlight. "Are you saying it's not true that you'd make jokes about things many of us take seriously?"

"Oh, no, I'd do that for sure." She waved off Gayle's insulting question, then placed one hand on the woman's shoulder. "I'm saying it's not true that I made fun of debutantes. Not yet, anyway." She glanced at Rose and winked. "But if you'd care to give me a minute, I'm sure I could come up with something—"

"This is a waste of all our time!" Gayle stepped away from Naomi's touch and from the small cluster the four of them made in the quiet, empty spot at the edge of all the trees.

"I couldn't agree with you more, Gayle."

"Thank you, Rose." Gayle gave the woman a courteous nod.

"Your temper fit has wasted *all* our time." Rose literally and figuratively put down her foot, calling Naomi's attention to her deceptively plain looking slip-on shoes.

Naomi knew, as did any good woman of the South, good shoes were the hallmark of good upbringing. Whether clean or filthy, appropriate to the season and situation or out-of-style, worn-out or worn with the wrong outfit—all such details told absolutely anyone taking note—and, don't kid yourself, people *would be* taking note—just what kind of woman they were dealing with.

Rose's shoes, all fine leather of understated beige with just a flash of burnished gold, proclaimed her a woman of uncompromising taste who did not suffer fools gladly. Something she proved in point of fact when she turned her back on Gayle and stuck her hand out to Naomi. "Welcome to the prayer circle, sugar."

"Thank you, Rose."

Naomi gave Rose's hand a firm shake then let it slip away, unsure if this gesture made it all official or not. After all, Gayle clearly did not want her in the group, and Miz Lucy had not shown a deference either way. So the score remained one for, one against, one undecided.

Make that two undecided, she corrected in silence.

A cold heaviness sank into the pit of her stomach. Why was she here anyway?

Every mile on the way out to the grove, every landmark from childhood she passed along the way—and every melancholy scar where the landmarks no longer stood—made her question her actions. Yet she'd forced herself to make the journey—and even held out hope that she'd done the right thing when she overheard the other women praying for another member.

Then only a few moments with Gayle and she was a kid again. She felt a little less than good enough—a little dumb and a little dirty, though she had never been either.

Why had she thought it would be different now? What had possessed her to step outside her "place" and come here today? Naomi's answer filled her thoughts and tore at her emotions like a knife, and real and startling pain cut short her breath. She had come here today to join the circle for the very same reason she'd closed up her cottage in Maine, warehoused the supplies she used in creating her critically acclaimed folk art, pillaged her savings, and headed to Tennessee.

She had come to find a way to deal with the cruel tricks that age had played on her mother.

Naomi's mother had grown too infirm to remain in her own home. The time had come to put Mama in a nursing home. It was Naomi's only recourse. Logically, she knew that neither her prayers nor her proximity would turn back time and restore Mama's youthful spark, and she'd made her uneasy peace with it.

Her mother had led a good life, filled with love from childhood through motherhood, and even as a grandmother to Naomi's only son. From years of hard work at whatever she could find to serving on boards, committees, PTAs, juries, local campaigns, and any number of things that made her small community thrive, Naomi's mother had done them all. Now Naomi had come to tidy up the last loose ends of that life. For her, joining the prayer circle was part of that process, a coming full circle of something that had meant so much to her family, her town, and especially, her mother.

Mama had been in the very first prayer group, though many people did not realize that. Through the years as the folklore built up around the practice, the idea for the trees and all that followed became attributed to the wife of a seven-term mayor. But Naomi knew better.

She also knew there could be no finer tribute to her dear, wonderful mother than for Naomi to take part in what was rumored to be the very last prayer circle. If, that is, these women would allow it.

Naomi took a deep, aching breath. The humid air filled her lungs and senses with the almost gritty scent of trees and grass and fertile soil. She looked to Lucy, whose acceptance or denial would make the difference.

The girl pursed her bee-stung lips and her thin eyelashes narrowed over a gaze shifting from Rose to Gayle, then to Rose again.

To nudge things in her favor, Naomi offered her hand to Lucy, asking, in essence, for her confidence. Lucy huffed an enormous sigh.

"Yes, welcome, Naomi." Lucy, using just her thumb and forefinger—which were stiff as a crab's pinchers—nabbed Naomi's hand. "We can really use the extra body."

"'We can really use the extra body,'" Gayle grumbled under

her breath. Her face went red the instant she realized she'd been heard. She winced and turned her head, and Naomi wondered if poor Gayle was more upset at feeling angry and helpless or just ashamed of her immature behavior.

"Gayle!" Rose gave a stern *tsk-tsk* look.

Lucy blinked like a motherless calf.

Naomi couldn't help it. She hee-hawed out in triumph.

Gayle wanted to scream. Obviously, Naomi thought she could come in and run roughshod over this group. It was clear she believed Gayle posed no threat to that careless way of hers, that devil-give-a-darn way that usually ended up hurting someone—anyone—other than Naomi herself. Why did that woman have to come back? Why now, of all times?

"It *is* an answer to a prayer, Gayle," Rose said, as if she'd suddenly become privy to Gayle's thoughts.

"How on earth could *this* be an answer to prayer?" Gayle tightened her arms around her rib cage. "I can't see *this* bringing anything but trouble."

"Thank heaven answers to prayer don't originate on earth, Gayle. And it's what the Lord sees that matters, not you nor I. Nothing is hidden from his sight, not even our hearts. Now, Lucy and I are willing to trust him and welcome Naomi. How about you?"

Leave it to Rose to make this an issue of obedience to God. Nothing short of that could have pitted Gayle so against her own better judgement. Still, Rose and Lucy could operate out of a purity of faith that Gayle did not possess—at least not where Naomi Beauchamp was concerned.

Naomi swung her hand out, an irritatingly genuine smile on her lips.

Gayle flexed her fingertips against the fine fabric of her outfit, which despite all outward appearance, had her sweltering beneath the fresh, cool surface. Her rings nipped at the skin between her fingers.

"I don't understand why you're being so stubborn, Gayle." Rose swatted away a nonexistent bug.

"Yes, we've welcomed Naomi in, why can't you?" The childlike quality of Lucy's appeal, the obvious need to keep things pleasant, tugged at Gayle's guilt almost as much as Rose's call to submit to God in this matter.

"Please, y'all, don't scold Gayle for her reluctance. I, of all people, understand it."

Gayle tensed. The breeze caught a strand of her hair and sent it whipping against her temple. The lacquered end jabbed into the corner of her eye like a chiseled point. With a gesture as brassy as a belle slapping away a fresh upstart, she swept the lock away. She tried to push down the sickly sensation just as defiantly, but that scared, nauseous feeling—the disorienting terror one gets in the split second when a roller coaster tops a towering incline, hesitates, then begins its downward plummet—would not budge from her being.

More than Lucy's discomfort, more than Rose's reproach, more, perhaps, even than willful dismissal of her Christian duty, Gayle feared what Naomi could and *would* tell her friends about Gayle's past.

"Keep your friends close and your enemies closer." She'd heard it said many times. And while she did not consider Naomi an enemy in the strictest sense, her knowledge threatened everything Gayle had struggled to build and preserve these many years. Like it or not, she had to keep a close watch on Naomi Beauchamp—at least until she could figure out how to handle this whole horrid situation.

That was what finally propelled her forward.

"Fine, as far as I'm concerned she's in." She grasped Naomi's thin hand, enveloping it in both of hers. She pumped vigorously. "You're in. You're in. Are you happy now?"

"Not yet." Danger and a hint of mischief played in Naomi's smile. "But I will be happy if you ladies will consider my suggestion. That we choose an apple tree, as they did with the first circles, to represent what is likely the last circle."

"It's fine with me," Lucy rushed to say.

Rose put her hand to her remarkably smooth cheek. "It does sort of add a poetic touch, doesn't it?"

Gayle sucked her lips against her teeth. If she hoped to survive these crucial first encounters with Naomi, she'd have to pick her battles. She knew it—and by the glint in her old friend's eyes, Naomi knew it too.

"Yes, yes, that's fine with me. An apple tree it is." Funny, that didn't feel as bad as she'd expected. In fact, as she glanced at those four pathetic poplars sticking up as plain as light posts, Gayle warmed to the notion. "I'll call the nursery and have them deliver it out here this afternoon so it will be ready for tomorrow's service."

"Good." Rose tucked away her handkerchief. "Now that that's over, let's get in out of this heat."

Gayle sighed her agreement, looking forward to some air-conditioned quiet in which to think this mess through.

Rose turned on her heel and began back toward the cars, Lucy lumbering along behind.

"Wait!" Naomi ran one hand back through her short black hair.

Gayle moved on past her after the original members of the group.

Naomi did a double step to catch up. "Don't we have to pick a song, too?"

Rose stopped, and Lucy came up short behind her. "Oh, no, dear, the outgoing groups choose the song. We just choose the tree."

Gayle trudged on past, muttering loud to make herself heard and yet soft enough that she could deny any malcontent, "Oh, joyous day. I'll bet we get to hear something dazzlingly original from those circles. Does everyone have the words to 'Sweet Hour of Prayer' memorized yet?"

Naomi laughed.

"Sure, *you* think it's funny." Rose fluffed the thinning ends of her hair. "You haven't sat through decades of the same four or five songs sung over and over and over—"

"And *over* again." Lucy concurred. "They don't even have the decency to rotate them properly. I remember the very first time I came to the service, I was eight, they sang 'Morning Has Broken.' Then they proceeded to sing it year after year so that the first time they sang something different, I thought they'd made a mistake."

Gayle stopped to face the others, who had clustered near the parked cars.

"That and 'Amazing Grace.'" Rose's chuckle didn't quite disguise her weariness at the mere mention of the beautiful hymn. "I love that song, I truly do. But can it drag on. Specially when the weather doesn't cooperate and you have two dozen tone-deaf prima donnas droning out every last verse—all in full vibrato fervor."

"Do they still do 'In the Garden'?" Naomi asked.

"Of course." Gayle couldn't help chiming in. "'In the Garden' is a personal favorite of the unchurched and the unimaginative."

"Oh, really?" Naomi's diaphanous skirt fluttered around her slim legs. "I was going to say how much I like that song."

"Yeah, and I was going to sprout wings and fly from branch to branch chirping the tenor part to 'Victory in Jesus,'" Gayle shot back. She'd bowed to personal pressure in letting Naomi in, but that did not mean she'd let the woman embarrass her or make sport of her.

Naomi laughed lightly. "No, really, I mean it. I *do* like 'In the Garden.' I sort of hope they do sing it tomorrow. In fact, I'm willing to bet that they will."

"Bet?" Gayle cast her gaze heavenward. "This is hardly the kind of thing you wager on, Naomi."

"I didn't mean *bet* bet, although…" She gave a cat-eyed grin. "We could each guess what they will sing, purely for fun and speculation, and if anyone guesses right, that person receives the great honor of bringing the refreshments to our very first circle meeting."

"Dibs on 'Morning Has Broken.'" Lucy beamed.

"You're not seriously going to—"

"I can almost hear it now." Rose put her hand to her ear. "The sweet strains, and I do mean *strains,* of 'Amazing Grace.'"

"How do you do this, Naomi?" Gayle demanded.

"Do what?"

"*This,*" Gayle opened her arms. "The way you get normally reasonable people caught up in things that they'd never—"

"Are we talking hymns or history now, Gayle?" Naomi asked, her expression something between teasing and tenderness.

Gayle wanted to look away but she dared not.

Well? The question hung in the air unspoken as all three women looked at her and waited.

She wet her lips, dried her brow, then pulled her body up

straight but not rigid, saying simply, "'Sweet Hour of Prayer.'"

Naomi conceded her choice with one angled nod of her head. "Until tomorrow, then, ladies."

Four

I come to the garden alone…"
Naomi curved her arm around her mother's once indomitable shoulders. She sang a bit more softly than usual so that she could savor the now craggy timbre of her mother's voice. Someday, all too soon, that voice would go silent and she would never hear it—this side of heaven—again.

Her mother's footsteps wobbled over the uneven ground.

Naomi clutched her tighter, but not too tight. Her mother seemed so frail these days, not at all the feisty, bright-eyed woman she'd loved, admired, and often wished to emulate.

"Let's hang back, Nomi," Mama whispered, using the pet name from Naomi's childhood. "That way if I need to go sit in the car a spell, we won't disturb anyone."

"Sure, Mama," she murmured, halting beside her mother. She shut her eyes to let the words of the hymn, rough and sometimes garbled by her mother's faltering voice, wash over her.

She planted her new sandals in the dewy grass, then repositioned them, her naked feet chilled by the sudden change of weather that had come upon them overnight. She should not have worn sandals, she supposed, to church and then here to the prayer-circle ceremony. Sandals weren't, in the strictest Southern sense, a dressy shoe.

Naomi wriggled her toes. Still, she had so looked forward to allowing herself the freedom of wearing them after years of sensible hiking boots for fall, fur-lined boots in winter, cross-training athletic shoes for spring and summer, and black or white ballerina flats for whatever rare dress occasion might crop up. In Maine, she did not wear sandals that let the damp grass tickle her ankles. She did not do much of anything but what was expected of her as a single mother and member of her tourism-driven community.

Not that anyone would've said anything about it. Had she worn sandals in her new hometown, eyebrows would arch and she would be thought foolish, but not a single word would be spoken of it. Until, of course, it passed into the realm of local legend: "Eh-yup, once was a woman come up from Tennessee who took it in her mind to wear sandals. Hear tell she lost three toes to frostbite. That's what they say, anyways." So the story would go as it was told to out-of-towners years after Naomi had passed on.

She smiled at the thought, and glanced at her sandals. Wearing sandals here, she decided, only added to her image of being avant-garde and from another place. And that pleased her.

In Maine, she was not considered avant-garde but just another sturdy craftsperson who lived—and often looked, in her oversized parka or smock and wide-brimmed hats—like a hermit crab taking residence in a place not intended for her by birthright. How amused her stone-faced neighbors would be if they knew that here in New Bethany, Naomi had been considered a "wild child." She could picture how their lips would curl into tiny smirks and their eyes would crinkle ever-so-slightly at the corners at the thought of "The Pottery Lady," as they called her, as a teenaged hellion or even an extravagantly dressed, middle-aged Bohemian troublemaker.

The idea made Naomi smirk a bit, too. Not from amusement, mind you, but because she rather liked the idea that the old guard might still find something in her to click their tongues at and shake their frosted domes of lacquered hair over. Naomi did not think God intended for everything in life to be roses—and sometimes she purely embraced her role as a thorn.

The breeze stirred. Naomi inhaled the heavy floral scent of the Sunday cologne that clung to her mother's last good dress. "Cologne is for Sunday, perfume is for Saturday night," her mother used to say. "Eau de toilette is for cheap, fast women, who all but bathe in it to hide the odor of their repulsive lifestyles—and for little girls under twelve, of course."

The outdated rules to which Naomi suspected her mother still adhered warmed her heart. Everything about her return to New Bethany was having that effect on her. The smells, the sounds, the sights…

She lifted her gaze to take in the familiar surroundings as the verses of the old hymn flowed from the gathered women.

The grove seemed so much fuller than it had when she'd last seen it, on the day she'd last driven away from New Bethany, almost a decade ago. She hadn't intended to stay away so long. Caught up in her new life, she had hardly realized so much time had passed. But the transformation of the grove gave testimony to the length of her absence.

Trees that had been saplings when she'd last visited now towered above them. Rows of new trees, each representing a new year of prayer circles, stretched toward the opening where the attendees now stood. Each year's living memorial to service—fewer in number and planted further and further apart to impart the illusion of taking up more space—told the story of the decline of the cherished tradition.

On knobs that reached into the smoky distance, on the other side of the clearing, ponderous tendrils of menacing kudzu stretched toward the grove. Fat green leaves, shaped like the spade on a deck of cards, quivered as if time around them had slowed so that anyone might observe the plants in the very act of creeping deliberately forward. The Japanese vine, having found a home south of the Mason/Dixon line—and for some incomprehensible reason, nowhere else—overtook fences, tree stumps, abandoned farm machinery, even whole hillsides in short order. The invasive plant often caused even the most ardent watchdog trying to keep it at bay to simply surrender to the inevitable and let it grow.

That kudzu served as a chilling reminder, Naomi thought. *This, too, shall pass,* the vine seemed to say. *This, all you have loved and known and labored over, can be swallowed up before you know it by neglect, apathy, or—worst of all—discouragement.*

Naomi shuddered. She drew her mother closer, hoping to protect her from the chill, both real and imagined.

"Brrr-rabbit," Naomi whispered the phrase Mama had often said to her when Naomi was young. She used the exact same intonation, too, and added a little squeeze of her hand, just as her mother had always done for her. Mama nestled close, almost clinging.

Naomi's throat was parched. Her heart thudded like that of a small hare snared in an unfamiliar briar patch. Things would be different now. No, everything would be different. The roles of mother and daughter had begun their shift.

"Blackberry winter," Mama rasped back at her, interrupting Naomi's concerns and the final verse of the hymn.

The beginning consonants in Mama's speech remained crisp, despite the slight slurring of her words, owed to the mix of her Southern accent and her age. It gave her speech the sense of having begun with a purpose that could not be carried off, surrendering instead to the weight of enunciating each syllable clearly.

"What, Mama?"

"Blackberry winter, Nomi." She patted her daughter's hand. "That's why it's so cool this morning. Won't be long we'll be blackberry picking, you know."

Blackberry winter. Naomi had not heard that term in years. They did not have blackberry winters in Maine, or strawberry winters, or dogwood winters—all terms used to refer to three cool snaps that folks expected here each spring.

That blackberry winter still existed, that she had come home in time to experience it, bolstered Naomi's spirits. And something in her mother's touch—something subtle that conveyed, "I'm still your mother, I still have something to contribute to you," did much to set Naomi's world right again.

"You'll see, Nomi. Few weeks from now, we'll get us some pails and go out and pick enough blackberries for a fine cobbler. You'll have to do most the work, though, but I can tell you how, and it'll come back to you." Mama straightened away, as much as her bent little body would allow. "You'll see. Won't stay blackberry winter for long, then comes the sweet reward."

Drawing the refreshingly cool air in, Naomi raised her voice to conclude the old hymn with a resounding, "Amen."

Unoriginal or not, Naomi still loved that hymn. Despite her joking about it, she'd really hoped that the past year's prayer groups—if they insisted on going traditional—would choose it. She would've picked something far more tailored to the group and the occasion, yet hearing these women's voices weaving together in this song certainly filled the bill. It set a mood and reverence for the occasion that uplifted the soul. Naomi gazed from the small girls pretending to read from the thin, wind-fluttered pages to the old women, who had sung the song so many times that they ignored the hymnals altogether, their faces upturned and eyes shut. Then she looked at her mother's face, altered by age but still so sweetly serene at being here to participate in something that held such meaning.

Yes, it was a good choice of songs. Just as her choice to come here had been good. Somehow, it would all work out all right.

"I'd like to welcome you all here today." A stout little man in a pale blue suit and gold-and-royal-blue tie spoke up, making himself heard above the murmur and shuffling of the small crowd. He thrust his hands out and upward, his stubby arms looking like plump rolls of sausage encased in tight polyester. "Can I…can I have your attention here, ladies?"

"That's the Baptist minister caused all the commotion." Mama's head nodded against Naomi's shoulder.

The man waited for a moment to allow things to settle a bit.

Naomi squinted to try to get a better view of the minister's ruddy face. "What commotion?"

"We're going to get started in just a moment here," the minister shouted. "But first I have been asked to tell whatever flighty little gal that parked in front of the entrance road up there, that you have got to move your car. And I mean right now."

Naomi secretly wondered if whatever "commotion" this man had caused could be traced back to his winning ways in handling people. "What commotion are you talking about, Mama? Just what happened?"

"Oh, who knows for certain." Mama sputtered something like "pshaw" and rolled her eyes. "You know how it is in small towns and small churches. New minister comes in, has some new ways, new ideas. Words fly, everyone takes affront, and before too long four or five fine, upstanding families have left the flock to take their pew-filling and their pocketbooks elsewhere."

"So they joined another Baptist church?"

"Clean over in Wilmont. Yes, they sure did. Drove right past the new Antioch Baptist Church, their cars shining in the Sunday morning sun like floats in a homecoming parade, and headed straight out to the Victory Baptist Church in Wilmont. The whole lot of 'em—'cept Rose, of course."

"Rose?"

"Rose Holcolmb." Mama made a waggling gesture with her hand in the general direction of one of the women Naomi had met the day before. "She didn't just up and quit the minister or Antioch Baptist. No, ma'am, she left everything."

"Everything?" What did Mama mean by that? "Was it that serious a flap?"

"Can't say."

"You can't? Or you won't?"

"Can't. Don't know the lady to her face. Never heard, exactly, what went on." Mama shrugged. "Plenty of speculation, though. You know how Baptists like to…speculate."

Naomi tried not to grin. "I know that Baptists are human, and that all humans fall short of the glory of God—and sometimes they accomplish that by gossiping."

"Not Congregationalists," Mama hissed.

There hadn't been a Congregationalist church in New Bethany since Moses wore knee pants, as Naomi's grandmother might have said. But Mama's grandpa was a Congregationalist minister, so Mama held a deep abiding respect for the denomination based solely on family adoration and folklore about the ways of the stalwart practitioners. Knowing that, Naomi supposed, it seemed safe enough for her mother to extol the many virtues of the long passed over or otherwise converted disciples above those of the living, breathing—and obviously talking—Baptists.

"I'm sure you don't mean that as an indictment of Baptists as a whole, though," Naomi said, hoping to steer the conversation gently back to Rose's situation.

"No, no. Just an observation. I think Baptists are fine people, good people. They're not Congregationalists, but then, no one really is anymore around these parts."

"What about Rose?"

"Rose?" Her mother's face became a crepey mask of bewilderment. "I didn't know Rose was a Congregational—"

"Never mind, Mama." Naomi sighed.

About then the minister, who stood on a collapsible stage brought over from the high school—just six choir bleachers arranged to make a sort of low table, actually—cleared his throat and tussled with the buttons on his suit jacket.

"Got no business here, that man," Mama grumbled.

"Because of the commotion?" Naomi asked, all innocence and curiosity.

"What commotion?" Mama frowned.

"The—" Naomi cut herself off. No point in chewing the same meal twice. Obviously Mama had already forgotten about Rose and the preacher and the Sunday parade to join the Free Baptist church. Her heart heavy with the realization, she brushed back Mama's soft silver hair and asked indulgently, "Why doesn't that man have any business here?"

"Well, aside from the fact that he looks and talks like that big ol' cartoon rooster—"

Naomi chuckled at the surprisingly apt comparison.

"This isn't a man's place." Mama's voice rose. "Isn't any man's place to be here. This grove, this ceremony, these trees, and the thousands of prayers they represent are *women's* work."

"Uh-huh. Yes, that's right."

"Tell it, Miz Beauchamp. You tell it right."

Naomi turned to find two familiar faces, with skin like fine, polished mahogany and twinkling brown eyes.

Naomi gave a little nod. "Morning, Sister Marguerite, Sister Princess."

Marguerite and Princess Johnson, sisters in title to everyone in town and in blood to one another, were a mainstay of the small town's religious conscience. They had participated in the first "black" prayer circle in 1968 and in the first integrated circle in the early nineties. Naomi had always held them in highest esteem because they were first in service to God and first to speak out to confront injustice, no matter whom they had to go up against.

"Let yourself be heard, Miz Beauchamp," Princess commanded, her hand upheld.

Naomi winced, her gaze darting to the many faces that were turning to witness the excitement. Suddenly she wished the Johnson sisters would mind their own business. Her pulse quickened and her cheeks grew hot. This was definitely *not* the way to begin her reentry into the community.

"Women started this tradition so we could have something our own. *Our own*," Mama called back to the sisters with a passion that startled Naomi.

Pride in her mother's conviction mingled with chagrin at suddenly finding herself at the center of controversy. And here she had not been back a whole week. What would everyone think? A buzz began to work its way over the crowd, and more heads turned. To be suspected of being avant-garde was one thing, Naomi thought, to be taken off guard quite another.

"Now, if y'all will all quieten down a bit here…" The preacher patted the air in downward motion. "Ladies! Quieten down, now. How's a man s'posed to make himself heard here?"

"A man *isn't* supposed to make himself heard here," Mama

grumbled just loud enough for the handful of women closest to them to hear.

Someone a few feet away repeated Mama's concern, and like a peculiar echo, another voice and then another took up the phrase, "A man *isn't* supposed to make himself heard here."

Naomi started to remind her mother of some antiquated rule—"A lady doesn't create a scene"—but she wasn't ready to swap the roles of chiding parent and disobedient child out loud. Not just yet.

"Now, Mama, things have changed over the years. It's not like all the men are off at war now like they were in the early days. Look here, there are a lot of nice men come out here to lend support," Naomi whispered as she made a flitting motion with her hand toward the few men scattered among the three dozen or so women.

She didn't recognize a one of them to name names to her mother, but one man gave her a wry grin as though he was quite enjoying her predicament, not in a mean way but in a way of subtle appreciation of it all. A tall, lean fellow—more balding than a man of his apparent age should be—he gave her a nod much like a greeting, a push forward, and a stamp of approval all in one. She tried to swallow, but there was a lump in her throat in a gut response to the man's engaging attention. She wasn't used to drawing men's notice and she didn't seek it. She'd had a lousy marriage and an even lousier divorce. So lousy, in fact, that she'd taken back her maiden name and had her son's name legally changed as well.

After that, it took her years to get up the nerve to dab her toe into the relationship waters again. "More than one fish in the sea," she'd heard over and over. When she finally got up the nerve to try, it didn't take long for her to conclude that her scheming, cheating, no-account husband *had* been a bad catch—and just one in an entire ocean of bad catches.

Most men, she thought, her eyes still on this one man with the charming presence about him, always seemed to have one-track minds. That track was not, as the old wives' tales would have you believe, sex. It was themselves. What effect will this have on *me?* How will *I* benefit?

Mama had always teased that men never matured emotionally past the terrible twos. In Naomi's experience, that was giving them more credit than they deserved.

Still, she found herself returning this man's smile as she said, "See, Mama, there are plenty of nice men here to stand with us today. Nothing wrong with that, is there?"

"Standing with us is one thing, taking lead is another," Mama insisted. "That's not how this was started. It sure as shootin' isn't how it should end."

"Amen," someone nearby added.

"That's true," another resounded.

Mama made sense. Naomi sighed. Mama almost always made sense.

"Now, listen here…listen, ladies," The minister moved to the edge of the stage, on the same side where Naomi and Mama stood at the back of the crowd. He stepped down into the grass with a huffing grunt. "The four prayer groups that served this past year invited me to conduct the ceremony, and I do think it only courteous to respect their wishes in the matter." The minister made sense as well. "Now what do you say, ladies, can we get on with this?"

A cumbersome quiet fell over the crowd.

Naomi wet her lips and shifted her feet in the stabbing, scratchy grass. She made a point to seek out the faces of the women she agreed to serve with this year. The cool glare from Gayle's eyes was no less than she expected, and it did not surprise her, either, that the exact instant her eyes found Lucy, the young woman looked away. But when she moved her gaze to where Rose had been standing, she found it empty.

A knot twisted the muscles between her shoulder blades. Had Mama's protest caused Rose to leave? Had the fleeting hint of strife churned too many bad feelings to the surface for the older woman?

"Rose left everything," Mama had said. It worried Naomi that Rose had just left them as well.

"It's all right, sugar." The feel of a strong arm over her tension-pinched shoulders, accompanied by Rose's husky voice, soothed Naomi like cool aloe on sun-blistered skin. "It's all right, Miss Ida."

That Rose used the endearment reserved for sweet old relatives or as a loving homage to a woman of significance spoke volumes of her support for both Mama and Naomi. Particularly in light of the fact that Rose probably only knew Mama as a nodding acquaintance.

"Miss Ida," Rose began again. "Let's us allow these other groups their way today. This won't be the last ceremony, and next year we'll see that it's done right, won't we, Naomi?"

"Of course, we will, Mama." She took her mother's hand. "You'll see."

"Do you promise?" Mama's intense focus fell on Naomi.

"I promise," she whispered. "I promise, Mama."

"Is everything resolved now?" In no way could the minister have overheard their conversation, but Naomi imagined he took the silence as concession. "Can we...can we get on with this ceremony now? I have a lot to do today, ladies."

No one seemed to want to speak for the whole of the crowd, but since no one objected either, the minister blustered a cough, then turned to climb his platform again.

The tension that had coiled in Naomi's neck and shoulders eased, though a twinge of guilt did grip her right through the middle at how badly she had wanted to smooth things over for the sake of convention and personal comfort. And she could see that giving in had rankled Rose, as well.

Still, it probably wasn't very Christian of them both to snicker when the chubby little preacher strode to the center of the bleachers, tipped the delicate balance of the makeshift floor, and almost went crashing through to the ground.

But since Naomi herself had to stifle a quick giggle, she could hardly chastise them.

"That Ida Beauchamp has lost her senses, you know."

"Mother, please!" Lucy fixed her gaze forward and hiked up the bird-boned little girl planted on her left hip.

"Well, she has!" Her mother bent her elbow, her stiff pocket-book sliding down to bump to a stop in the crook of her arm, and gave Naomi and Ida a little wave like the Queen of England on her royal balcony. "Carrying on like that—" Mother mouthed something that seemed warm and welcoming at the Beauchamp women, then tilted her head toward Lucy to conclude from the side of her mouth, "Not that one expects better from a Beauchamp, mind you."

"Well, I thought that Naomi woman was very nice," Lucy countered. "She's going to be in our circle, you know."

"She is?"

"Uh-huh."

"How did *that* come about?"

"It was an answer to prayer," Lucy said with far more conviction than she felt. She tugged at her pink jersey dress, which had bunched beneath one knobby knee of the child clinging to her, and pretended a sudden fascination with the preacher's rambling remarks.

"An answer to—Mary Lucille Jewell, that is the most ridi—"

"Shh." Lucy put one finger to her lips, never taking her eyes from the fat man spinning out some incomprehensible tale in the classic Southern preacher pattern, with undue emphasis on the last word of each sequence. "Don't raise your voice here and cause a scene, Mother. Else folks might think you're as dotty as Mrs. Beauchamp there."

Her mother harrumphed.

Lucy fiddled with the pale blonde hair of the child in her arms, pleased as punch to have gotten one over on her mother. It didn't happen often, but when it did, it gave Lucy a powerful delectation that she dared not openly relish.

Dare it or not, her mother wouldn't permit her to wallow in her satisfaction for long.

"Would you put that child down, Mary Lucille? You're spoiling her, carrying her around like that."

"How can I be spoiling her?" Lucy stroked her knuckles across the child's velvet cheek. "This is the first time ever I've looked after her."

"Then you're spoiling her mama. I sworn, Lucille, you only hired that gal yesterday and already you're taking care of her little girl—" Her mother leaned in close and lowered her voice, amending—"her *illegitimate* little girl."

Lucy curved one hand protectively over the child's ear, pressing the small head close. She narrowed her eyes at her mother and mashed her lips so tightly closed that they tingled and burned. She had nothing to say to that. What could she say? Mother was absolutely right.

Nikki Herndon, new in town and in need of work, had shown up yesterday with excellent child-care references and enough brass to ask Lucy to baby-sit within moments of accepting the job as Lucy's assistant.

"What was Nikki supposed to do, Mother? She had to move her things into her new apartment and a toddler would have just gotten in the way." Better to use her new employee's justifications than to admit the truth, especially to her mother, that Lucy had jumped at the chance to have the cherub-faced child all to herself for the day.

She curled the tiny body into a gentle embrace and drew in the smell of animal crackers and apple juice. Lucy couldn't remember when—or if—she had ever felt so content. A beautiful day, a beautiful child in her arms, the priceless opportunity to play at mommy if only for a few hours…she shut her eyes and sighed.

"Isn't it enough that you *loaned* her your boyfriend to help move her things?" Mother said it like she suspected the woman's *things* to consist of dump-salvaged furniture, second-hand lingerie, and a trunkful of plastic jewelry and stiletto heels. "Isn't that how you put it, sweetheart? You *loaned* her Ray to help her move?"

"Yes, Mother."

Mother let out a low, pathetic moan of a sigh. "Do you really think that's wise? I mean, a woman like that?"

"Like what? Nikki had wonderful references—which I checked, thank you—and I found her genuinely sweet."

"So is taffy, but if you aren't careful, it will pull the fillings right out of your head."

"Oh, Mother."

"Don't 'Oh, Mother' me, young lady. You're the one who sent your boyfriend off with a slim, attractive gal, who already has one illegitimate child, might I remind you—"

"I was just doing my Christian duty. So she spends the day with Ray and I spend the day with her baby, what does that matter to you?" Lucy stopped short of telling her mother that she considered herself to have gotten the better end of the deal. "Besides," she added, nuzzling the downy hair on the side of the child's head. "I'm enjoying my time with Tiffany Crystal."

"Tiffany Crystal," Mother muttered. "What kind of a woman gives a child a name like—"

Lucy laid her cheek against Tiffany's and began to hum softly, drowning out whatever criticism her mother felt compelled to share.

Somewhere beyond them, the voice of the minister droned on. "And in this time of renewal and new beginnings—"

Lucy touched the tiny fingers entwining in the soft folds of her short sleeve. She hummed some more.

"We gather here today—"

She took one tiny pink canvas shoe in her hand and gave Tiffany's thin little leg a playful swing. Her heart filled with imaginings of how it must feel to have your own baby, with hands that reached out just for you and plump legs that jumped and danced when mommy came into the room.

"To thank the women who served—"

Lucy began to sway as she hummed.

"And to encourage those who will serve—"

She wished this moment could go on forever.

"If those ladies would kindly come up here now."

"Lucy, that's you." Mother's well-padded elbow still delivered quite a jab. "That's you. Go up on the stage."

Lucy started, took one step forward, then realized she still had Tiffany. "Here, Mother, watch after Tiffany for a minute, would you?"

"No, no, Lucy. On the ground, on the ground." Mother waved her hand downward. "I can't hold a child that size. Put her down, and I'll just grab a hold of her arm."

Lucy lowered the child until the grass fringed the sides of Tiffany's pink shoes. She backed away a step.

Mother latched on to the girl's upper arm, leaving her small forearm and hand dangling like some sad marionette's.

Tiffany looked from Lucy to Mother then back again with the unreadable expression of a toddler trying to make sense of a world that she could not possibly understand.

"Go on now, Lucy, they're waiting on you."

Lucy took one step backward, wondering how much people would talk if she marched up to join the others carrying the newcomer's toddler. Too much, was the answer, and Lucy, as usual, gave over to convention and headed toward the stage, her shoulders slouched and her eyes on the path opening in front of her.

She moved onto the stage with the caution of someone stepping into an unsecured rowboat. The last thing she needed was to repeat the minister's gaffe in tipping down one corner of the creaking bleachers.

Gayle was already waiting there, her dark skin a dazzling contrast to her pale peach suit. She stood with the toe of one of her perfectly color-coordinated pumps pointed frontward. Her other shoe pointed to the side, putting her hips in slenderizing profile; her upper body twisted at the waist to emphasize its smallness in contrast to her shoulders.

Lucy recognized that pose. It was pure beauty queen. She took her spot beside Gayle and tried to imitate the elegant posture, but a flash of discomfort in her turned knee and a twinge of protest in the small of her back mocked her attempt to be something she was not. She shuffled her feet until they both pointed the same direction, folded her hands in front of her, and watched Naomi help Rose up onto the platform.

When they all stood in a line, with everyone gawking at them, Lucy could not help but wonder if this was how the final contestants in a pageant must feel. She tried to enjoy the fantasy but could not. She just kept thinking how, if this *were* a contest with these three other women, that she would come in dead last—last in looks, last in poise, last in congeniality.

Lucy drew a ragged breath against the slashing pain of her own truth but could not conceal herself from it. She would always be that stubby-legged, broad-hipped, double-chinned child that never could win her daddy's approval.

It clawed at her even now, the memory of the cold disappointment in Odel Jewell's eyes when he looked at her. She could still hear his slick, contemptuous tone each time he'd read aloud from the paper that a friend's daughter had taken the Miss Peach Blossom or Sweet Corn Queen, or some such contrived title bestowed on every other girl in the community.

Daddy liked beauty queens. And former beauty queens. The more titles—and the fewer morals—the better. Of course, being the successful, handsome man that he was, he attracted plenty. And they attracted him, much to her mother's humiliation.

Perhaps if Lucy had been a better daughter, if she'd been pretty and refined and someone to be proud of—

The burst of applause from the gathering took her completely aback and signaled to Lucy that this year's service had reached its conclusion.

"So, it looks like I'll be bringing the goodies to our first meeting." Naomi wrung her hands together as the crowd around them began to break up. "When and where will it be and what shall I bring?"

"My house," Rose said. "This Thursday, seven o'clock. It's only our organizational meeting, you know, to compare schedules, elect a secretary to take notes, go over the loose ends and suggestions from last year's groups. That kind of thing."

"Really?" Naomi blinked. "They do all that? Notes and a secretary? I never imagined."

"It isn't a big party, if that's what you thought—"

"Gayle, don't start," Rose said, placing one hand on Gayle's arm. Keeping her hand there, she faced Naomi. "We also have to decide how we're going to look after our tree."

"It's a lovely tree, isn't it?" Naomi asked. The sincerity in her tone and the pure sentimental longing in her eyes made them all follow the line of her gaze to the small sapling planted just a few feet from the stage.

"It was a good choice," Gayle was the first to admit.

"It's lovely," Rose concurred.

"Yes." To her surprise Lucy actually did think the sweet little tree quite compelling as it stood in a row by itself at the end of the tree-cluttered grove.

"I think I'd like to look after it, if y'all don't mind," Naomi said. Her chin dipped even as her gaze stayed locked on their fragile, new contribution to the town custom. "I think I'll need the distraction, what with Mama being…the way she is now and all."

"Taylor Boatwright'll help you all you need. He's the nurseryman." Gayle almost sounded conciliatory.

"So, what kinds of refreshments shall I bring to the first meeting?" The high, bright sun accented the few silver threads in Naomi's gleaming blue-black hair.

"Cake is always nice, or cookies," Rose said. "But don't go to too much trouble. Just something you can pick up ready-made will do fine."

"You could bring frozen pie," Lucy heard herself volunteer without having willed her voice to do so. Still, now that she'd spoken up and all eyes had fixed on her, she had to finish the thought. "I'm sure Ray will give you a discount, and his place's pecan-turtle brownie crust, chocolate-swirl cheesecake ice-cream pies are the best in town."

"Well, now that *is* true," Rose said as Gayle nodded in sluggish agreement.

"Oh? I thought I'd just stop by the Piggly Wiggly and pick up some decorative plates and napkins, maybe some brownies—"

"Oh, Naomi, the Piggly Wiggly has been gone for *years.*" Gayle shook her head.

"Really? What a shame." Naomi looked and sounded kind of distant and dreamy at the news. "I used to love to tell the folks in Maine about shopping at the Piggly Wiggly. Just mentioning the name would make their faces light up."

"I'm sure they did, and I'm sure you got quite a kick out of making us all sound like silly Southern hicks, with Southern hick names for our stores and shops—"

"It's not like that at all, Gayle."

"You bet it's not. It's not like that at *all* around here anymore. Believe it or not, we have the same stores and products down here as they do all over the country. Oh, sure, we *do,* some of us, still get our hair done at Frankly, My Shear Beauty Parlor or send our daughters to Miss Trudi's School of Charm and Dance. But on the whole, we live and shop and patronize places with generic, purposeful names, just like they do in the rest of the country."

The moment Gayle paused to take a breath, Naomi laughed and held up her hands in surrender. "I believe you. I believe you. Now, where is it I should go to get the paper goods and this pecan-turtle brownie crust, chocolate-swirl cheesecake ice-cream pie?"

"Get your plates and such at the Dixie Dazzler Party Mart and Bait Shop," Gayle suggested, so serious she was almost grim. "They have the best selection. Best prices, too, if that matters to you."

Naomi transformed a reactionary laugh into a cough, but not well.

Gayle ignored it valiantly, adding with cool aplomb, "And you can pick up the ice-cream pie at Ray's Bob's Cone and Coney King."

Naomi's brow crimped down. "You mean *Ray* Bob's—"

"No," Lucy jumped in, her tone adamant. "It's Ray's Bob's—"

"Used to be just Bob's Cone and Coney King," Rose explained, the phrase intoned like a person giving a leading clue on a TV game show.

"Oh, I remember that." Naomi nodded.

"My boyfriend Ray took it over a while back." Lucy smiled with pride.

Naomi gave a squinty-eyed look. "Why didn't he change the name to just his?"

"Well, he said Bob's already had the reputation and the customers, why lose out on that? He said it only made sense to take advantage—"

"And believe me, when it comes to taking advantage of someone else's hard work, Ray's the best."

Lucy pretended to ignore Gayle's unkind, but bitingly true, observation.

Naomi jumped in and rescued them from the potentially awkward moment. "Well, Ray's Bob's it is then. Now if you'll excuse me, I've got other things to see to."

Naomi motioned toward her mama, who looked even frailer standing between the flamboyant Johnson sisters.

Lucy heard her own mother chiding Tiffany for taking off a shoe. "Yes, I'd better go, too."

"Until Thursday, then." Naomi tossed off a causal wave. "I'm looking forward to getting started. It should be fun."

"Oh sure," Gayle muttered, as she took Rose's arm and gave a guiding nudge to Lucy to lead the way off the stage. "It should be a real riot."

Five

I don't see why you can't come home for a few weeks after graduation, Kelley. Just to get your bearings and—" Rose moved through her quiet house with the cordless phone pressed to her ear. "Yes, yes. I understand. I do, sweetheart. I do. You're young and—"

She paused to swipe at a spotless end table, ruffling one of her grandmother's yellowed doilies as she did. On the other end of the line the younger of her two daughters was explaining why she wouldn't be coming back to New Bethany after graduating from college in June.

"And so you say this friend of a friend has what kind of apartment in Nashville?" Rose tried to focus on her daughter's enthusiastic answer, but a subtle throbbing in her temples fogged her thoughts. She wandered across the living-room floor, murmuring *uh-huh*s and *oh?*s into the receiver, her gaze flitting from object to object searching for something, anything, to tidy up before tonight's prayer-group organizational meeting.

Not so much as a magazine on the coffee table lay askew, not a coaster or knickknack was out of place. How could there be? Who was there but she to bring disorder to her house? For the past few weeks she had hoped that Kelley would come home soon to leave clothes strewn in the bathroom and dishes on the porch, if only for a while, but now…

Rose poked at the tangled fringe of the hearth rug with the toe of her shoe. Her daughter chattered on about new friends—*All of whom I've yet to meet,* Rose thought with a pang—and how her favorite professor had given her a hand-written letter of reference and a lead on a promising job in Nashville.

Leaning her elbow on the mantle, Rose adjusted the array of picture frames a fraction in one direction only to set them precisely back where they had rested before. When her finger-tips brushed over the intricate silver oval that ringed her late husband's picture, she paused.

J. Curran "Curry" Holcolmb. A handsome man who wore his smile as much in his eyes as on his lips, had a well-deserved and unchallenged reputation as an honorable man. A bank president who did not let his position in the community blind him to the real values of life, Curry supported Rose and the girls in comfortable fashion, as their stately old home in the heart of the town attested.

But Curry had given them so much more than money and status. He never hesitated to give his family something that so many men neglected: himself.

Rose had waited to marry. "I prefer to take my time in find-ing a mate," was her response to those who asked what she was waiting for, and wasn't she worried about being "an old maid"? She'd been sure, when the time—and the man—was right, God would help her know. Besides, waiting had paid off, for she had learned much about herself in the process. So when she finally found Curry in her late twenties, she knew she had found the one man who could be her husband, her lover, the father of her children, and her very best friend. He was some-one, she was sure, who would share her faith and her life, enriching both. Curry had been all that and more. She owed much of the happiness she'd known in her life to this one man.

As Rose fingered the gleaming, cool frame, she wondered when, if ever, she would find it in herself to forgive him for dying and leaving her so very, very alone.

Kelley's plaintive voice drew her attention. "I understand, honey. No, I'm not mad at you. I raised you to spread your wings and fly. How could I get mad when you actually did it? I'm proud—" Rose flattened her hand over Curry's black-and-white photo—"and, well, just a little bit disappointed that I won't have my baby back home with me, even if for just a bit. But I'm a big girl, I'll get over it."

Rose laughed, making sure it rang nice and light so as not to give away the heaviness in her heart.

Apparently the act did not convince Rose's astute child, who pleaded with her mother not to be upset with the obviously hasty decision.

"Kelley, honey, I'm not mad, honest. I'm—"

"Knock, knock!"

Gayle's voice, accompanied by a sharp rapping on the kitchen's old wooden screen door, cut Rose short.

"Come on in, Gayle," Rose called out. "Oh, Kelley, honey, it's Gayle Barrett at the door. Yes, Gayle Shorter, your very own Miss Gayle-y Girl."

Rose gave her guest a smile at the decades-old nickname given by Curry, who'd thought up an imaginative pet name for almost everyone. She lowered the mouthpiece an inch and whispered to her guest, "It's Kelley."

"Tell her I say 'hi,'" Gayle gave a wave as though Kelley might see it.

"Gayle says 'hi,'" Rose repeated, even adding the wave as it would have seemed rude not to, then lowered the mouthpiece again. "Kelley says 'hi back' and…"

Rose felt the folds around her eyes furrow as she tried to concentrate on everything Kelley wanted passed along. "Slow down a bit, honey, I—" She sighed and extended the phone to

Gayle. "She'd rather just tell you herself."

"Me?" Gayle buried one immaculately manicured fingernail into the folds of a sheer silk scarf thrown casually—with intricate care—around her neck. "What would Kelley have to say to me?"

Rose shrugged and waggled the receiver in Gayle's direction.

"Well, I—" Gayle gave a flourish with her hand, perhaps hoping to magically conjure the perfect response from thin air. When none came, she extended that hand toward Rose to take the portable phone.

As Rose laid the heavy black phone in her palm, she noticed that Gayle's nail polish was actually chipped and cracked at the tips. On anyone else she would have thought nothing of it. She'd attribute it to some last-minute gardening impulse or a rushed schedule that prohibited flawless grooming or, in some women, even an oversight or lack of concern. But Gayle? Even this kind of tiny chink in her veneer was not only highly uncharacteristic, it was downright disturbing. It was like finding a tiny thread loose on an exquisite designer gown and wondering if it was just a stray snippet or the foretelling of something about to come unraveled at the seams.

Rose had known Gayle most of Gayle's thirty-nine years. Not being contemporaries, she did not consider her a friend, but more a fixture, a part of her life she pretty much took for granted. When Gayle was a teenager, she had baby-sat both Rose's girls. They'd worked side by side on various bake sales and charity projects in the last fifteen years or so. After Rose's falling out with the new Baptist minister, it was Gayle's father, now retired from the Methodist pulpit three years, who had officiated at Curry's funeral.

And if there was one thing she'd learned about Gayle Shorter Barrett, it was that the woman was always—*always,* mind you—perfectly put together and perfectly in control.

Rose pulled her own hand slowly away from the receiver, dipped her head toward it and, with more curious concern for Gayle than for Kelley, said, "Tell her I'll talk to her before graduation...and that I love her."

Gayle nodded.

"I have to check on the...things..." Rose gave a hapless gesture toward the kitchen. "You know, before the meeting."

Rose blotted out the buzz of Gayle's one-sided conversation by puttering around the kitchen. She opened cabinets, then drawers, all without having to take more than a few steps in either direction in the cramped quarters.

She and Curry had bought this house because of its desirable location, architectural soundness, and prize-winning landscaping—the gem of which was a walled garden that Rose maintained with the untiring help of Boatwright Nursery. The size of the kitchen—in fact, the size or comfort or livability of any room—had never been a consideration to Curry. He'd loved this place, the prestige of it, the spirit that Rose and the girls had infused in it. He'd loved it and insisted they keep it even when Kelley had moved off to college and it seemed far too much house for the two of them.

He had promised her that she'd feel different when the place was filled with the sights and sounds of kids and grandkids laughing over holiday meals and gathered 'round the Christmas tree. They'd have grand affairs here, he'd said, Fourth of July picnics and an elegant New Year's eve party. And guests! Without children underfoot they could invite distant cousins and old school chums to come and stay and stay. So he'd promised.

Why did it happen this way, Lord? Why was that man so stubborn he didn't let me know how serious his condition was? Why did he let me think it was just a routine bit of surgery?

Rose opened a cabinet, then banged it shut again. Now she was stuck in a two-story, turn-of-the-century showcase house. Stuck with a kitchen too small to become the kind of warm hub of friendship she'd always longed for. Stuck with a monstrosity of hallways and tiny dark rooms that only served to remind her how empty her life had become.

"Your little girl is worried about you, Rommy."

Rose jumped at the intrusion of Gayle's gentle voice.

"Rommy," Gayle repeated, something wistful in her tone. "I'd forgotten your girls called you that. Oh, and so did Mr. Holcolmb."

"Yes, well…" Rose forced a smile. *Rommy*. Curry had dubbed her that when she had flailed against the idea of her own husband calling her "Mama" after the birth of their first baby. Curry's solution—to combine her name and the sweet title of Mommy—had been offered in utmost respect and kind affection. How she had thrilled to hear the endearment on the lips of her loved ones. *Had* thrilled.

Lately, Rose had begun to realize how the intertwining of her name with her role as mother had forever fixed her as a single identity in Curry's mind, as well as in her own. Another cruel reminder of all she had lost these last few years as the children moved away and no longer needed their Rommy to nurture and guide them.

"Anyway, Kelley asked me to look out for you. She has the wild idea that you're lonely here and likely to do something—" Gayle cocked an eyebrow and drew in her cheeks to underscore her mocking of the seriousness of Kelley's anxiety, then concluded in a husky drawl—"rash."

"She needn't worry herself over *that*."

"I didn't think—"

"Because I already have."

"Have what?"

"Why, done something rash, of course, Gayle-y Girl."

"You have?" Gayle batted her just-sparse-enough-to-pass-for-real false eyelashes. "Why, whatever rash thing have you done, Rose?"

"I joined the prayer group, didn't I?" Before Gayle could refute or question that, Rose turned away and began riffling through the silver drawer. "And on that very subject, you certainly are here early for the first meeting."

"I wanted to see if there was anything I could do to help you get ready." She said it so fast the words almost collided and tumbled over one another.

"Oh?" Rose pulled free four long, elegant iced tea spoons, and pivoted to face Gayle. "Is that so?"

"Well, partly." She gave out a long sigh that did not relieve one iota of the steel and starch in her body. "See, my youngest had a play date, and the middle one had a ball game across town. The oldest is spending the evening stuffing little colored squares of tissue paper into chicken wire up at the high school—she's head of the junior prom decorating committee and no one else has the vision and commitment to do it right—"

"Like mother like daughter." Rose lifted the silver spoons in a kind of salute to prevent the remark from seeming mean-spirited.

"Lord help her, I hope not," Gayle muttered through clenched teeth as she slumped into a straight-backed kitchen chair.

Rose opened her mouth to question the off-handed declaration but Gayle rallied, pulling herself up to charm-school-graduate posture and going on.

"The point is that my kids are scattered to the four corners

79

of New Bethany, and once I had them all neatly delivered and arrangements in place for their safe return, it was already so late that I just couldn't go home."

"Couldn't?" Rose set the spoons down with a gentle tapping on the table.

Gayle did not answer right away but placed both hands at her temples and pushed her fingers back through her hairline.

Rose had never thought of Gayle as looking any older than she had when she'd taken care of the girls—until this moment. With the added lift to her face from her fingertips, Rose saw for one fleeting moment the young, vibrant woman Gayle had once been.

Then Gayle winced, took away her hands, and fixed her leaden gaze out the window. "Couldn't. Wouldn't. Didn't. I'm here now, a bit early, but here." She turned to Rose, her smile tight but sincere. "Now, tell me, what can I do to help you get ready?"

Rose thought of telling her to just sit and do nothing for a change, but the niggling mix of fear and anxious energy in Gayle's demeanor made Rose think that was the worst possible idea.

"I already have a big pitcher of tea chilling in the icebox, but if you like you can slice lemons and then go into the garden and pick some fresh mint for a garnish. By that time the other ladies should have joined us."

"One pecan-turtle brownie crust, chocolate-swirl cheesecake ice-cream pie." Naomi repeated the lengthy order just as Lucy had told it to her over the car phone moments earlier.

Naomi had, in fact, been chanting the order like a mantra with every step from the parking lot to the counter of the white brick eatery, complete with a huge picture window and gleaming chrome. She'd added a good ten miles and endless minutes to her premeeting errands trying to collect the exact refreshments and supplies she'd promised. Heaven help her if she'd withstood roadwork that detoured way out to Old Seminole Park Cemetery Road, then braved the incongruous odors of live bait, diesel fuel, spit cups, and overbrimming bins of fresh produce at the Dixie Dazzler Party Mart only to pick up the wrong dessert at Ray's Bob's Cone and Coney King.

"Pecan-turtle brownie crust, chocolate-swirl cheesecake ice-cream pie," Naomi whispered again, ticking off each component of the supposed delicacy on her fingers to check her recollection.

"With or without hot fudge?"

"Come again?" Naomi blinked, then blinked again. Lucy had given her the detailed list to order. *And* she'd told Naomi to ask for Ray so she'd get a substantial discount. But she had never mentioned *anything* about hot fudge.

Naomi thought to call Lucy and ask again, but that would mean a trip to the car to use the cell phone, which wouldn't do any good anyway. Even as they'd spoken minutes ago, Lucy was expecting the newest day-care worker, who'd taken the afternoon off to wait for the cable man, to show up momentarily and claim her daughter from Lucy's care. Then Lucy would be off to Rose's.

What to do? What to do?

The teenager behind the counter rolled her eyes and gave Naomi a look that left no doubt that the child thought she was witnessing the first stages of senility. The girl raised her voice to enunciate each word as if that might help Naomi comprehend and thereby come to a quicker decision. "*With* or with*out*—"

"You'd better get it with." The deep, lazy drawl—which put Naomi in mind of warm honey and melted butter—had a strange prickling effect on her frazzled nerves.

She made a smart, sharp turn the entire aim of which would convey her pique with the meddlesome intruder without so much as a sound from her lips. But a sound did slip from them. A tiny, gasping "oh" came up like a hiccup and left her mouth in an astonished, rounded pout as she stared straight into the eyes of the man from the grove.

"Take my word for it, ma'am, get the hot fudge. No sense giving the ladies any other reasons to hold something against you."

"The ladies?" She narrowed her eyes, her heart pumping hard at the realization that this man might know the nature of her errand.

"The ladies from the prayer group, ma'am." His smile came slow and easy, as though it poured out rich and irresistible from some wellspring deep inside the man. "First meeting's tonight, isn't it?"

"I…uh…um…yes. Uh-huh."

"Thought so." He gave a knowing nod. "Now, I can't speak for the others, but I do know that Ms. Rose Tancy Holcolmb does like her chocolate. Chocolate and white roses. Curry used to cart them home to her every anniversary and after every spat. Heard a time or two of the roses taking flight right into the old man's face, but never once has it been said that she refused the chocolate."

Naomi shook her head, her eyes downcast in disgust. New Bethany. She'd forgotten how claustrophobic life here could be with everyone knowing about everyone else's business and feeling free to wade knee-deep into it whenever the spirit so moved. She could not wait to get out of here—out of this town and more immediately out of this shop—without any further interference from well-intentioned strangers.

"With or without hot fudge?" The girl behind the counter shifted her boyish hips.

Naomi drew up her shoulders tight. Much as she longed to defy the busybody's recommendation, she could not ignore his good advice. Teeth on edge, she half-growled: "With."

"A pint on the side," he told the girl waiting on Naomi, indicating the proper size by the space between his hands.

A working man's hands, Naomi noted, trying to avoid acknowledging him with eye contact. Short, clean nails that she suspected didn't stay clean during the course of a day and long, supple fingers that could fit around a tool or stroke a woman's hair with equal confidence.

Metal clacked on metal as the store clerk flipped open the lid of a well-like container beneath the sneeze guard. With a Styrofoam cup waiting in one hand, the girl plunged a stainless-steel ladle into the steaming brown liquid. The stinging cold of the air-conditioned room filled instantly with the aroma of chocolate fudge.

Naomi inhaled until her toes curled against the leather of her sandals. Her thoughts and the day's tensions might have just up and drifted away right then and there—detour, decisions, nearby disconcerting man and all—if she could have just made herself ignore the gnawing of her upbringing. But she couldn't.

As she watched the glistening ribbon of chocolate fold and disappear into a pool inside the cup, she had to admit he was right. Bringing the extra fudge on the side would set well with the other women, even if they didn't indulge in it. It was the kind of thoughtful gesture that made life more pleasant, and she owed the man a thank-you for suggesting it.

Her cheeks ached around the controlled lift of her lips. She twisted her head to the side and, completely in profile, gave him a nod of thanks, relenting to civility in the very last moment to finish the gesture with a flashing, sidelong glance.

His eyes were blue. Carolina blue, like the Southern summer sky, and uncommonly beautiful in that way of a ruggedly masculine man with a single softening—almost feminine—feature. Deep creases lined his tanned cheek, more so on the left side of his face than the right. His lips twitched. Either the man was going to speak or smile or…well, she didn't know what else.

Like a partner drawn into a dance of glances and unspoken thoughts, hinting—never broadcasting—at the undercurrent suddenly sprung to life between them, she ventured a tentative, closed-mouth smile.

He dipped his squared chin, his eyelids became heavy hoods over those unwavering blue eyes as if to say, "I'm looking you over and I like what I see."

She angled her own chin up. *Oh, there's so much more to me than you can see.*

He dragged one callused thumb down his jawline. *So, you're a woman of depth.*

She ruffled her short nails through her feathery bangs. *That's the kind of thing a man would have to discern for himself.*

His gaze burned a bit too long in hers. *Is that an invitation?*

She folded her arms and cocked her head. *Could be, then again…*

"Will that be all, lady?" The sales clerk clunked down a thin cardboard-and-cellophane box next to the pint cup of hot fudge.

"Wha—?" Naomi felt awakened from a trance.

"Will that be all?" the girl repeated.

Heat flooded Naomi's cheeks, chin, even the tip of her nose and the rims of her ears as she thought of her blatant, uncharacteristic, come-hither behavior with this strange man. "That will be *quite* enough, yes, thank you."

Naomi put her back to the man, still vividly aware of his presence, of his eyes on her, of the assured smile stretched in idle amusement over his face.

The clerk stabbed absently at the keys of the cash register, then quoted the price.

Naomi fumbled with her wallet. She'd budgeted carefully to afford her extended leave of absence from her pottery business. Extravagances such as ridiculously rich desserts for four certainly did not fit into that budget. She weighed that reality against the certainty that the man she had flirted with so openly was now listening with interest to her conversation. The very notion of his nearness, of his likely curiosity about her, made her squirm.

Asking for Ray and going through the process of explaining herself and obtaining the discount would only prolong her discomfort. Yet, while one part of her wanted simply to pay the bill and slip away with the shred of dignity she still possessed, the pragmatic side of her held firm. She cleared her throat. "May I ask if Ray is here? That is—perhaps I should have mentioned this earlier—but Lucy Jewell told me to speak to Ray about a—"

"You're a friend of Lucy's?"

"I know her, yes."

The clerk staggered backward a step, her face screwed into a look of patronizing disbelief. "Listen, lady, I don't know why you want Ray, but I need this job and I don't see no way to keep it if I go telling some friend of Lucy's what he's up to right now."

"Oh?"

The gentleman behind her cleared his throat. Loudly.

Naomi decided in that split second that he *was* a gentleman. Only someone raised properly would have had the fine manners to feign choking in order to appear not to have heard something as private and awkward as the clerk's remark.

"Well, I—" Naomi gave a bit of a cough herself. "That is, it's not important. I'll just pay my bill then."

She dipped her fingers into her wallet and withdrew a crisp bill, following it with some disappointment until it disappeared inside the cash drawer. She held her hand out to cup the handful of coins she got in return. They made a sad sort of jingling as they slid into her empty change purse, Naomi thought, not so much in relation to the lost discount as to Lucy and what the clerk had said.

Naomi did not know Ray—or Lucy, for that matter—and she knew better than to draw any conclusions from some young girl's inferences. Still, her experiences with men, and something about the way Lucy wore her vulnerability like a fresh bruise that she refused to acknowledge, made Naomi worry. It didn't take a genius to figure out what Ray was up to that he would want to hide from Lucy. Most likely it was *not* anonymous charity work.

She bent at the knees to cradle the chilled pie box in her arms, then reached for the hot fudge.

"Here, let me."

The sudden coolness constricting Naomi's chest had more to do with the reemergence of common sense than the frozen delicacy pressed to her body. "I can manage fine on my own, thank you."

"But I'd like to—"

"I can well imagine what you'd like, sir." She swept past him, her head high. "And I'm telling you now, I am not interested."

He laughed. A chuckle really, one of those under-the-breath chuckles, all husky intimacy and pure humor that tweaked at her already agitated state.

To his credit, he did not try to wrest the pie box, nor the fudge perched precariously on top of it, from her. He did—also to his credit—however, step lively. Seconds before she reached it, he pushed open the shop's door with one hand, his fingers splayed to provide the needed oomph to swing the door wide enough to let her whisk by without even their shirtsleeves touching.

"You enjoy that, now, you hear?" he called after her, a hint of mirth lingering in his tone.

"Oh, I'll enjoy it all right," she kept her tone frosty and formal so as not to give him any foresight as to her parting shot. "I'll enjoy it just as much as you seem to have enjoyed badgering me just now with your uninvited advice and presumptuous behavior couched as polite helpfulness."

"Ah," his voice trailed after her, "then you will enjoy it a great deal, I'd venture. A great deal, indeed."

He was laughing at her and she didn't have to see him to know it. Still, she walked on, her forgotten belle-ish tendencies welling up within her like Scarlett with her fist raised to the fiery skies. How *dare* he? Why, who did he think he was?

The brilliant sun glinted off the windshields and bumpers of the row of cars parked in front of the Cone and Coney, obscuring her view of anything but her own nondescript blue compact. She popped open the passenger side door, intent on nestling the pie and fudge in the seat, wedging them in with the sack of napkins and paper plates. She was late as it was and exasperated to boot.

Rattled. That was the word for it, she corrected in silence as she fit the fudge cup into the built-in drink holder between the bucket seats. She felt rattled and flustered and…excited. And all over a man she'd never met before and would probably never see again.

A man, she scolded herself. Of all the things to let rattle her! She wasn't some doe-eyed darling to have her head turned even by a man with strong hands, a gentleman's demeanor, and compelling eyes. Nor was she some anxious female hoping for a man's attention to make her feel good about herself. She wasn't someone who needed a man to show everyone that she was a person of merit, to validate her worth as it were. She wasn't Lucy, for goodness sake.

A sudden flash of shame at her one-dimensional summation of a girl she hardly knew made Naomi hang her head as she slammed the car door. That man had made her do it, she decided, he'd…well, he'd just plain rattled her.

"Men," she muttered, coming around the back of her car to the driver's side. "Can't live with the decent ones, can't seem to go more than a few feet without running into a rotten one."

"Oh, Raymond, really!" A giggle bubbled up from somewhere behind her in the lot.

If Naomi had to attach a description to that giggle it would be 'blonde.' Something from a male-fantasy-beach-bimbo-movie blonde, to be exact. And it had wrapped itself around the one name she wished she had slipped away without hearing. In fact, she determined to try to do just that before she heard anything further.

"Now, stop, Ray. I mean it. I have to get going."

"You've already got me going," a man's voice replied.

More giggling.

Naomi's stomach roiled. The clerk's conjecture, the fact that this was the business owned by Lucy's boyfriend, and the man's name purred out again and again allowed Naomi little room for denial. She yanked open her car door, her gaze fixed forward so she couldn't, even by accident, confirm her suspicions.

Confirm them how? the thought suddenly sprang to mind. She wouldn't know Ray from Adam—or from Bob, the former owner of the Cone and Coney King, for that matter. For all she knew, this was an entirely different Ray. Even if it was Lucy's Ray, perhaps the interchange was entirely innocent or had a reasonable explanation beyond the obvious. She'd heard nothing to prove otherwise.

Her anxiety assuaged, she sighed and eased herself into the driver's seat, confident that she had overheard nothing but circumstantial evidence, nothing to concern her or Lucy. Just a woman using a very common name, no reason to connect it to her fellow participant in the prayer circle, no proof of that at—

"Now, Ray, you've got to get back inside to your business, and I have to go pick up Tiffany Crystal. If I'm too late, Lucy won't baby-sit for her anymore, and then I can't sneak off and spend time with you no more. And you know what that means."

Naomi did not *want* to know what that meant. She slammed her car door, gouged the key into place, and started the engine revving. She was late, she was rattled, and now—through no fault of her own—she was privy to something that could crush the fragile heart of a woman with whom she'd pledged to spend a year in spiritual unity and mutual support.

Now if that wasn't a fitting welcome home to New Bethany, she didn't know what was.

ix

"N̲o one said for sure, so as an added precaution, I picked up a half-pint of hot fudge on the side, you know, just in case someone wanted it." Naomi handed the heavy white cup to Rose, who accepted it as though it were brimming with liquid gold.

"Hot fudge?" Gayle clucked her tongue before she could stop herself from acting like a total prissy-pants. She crossed her arms. "Hot fudge on top of ice cream, brownies with pecans, and what have you? Seems a bit…excessive, doesn't it?"

Excessive. On the word, Gayle imparted a look that figuratively jabbed an accusing finger at Naomi. Gayle took in Naomi's appearance: unruly hair, a rayon skirt that flapped about her ankles yet was slit to above her knees, and those sandals. In spring, yet, sandals. Gayle set her jaw.

Naomi *was* excessive—in her appearance, her personality, even her presence in this group. Excess, as in excess baggage, and Gayle had no intention of letting her forget it.

Rose, on the other hand…

"Ummm." Rose sniffed the chocolate-laced air, her eyes shut in a display of pure ecstasy. "What a thoughtful thing to do, Naomi. You come right on in this house and set yourself down. We're so glad to have you."

"Thank you, Rose." Naomi wound her way through the kitchen, the pie box held up high in both hands until she could place it dead center on the round oak table. "I heard how much you like chocolate—"

"You did?" Rose placed the hot fudge just so beside the pie box. "From whom?"

"Well, from…" Naomi cleared her throat. She fumbled with the braided scarves wound around her waist.

So, Naomi Beauchamp could be flustered, Gayle noted with piqued surprise. But by what? Who could Naomi have spoken to that it made her cheeks tinge at the mere mention of it? That might be something worth knowing.

"Yes, Naomi, tell us, whom have you been talking to about Rose and her…culinary vices?"

"Oh, really, Gayle. It wasn't as though I was gossiping or *trying* to gather dirt on Rose. Or on any member of the group, for that matter."

Gayle stiffened.

"A total stranger standing behind me at the Cone and Coney King simply mentioned that they knew Rose liked chocolate. And so I thought it might be a *welcome* addition to the evening's refreshments."

"Oh, it will be an addition all right," Gayle said, ignoring the sarcastic emphasis on the word *welcome* to keep Naomi from ingratiating herself too much to their hostess. Pointing appropriately, she concluded, "An addition to the hips, thighs, and tummy. Why even bother eating the stuff? In the spirit of efficiency, I should just slather my whole backside in hot fudge."

"Why, Gayle." Naomi's eyebrows raised in mock shock as she chided, "I only brought a half-pint, but if it will make you happy, be my guest."

Gayle's jaw dropped.

"Oh, no you don't! That would be a waste of good chocolate." Rose plunked herself down at the table.

Naomi laughed above the squawking scrape of the chair she

pulled back before she sat directly beside Gayle.

Gayle saw the humor in it, she really did, and if anyone else in the entire world had settled next to her at the kitchen table tonight she would have joined in the joke. Instead she folded her hands on top of the table and looked at the Proverbs-in-Daily-Life, two-year calendar tacked to Rose's kitchen wall.

The month's verse stared back at her. Proverbs 15:1: "A gentle answer turns away wrath."

"My point is," she said, "I simply can't eat chocolate and keep my weight under control."

"And everyone knows there mustn't be a thing about you that isn't under control." The warmth of Naomi's smile made the dig seem almost friendly.

"I read once that chocolate contains the same chemicals your body produces when you fall in love." Rose snatched up a teaspoon, pointing the rounded tip of it toward the container she had placed on the table.

"There is something almost heady about it, isn't there?" Naomi, too, picked up a spoon.

Clearly, they intended to steal a taste of the topping any moment now.

"My word," Gayle said. "You two wouldn't! You're not going to spoon yourselves up some of that straight from the container, are you?"

Naomi waved her spoon with an arrogant flare. "Why not? Whether we have it alone now or on top of our pie, it all gets mixed up in our tummies by and by."

"I don't believe it."

"Believe it." Naomi copied Gayle's quiet intensity, then brightened. "It's a simple fact of biology."

Gayle started to clarify that she did not believe their actions, but Naomi knew that already, so Gayle set her face in what she hoped depicted wry observation. "It's also a fact of biology that unnecessary calories turn to body fat."

"I don't see how one little dollop of creamy, rich, melted chocolate would do any harm." Naomi feigned checking her reflection in the gleaming bowl of the silver spoon. "Besides, we all look like we could use the sugar rush before we get started."

"Naomi's right, Gayle. I, for one, could use that energy surge. You really should join us in our indulgence. After all, for we women, chocolate is the *high* that binds."

"That makes our *clothes* bind," Gayle corrected.

"Rose is right, Gayle. What playing sports and high-fiving one another is to men, what becoming blood brothers is to little boys, that's what sharing chocolate over the kitchen table is to women."

"You mean a ridiculous act of immaturity?" Gayle cocked her head.

"It's a bonding thing, Gayle," Naomi said.

"So is rubber cement, but I don't want *that* on my dessert, either."

"Yes, well, rubber cement never smelled like this." Rose lifted the lid to the container and fanned a damp curl of steam in Gayle's direction.

It did smell like heaven—deep, dark, coat-your-tongue-with-sweetest-pleasure heaven. And the ladies did have a point. Sharing something so wonderful and almost decadent and, well, out of the everyday, with these women would probably make them all feel closer. What a noticeable advantage to a newcomer like Naomi. The last thought shut down any leaning Gayle might have had toward the idea.

"Your attempts to provoke me are not going to work today,

Naomi," Gayle warned. She tipped her nose up. "I won't be bribed by chocolate."

"Aw, you're just an old stick-in-the-fudge, Gayle." Rose wagged one finger, then finished up her sham of a scolding with a wink. "But we love you anyway."

"And you don't know what a comfort that knowledge is to me, Rose." Gayle rolled her eyes in an exaggerated way to underscore her droll delivery.

Both Rose and Naomi laughed, as she had hoped they would, then Rose said, "Guess we'll have to make do with some nice, cold, sweet tea instead, then. Can I bribe you with a glass of that, Gayle?"

"I'd be obliged, thank you."

In an economy of movement, Rose gathered the ice from the ice bucket and dropped it from ornate silver tongs with a melodic *clink, clink, clink* into tall, slim glasses. The tea sluiced over the crystal clear cubes causing them to pop and crackle. That they would all take a lemon wedge seemed taken for granted, but Rose did pause to wave a mint sprig like some delicate temptation and get their approval before spearing it into the mixture.

She sat the glasses in front of each of them before sitting down again. They all took a long, refreshing sip and cooed their compliments over the drink before anyone spoke again.

"Ah, well. So much for enticing Gayle into the Sisterhood of Sugarhips." Naomi pushed the lid back down on the fudge container. "Maybe we'll have better luck with Lucy."

Upon saying the fourth in their group's name, Naomi tensed, her smooth cheek ticked as if catching a scowl half formed and subduing it. She narrowed her eyes. Her brows, with a natural arch that even without careful waxing and sculpting looked quite dramatic, crimped downward.

For the first time, Gayle saw signs of the passing years on Naomi's face in the tiny tucks and puckers along her lipline as she whispered, "Where is Miss Lucy anyway?"

"Late." Rose sighed, fingering the pie box.

"As usual," Gayle spoke out what she and Rose had both been thinking.

"Yes." Rose raised her hands in resignation, her eyes shut. "She'll pop in anytime now, agitated as a hummingbird in a windstorm, all apologies and excuses. Some child's parent didn't show up or she had to do this or that for her mother—"

"And don't forget Ray." Gayle hit his name hard and harsh, but she suspected that the name itself and not her spin on it made Naomi's knee go to jiggling under the table. "There's always some excuse involving Ray."

The thumping beneath the table became more pronounced.

"That *man*." Rose shook her head. "If I were Lucy…well, as I used to tell my Curry, if I ever caught him being unfaithful to me, I'd apply my boot to his posterior so forcefully he'd be wearing his boxers for a party hat."

"And I'll bet you said it just like that." Gayle couldn't help but grin at the woman she'd known most of her life.

"You'd lose that bet," Rose muttered, lifting her tea glass but not drinking from it. "When I said it to Curry I did not mince words. But here with company…well, I was just trying to be gracious."

"And that's exactly what I thought, Rose," Naomi assured her with a pat on the hand. "Gracious!"

Gayle snickered at Naomi's contribution despite herself.

Then the three of them fell into awkward silence.

Rose raised her glass again, cocking it to the left and then to the right until the ice tumbled over itself and clattered against the side.

Gayle watched the fine gray mesh framed by Rose's ornate wooden screen door, waiting for Lucy's round face to appear so they could get on with the night's business.

Naomi toyed with her bangs.

Rose tapped her long teaspoon against the rim of her glass. "Yep. Uh-huh. If I was Lucy, that's just what I'd do. I certainly wouldn't take what she does from any man. And certainly not that Raymond Griggs."

The nervous tapping from under the table resumed, faster and faster like a raging heartbeat. *Thumpity-thumpity-thumpity-thump-thump*.

"No, me neither," Gayle murmured, testing her theory that Naomi's jitters had some direct connection to the mention of Lucy's boyfriend. "If she had a stronger sense of self-esteem, she'd rid herself once and for all of that Ray."

Thumpity-thumpity-thud. Naomi slapped both palms down on the tabletop. "It's a known fact, then?"

"What?" Rose sipped at her tea.

"This Ray. That he…" she broke off, then started again. "Everybody knows, right?"

"I can't speak for everybody." Gayle leaned back in her chair, a slow foreboding welling within her over her own tactics to discover what had Naomi so skittish. "But it does seem that *you* know something."

"I *saw* something."

Gayle stretched her back up taut and proper.

"Or…or rather *heard* something." Naomi's leg started at it again. "At the Cone and Coney King. I…" She looked off through the huge arched doorway to her left and into Rose's dimly lit living room. "I didn't want to overhear, but now I have."

Rose shot Gayle a look.

"And I didn't know if I should keep my peace, it's really none of my business, after all. But then…"

Secrets. Gayle alone fully appreciated what Naomi could not bring herself to ask outright: should she keep this secret from and about her fellow member of the prayer circle? She wanted Rose and, in an act of more poignant irony, Gayle herself to tell her what to do.

Too late Gayle wished she'd never let the conversation go this way. She pushed down a heavy knot in her throat with a painful swallow. Why hadn't she chatted stupidly on about the tea or the weather or even eaten a mouthful of that calorie-laden fudge? Anything but to have to deal with this now.

Feeling alternately confused, frightened, and numb—feelings that had grown far too familiar these last few weeks—she was in no frame of mind for this. It seemed to Gayle that lately she'd struggled almost daily to keep the well-oiled machinery of her life whirring without spinning out of control. Now the prayer group and Naomi's return had only added to the sense of impending chaos.

Why hadn't she insisted that Naomi not be brought into their circle, or even resigned from participating herself when the women made clear they would accept the woman who had been gone for so long? She wrung her hands. If she had had the good sense to walk away from the group then, she would not be sitting here wondering when her own secrets would surface. Would she, as Lucy did, inspire pity from others? Or scorn? Or worse?

Well, she *hadn't* resigned, she told herself in a kind of mental slap worthy of a proud Southern heroine. And now Naomi was staring at her, waiting for her advice. Gayle had to do something, say something.

In her heart, she thought that Lucy, though not she and Rose, had a right to know about whatever Naomi had seen or heard. But for herself, she wanted nothing more than to protect her own shame, the extent of which only Naomi and one other person knew. She did not want her secrets brought to light even between Naomi and herself.

That, of course, is exactly what she had to do, she realized as she tucked a stiff strand of hair behind her ear. She had to meet with Naomi. That decision colored her tone as she crossed her legs and folded her hands in her lap.

"It's none of our business, Naomi, what Raymond Griggs does or how Lucy Jewell chooses to deal with it. I wouldn't be surprised, though, if she had her own suspicions already. That doesn't mean anyone has the right to throw it in her face." Gayle wet her lips, then went on. "However, if she were ever to come to you with those suspicions, to ask you outright what you thought or even to plead with you for your silence on the matter…"

Gayle stopped to take a breath and the look that passed between her and her one-time best friend confirmed that they were not only talking about Lucy and Ray anymore.

"Then I'd do whatever she wished in the matter, Gayle. Whether that might be—to speak the truth or to say nothing at all."

Gayle wanted to whisper a thank you, but knew it would have to wait until she and Naomi were alone and they could speak in earnest about everything that stood between them.

Rose eyed Gayle and Naomi with interest. Whatever history these two shared, it wasn't resolved. Not by a long shot. And this business with Ray only seemed to have stirred it up.

She opened her mouth to add her thoughts on the issue, but a thunderous crash on the back porch stunned them all into silence.

"I've dropped my…" Lucy's blonde head bobbed up then down again at the back door. Then she stood and beamed a pink-cheeked smile, her nose pressed to the screen, one hand shading her eyes so she could peer inside. "Oh, well, I'm here now. I'm here."

"Come in already then," Gayle called out.

No doubt Gayle's impatience with Lucy, mixed with the same guilt Rose herself felt at having just been discussing the girl, made Gayle issue an invitation as though this were *her* house. Though Rose doubted Gayle would ever have been so curt in her own home.

"Yes, honey, come on in here," Rose said, motioning Lucy into action.

The screen creaked. Lucy shuffled inside. The door banged shut. Her huge handbag fell to the glossy vinyl floor with a *whomp*. She blew out a long, silent whistle.

"Sorry to be late. The girl I hired, Nikki—that's her name—took the afternoon off to wait for the cable man. Of course he came at the very last minute and then didn't have the right tool or connectors or something and—" Her hands beat back and forth like two flashing fishtails, as if she could whisk away the conclusion to that sentence and any other conclusions likely to be drawn. "Anyway, I'm here now. Hope you didn't start without me."

"Course not, darling, you come and sit yourself down."

Rose stood and pulled out a chair. She hurried to the counter, having to wedge herself behind a chair to reach it in the close quarters. Then the smooth, cool handle of her grandmother's etched crystal pitcher filled her warm palm. "Tea?"

"Please." Lucy sort of slopped into her chair.

While Rose poured the tea into the fourth glass, it dawned on her that in all the days leading up to it—and even as she prepared her home today—she had not wasted a solitary ounce of worry over this meeting. Not until this precise moment. Now, having all of the women here sitting in her kitchen poised, as one might say, on the precipice, a nervous quiver began in the pit of her stomach.

This was it. For years she had formed very definite opinions about the prayer circles, opinions which had run the gamut from admiration in the beginning to scorn these later years. She'd spoken against the very notion of continuing the circles, given what they had become. In her grief over her husband's death, she had even ridiculed the circle that had reached out to help her.

Now she'd hung her hope on this final circle, this small gathering of practical strangers. What if it didn't work? What if it all fell apart and didn't even make it through the year intact? Or worse, if they did make it through but it didn't change anything? What if it effected no one in New Bethany? What if, this time next year, Rose still felt empty and lost and longing for something she could not articulate?

Heavenly Father, don't let that happen. Don't let what we start today end in disappointment.

She lifted the lid from the ice bucket, and the swirling cold inside nipped at her fingertips. She shivered, but not from the chill.

"Will you have some mint in your tea, Lucy?" Her words

sounded dry and scratchy even to her own ears.

"If it's no trouble."

Rose pinched up a sprig, the fragrant mint making her nose twitch as she considered Lucy's predictable comment. Poor Lucy. She needed the support and foundation of prayer and friendship this group could provide. She needed it every bit as much, perhaps more, than Rose did.

She set the glass down before Lucy and, giving the girl's round shoulders a maternal squeeze, whispered, "No trouble at all, dear. If you need anything else don't be afraid to ask, you hear?"

Lucy mumbled her thanks through a watery smile.

"And Gayle? Naomi?" Rose clasped her hands with a soft clap. "What will it be for you?"

Refuge from whatever has your picture-perfect life out of focus, Gayle? A friend, Naomi? "More tea?"

As Rose refilled the glasses, she renewed the vow she had made to herself after her husband's death: this last prayer circle would succeed. It would be returned to its original intent to serve others, praise God, and replenish the spirits of those who participated.

O God, please, let it be so.

"Now," she said as she drew her chair up to the table. "Let's decide how we can all pitch in to make this thing work. Naomi has agreed to care for the tree—"

"Have you contacted Taylor Boatwright about that yet?" Gayle dove one hand into her designer purse to withdraw a matching leather datebook, well used and held shut with an ornate silver snap.

"No, I'm embarrassed to say I haven't," Naomi admitted. "I've been…distracted."

"Well, no matter. You can go tomorrow." The snap on

Gayle's book made a crisp pop. "If not then perhaps early next week. Mornings are best, but weekends are far too hectic. Now, you do know where the nursery is, don't you?"

"Well, I—"

"It's way out Old Seminole Cemetery Road, about a mile past the West Harding turnoff. That's the back way to Ray's store." Lucy paused to caress the corner of the pie box with the *Ray's Bob's Cone and Coney King* label.

Rose could feel the other women tense. She held her breath and knew they did the same as they waited for Lucy to ask about the man.

I hope it's not a sin to ask this, Lord, but could you please keep Lucy from talking about Ray? The last thing they needed to have to deal with today was even a hint of Naomi's discovery. Not now—not with things so new and fragile between them. Rose dabbed a napkin at the beaded water trickling down her tea glass.

"Anyway, don't take West Harding," Lucy went on, seemingly unaware of the wave of relief that washed over her companions at the direction of the conversation. "Go on about a quarter mile and you'll see the white-and-green sign for Boatwright's Nursery, big as day."

"Ask for Taylor," Gayle instructed. The leather of her appointment book crackled as she pushed the spine down flat. "He'll know what to do."

"So, now that that is settled, we'll need a secretary." Rose rushed in to help defray the discussion from any further mention of Ray. "As I see it, Naomi's doing her part with the tree, so—"

"I'll do it." Lucy's overture lacked a certain enthusiasm. It sounded, in fact, like someone surrendering to the inevitable, only lacking the "if nobody else will" to make it ring of stoic, downtrodden self-sacrifice.

Rose swatted away Lucy's offer with good humor, seizing the chance to shore up the girl's wobbling self-esteem in the bargain. "You, of all people, shouldn't get stuck with this, Lucy. Why, a savvy, hard-working, independent businesswoman like you has so many other things to deal with in the course of her day—"

"I do?" She kind of perked up.

"Yes, you do. Of course, you do," Rose assured her, gushing a bit. "But I was thinking that since the meetings are already being held at *my* house and—"

"Say no more." Gayle slid the skinny black pen from its place in the book and began searching for a blank spot in the tiny crablike writing covering each compartmentalized day. "I've got this covered. I can do it."

"Oh, no." Rose laid her hand over both open pages in front of Gayle. "Honey, you have more than enough on your plate without heaping this on, too. Now, if you'd just hear me out."

Gayle gripped the pen with both hands, holding it like a safety bar in front of her.

"As I said, we're already meeting at my house, and it's the secretary's job to bring the prayer requests, to keep a journal of them for review, and to be a contact for the group. In the spirit of efficiency, I volunteer to act as secretary."

"But Rose, just having it at your house is enough," Naomi protested above the similar remarks by the others.

"Oh, pooh. What does that take? To open the screen door with a smile and have a pitcher of tea in the icebox? If I wasn't already doing that whenever the situation arose, I wouldn't be much of an example of fine Southern womanhood, now would I?" She gave them a wicked grin. "No, I'll be in charge of the prayer requests."

"If you really don't mind," Lucy ventured.

"I'll do it," Rose said more adamantly than before. "And I'll be *glad* to do it."

And to her own surprise, she actually meant that.

Seven

I don't care if it *is* the biggest pool party of summer, no staying out 'til all hours tonight, young lady. Church tomorrow." Gayle gripped the honey-colored wood of her handrubbed banister. It was not her style to "go a-hollerin' up the hillside" as her paternal grandmother might have put it. But if she did not shout her edicts up the staircase, she had little chance of getting her oldest child to hear them at all.

Her daughter's bedroom door whooshed open, as did the door to the upstairs guest bath, then they both slammed shut, like thunder coming down from the mountaintop.

"Mathina?" She used her child's legal first name instead of the more common nickname "Max," which Gayle abhorred, no doubt giving it more appeal to her headstrong firstborn. "Mathina, do you hear me?"

"Lighten up, Mom, we *all* hear you." Her middle child, twelve-year-old Nathan, brushed against her as he clomped his way up the stairs.

Tomorrow the boy would head off for a week of church camp. Gayle felt at once relieved to have one less responsibility around the house and guilty over that unmaternal emotion. Not that the lessened responsibility would last more than a few hours, as tomorrow her eight-year-old, Lillith, returned from her turn roughing it with the air-conditioned cottages, planned activities, and a canteen full of junk food from the Methodist camp in rural Tennessee.

Gayle felt the muscles of her face pinch. It was already mid-June. Where had the time gone?

"Are you packed for camp, mister?" she asked the back of Nathan's head, which was the only thing she seemed to see of him these days. "I laid out clean underpants and—"

"Mo-oom!" he groaned in the universal code for "How could you talk to me about underwear? I'm not a kid, you know."

"All right!" She threw up her hands. "But don't blame me if you get to camp and have to spend the whole week in the same pair of disgusting briefs."

"He's twelve." Ted, who had just rounded the corner to take her by surprise in the small, dim space at the foot of the stairs, murmured against the shell of her ear.

A shiver snaked down her back.

Ted's strong hands kneaded her knotted shoulders. "Even if Nathan had a truckload of clean underwear, he'd just as soon wear the same pair until they had to be peeled off him like skin from a rotten peach."

Gayle looked straight ahead. "Now there's a lovely image."

Ted laughed, his breath tickling the hairs at the nape of her neck. He planted a warm, tender kiss there. "I, on the other hand, am not only wearing fresh drawers, but they're red—"

"Shhh." She put one finger to her lips to hush him, and made a show of tripping her gaze down his pressed, tailor-fit jeans. "It's bad enough you've got those things on to start with, Ted. But you don't have to practically announce it to the entire world—"

"You may be *my* world, Gayle, but you're not exactly the entire world." He laughed again and locked his arms around her waist. "Besides, why act so shocked, sweet wife? They were a present from you—Christmas two years ago, if memory serves."

"As a joke," she whispered. "A joke."

"As I recall the card said—"

"Ted!" She pushed his arms from her and shifted to shoot him a scathing look. "Don't you dare repeat that out loud! And right here in the foyer, for goodness sake!"

"How about later?"

"I…uh…" Her knuckles went white as she curled her fingers closed over the finial. She felt her cheeks tinge with heat.

Ted chuckled and feigned a smarmy accent, teasing, "I love it when ze woo-man blushes in my arms, ma petite cherie."

Blush? Gayle swallowed. *Blush?* She supposed she should be relieved that Ted mistook her reaction for anything other than what it was: frustration and distress. "Ted, no. This isn't the time or place," she found the composure to murmur, looking away.

"No, but later," he persisted, "when Max is off at her party, and Nathan is holed-up in his room with his TV up loud *and* his headphones on…"

"Well, I'm not sure that—"

"What with Lily gone until tomorrow and the other kids occupied at least for a time, we can finally be alone." His green eyes held a starkness, devoid of any guile or blame, and in his frank expression she could see that after all their years together, this man still wanted her, still loved her and only her. "Being alone with you is something I've looked forward to for a long time, Gayle."

Ted's tenderness and devotion should have made her feel terrific. Cherished. Whole. But they did none of those things. They only served as a biting reminder of her own failures as his wife.

She had tried so hard for so long not to falter and disappoint the people she cared for—her husband, her children and extended family, even her friends and all the people around town who relied on her. She set a high standard for herself, it was true, but she had fallen far, far short of that standard for a very long time. Only by sheer determination and gargantuan effort had she hidden her shortcomings, but for how long?

It certainly couldn't last much longer. Especially not now, with Naomi back in town. Naomi knew the ugliest truth of Gayle's flawed nature, and any day now Gayle's attempts to keep a positive face on everything would simply fall apart.

"Oh, Ted," she whispered. The tears felt trapped behind her eyes, burning and straining but unable to flow free. In her heart she felt a void, a great emptiness where joy and love should have welled up. She did not deserve this good man's love or any of the wonderful things that came from it.

"What is it, sweetie?" He reached out to her.

She turned away from him and gripped the finial like an anchor in a wind-tossed sea. "I haven't exactly been fair to you lately in…in that department, have I?"

"It has been a long time, Gayle." He pulled her back against him, folding her into an embrace that warmed her body but did not ignite her passion. "It's been since—"

"I know how long it's been." She could count back to the exact date in which she had started to avoid her husband's romantic overtures. It was the day that Naomi had come back into town. "And I'm sorry. I'll try to do better."

"Starting tonight?"

"Yes." She slipped her hand back to caress his cheek.

His five o'clock shadow felt like fine sandpaper to her palm. She closed her eyes, envisioning his face, the angular planes, his pale lips, the distinguished laugh lines that fanned out toward his cheeks and temples. She could see as clear as if she met his gaze the sparkle in his eyes. She could picture his hair, a compelling sweep of boyishly wayward sandy brown waves.

She could picture, as well as feel against her back, the body owed to years of good diet and slavish devotion to a running and cycling program, and to tennis at the club instead of golf. Ted's conviction that caring for his health was one way of caring for his family had paid off in other dividends as well. He had the physique of a much younger man, something many women in their circle and at Ted's law firm saw fit to point out to her, telling her how lucky she was.

Gayle did not believe in luck but she did count her blessings, and Ted was at the top of her list. She did not want to do anything to risk losing him one moment before she had to.

If she had to.

She curved her fingers to brush her knuckles along his firm jawline. "Yes," she whispered again, wishing with all her being that genuine longing for her husband and not fear and shame had prompted the reply. "Yes, Ted, tonight. I'll try to make it all up to you."

"Nomi, I took that cobbler out of the freezer as soon as I heard. Should be ready for you to pop into the oven about now."

"Cobbler? Pop into the…?" Naomi looked up from the pile of frayed and forgotten bedsheets and pillowcases she had been sorting in Mama's dusty linen closet to find her mother's tiny frame looming over her.

"Get up, Nomi." Mama made a shooing motion with both hands. "Can't be lollygagging. Lots to get done and little time to do it. Take care of that cobbler first."

"Excuse me, Mama, but what cobbler? What are you—"

"The cobbler!" She shook her head, a wisp of gray hair

undulating away from her face like a cobweb fanned by a faint breeze. "The blackberry cobbler. The one we made together, you remember."

Yes. Yes she did remember. She would always remember, for the rest of her life, Naomi thought, gazing up at the glimmer of familiarity haunting the eyes that were once so revealing.

Just as Mama had promised, blackberry winter had not lasted long. Then spring came to full bloom all through and all around New Bethany, with days so bright and air so clean they practically radiated contentment.

She and Mama had gone out into the glow of that brief season, wearing sturdy canvas gloves and carrying shiny metal pails, to collect the ripe, tempting berries. What a day they'd had. Naomi pictured it, even as it happened, like something from a faded home movie, where people with cheerful dispositions—which in these cynical times would be suspect of some maniacal disorder or at the very least, deep, deep denial—beamed toothy smiles as they clowned and hugged and made their everyday activities look engaging and festive and...wonderful.

Mama had been in good spirits that day, as usual, and in good health, something far from usual anymore. And she'd been sharp. No ramblings, no long pauses in which she had forgotten basically everything, if only for a moment. She'd been patient and charming, clearheaded, quick-witted and—well, she'd been Mama.

Then the mother she had always known and counted upon had slipped quietly back into the fog and frailty brought on by nearly eighty years of living.

In these last two weeks Naomi had walked on eggshells, never knowing from day to day, moment to moment, if things would deteriorate further. Would Mama be sick or weak or befuddled? Or might Naomi be granted at least one more day, one more glimpse, of the mother who had taught her how to love unconditionally, how to savor life, and how to be a good-hearted, smart, strong woman?

Each evening before she fell asleep and each morning before she opened her eyes, Naomi would lie in her bed and pray for time. She prayed for a few more minutes with the one who kissed away her tears and held her hand through everything from braces to boyfriends, through a life-affirming delivery and a consciousness-deadening divorce. In short, she prayed for miracles.

"I got that cobbler out soon as I heard, Nomi, now you go put it in the oven to warm."

But the miracles did not come.

Naomi pushed herself up from the floor, inhaling deep the musty scent of old sachets, starched cotton, and age. "Heard what, Mama?"

If she wasn't mistaken, a twinkle appeared in Mama's eye. "Heard that you were to have a gentleman caller, of course. That's what that phone call was about, wasn't it, sweetie?"

She dug her fingers into her temples. "No, Mama, you misunderstood. The man on the phone was Mr. Boatwright. Taylor Boatwright."

"Taylor Boatwright," Mama echoed, her head tipped and her gaze fixed in the distance.

"Mama, you say it like you think he's Elvis or something." Naomi laughed.

"Elvis?" Mama's whole face puckered up like she'd just chomped into a big ol' persimmon. "Never did care of him much. All that wiggling and grimacing."

Mama jerked her backside to and fro in a remarkably passable Elvis impersonation—had Elvis lived to be eighty and shrunk to the size of roughly, say, an elf.

Mama batted one hand and resumed her more ladylike posture. "No, I did not care for that."

"And I do not care for Taylor Boatwright, Mama. Fact is, I don't even *know* the man."

"Then what's he coming to the house for?" She said in the same tone she might have said, "Is that so, Miss smarty-pants?" when Naomi was younger.

"Oh, Mother. *Really!*" Naomi herself used an intonation from her past. "I told you all about this—how I volunteered to care for the prayer tree this year and how Mr. Boatwright graciously agreed to help? Remember?"

"Yes, yes."

"Well, I've been out to the nursery three times in the last month and never once caught him there. This is a very busy season for them, you understand. So he called to ask me if I would be around the house today and if I would, could he just drop in and we'd discuss our business here."

"Just as I said," Mama pursed her lips and tucked her trembling hands into the deep pockets of her gingham housecoat with lilacs embroidered on the collar. "A gentleman caller."

"Mama, he's not—" Naomi started to throw up her hands, censored the gesture and ended up making a halfhearted shrug. "It's business. Pure business. In fact, not only do I plan to talk to him about the prayer tree, you might as well know that I intend to ask his advice about the backyard."

"The backyard? Whatever for?"

"Because it's a mess, Mama." Naomi wagged her finger and made a preemptive warning: "And don't you go arguing with me that it's not. I can tell from the rust on the screen door hinges and the general shape of things out there that you haven't even *been* in the backyard this spring. Probably not last spring, either."

Mama pouted like a two-year-old but did not deny Naomi's assessment.

"Your flower beds are all grown over with weeds. And the hydrangea bush out by the storage shed?" Naomi tried not to sound scolding. "It's a monstrosity. Plain and simple. A monstrosity."

Mama angled her chin up until even the sagging skin along her neck grew taut—or as taut as it would ever get.

Naomi saw the wounded pride in her mother's watery eyes. She reached out to put her arm around Mama's brittle-boned shoulders. "And I'm not sure," she said in a way that would cajole a brooding child, "but I do think I saw some kudzu trying to creep over the back fence. Now we can't have *that*, can we?"

Mama sighed and it jarred her whole body.

"Good. I'll ask Mr. Boatwright what to do about it all, then." She kissed her mother's velvet-soft temple, burying her nose in the hair that smelled faintly of a light, floral day cologne. "Let's hope he has a few fast, simple, and *cheap* ways to deal with it all."

Mama patted her hand.

"After all, we don't have much time, nor any money, to waste in getting this house whipped into shape so we can put it on the market as soon as possible."

Mama's age-laxed muscles went rigid and her stooped posture jerked upward. "I'll thank you, missy, not to be selling my house while I'm still living in it."

"Mama, please." Naomi felt her jaw lock down over the last word. "We talked about this—"

"And I told you then that the only way I would be going

out of this house permanently was carried. Feet first."

"But Mama, you can't live here anymore by yourself. It's not safe. You can't see to do things like you used to and—"

"And what are you judging that on?" Mama pulled away from Naomi's touch. Her face took on a scowling, hard look. "Because my backyard is a disgrace? Let me tell you, missy, there's plenty of young healthy people with overgrown flower beds around these parts, and nobody tries to run them out of their homes for it. And *you* won't do it to me, either."

"Mama, it's not just the flower beds and you know it."

They stood, glowering at each other for what seemed like minutes. Naomi wanted to avoid reciting again the litany of reasons why her mother could not remain in the home that had been theirs for almost thirty-five years. She wasn't sure she had it in her to go through the list again, to hurt her mother by counting aloud each infraction, the many concerns, and every peril that her daily life had become.

"Don't make me go over all this again with you, Mama." There was an almost childlike pleading in Naomi's tone.

"Of course not, Nomi." Mama's whole demeanor softened. She crinkled up her nose, sending a cascade of wrinkles over her cheeks and alongside her smile. "You don't have time for that now, anyway."

"Don't have time?" Naomi's throat felt shriveled and burning, like she'd just tossed back pure lemon juice. "Why don't I have time now, Mama?"

"Because you've got to get ready for your gentleman caller." Her expression seemed dreamy and far away. "Got to get that cobbler in the oven. It's not good manners to have a gentleman caller and not have something sweet to extend to him. And since this *is* his first time coming around, the only sugar a lady would offer is of the baked goods variety."

"Mama, he's—" What was the use? She wouldn't hear any different, and the notion of Naomi having a caller did seem to give Mama a kind of contentment. Contentment was one thing sorely missing in most of their other exchanges these days, so why rob Mama of it now?

Naomi sighed, ran her hands back through her hair, and decided to wait for Taylor Boatwright on the back porch.

"Oh, no you don't." Naomi eyed a tenacious-looking lone kudzu vine that had not only scaled the back fence but had snaked along the grass a few feet. There it had wound itself around the fluted base of the cracked cement birdbath in the corner of the yard, as if anchoring itself to heave the massive blanket of tangled greenery that lay in its wake over the splintered wooden fence. The image gave her an eerie feeling.

The whole backyard gave her an eerie feeling. She hugged her arms close over her sleeveless knit top. A mosquito that seemed the size of a dragonfly whined around her head. It jounced in the air around her like a broken marionette until she jerked her leg to scare it away from feasting on the skin exposed by her walking shorts. No telling what kind of over-sized bugs lurked in the thigh-high weeds at the edges of the yard that had once been her childhood domain.

It looked so small now. Far smaller than her youthful memories of a vast expanse, a battlefield for games of Red Rover and Hide-and-Seek and Kick the Can.

It looked smaller, even, than ten years ago, the last time she had visited. She had watched her son, then ten, romp and play while she and Mama had sat together on the porch swing and comforted one another over the loss of Naomi's father.

Naomi ventured further into the yard, wading through the

117

ankle-deep grass, kept at bay by a kind-hearted neighbor, who mowed it when it got too out of hand and never took a dime for his work.

Yes, the old yard seemed smaller.

The trees and shrubs had grown so tall and thick that they gave the impression of walls closing in around her. And the summer air, warm and saturated as steam and thick with the smell of grass and growing things, did nothing to dissuade that sensation. Naomi forced out a long, weighty sigh.

Maybe she shouldn't have wandered out here. Maybe she should have just stayed on the porch until Boatwright showed up. Who was she kidding? Sitting and thinking, watching the occasional butterfly tumble drunkenly through the air in front of her...that wasn't Naomi's style.

She was a woman used to doing things, to taking action. Getting off her duff and taking charge—whether that meant leaving New Bethany for Maine or starting her own pottery business—that was Naomi's style. She'd never intended to do anything less, as evidenced by the way she'd horned her way into the last prayer circle despite Gayle's objections and the fact that no one else knew her. Or she them.

Since she'd done that, however, she'd become remarkably sedentary, both physically and emotionally. According to Naomi's original plans, she should have had the old house in order by now and should know enough about Mama's affairs and condition to begin the process of selecting a new home for her.

Instead, she sort of moped through her days, poking through Mama's cupboards and closets, even venturing up into the attic just to look at all the comforting clutter from her childhood. It was a kind of mourning, she realized, an attempt to let herself say good-bye to it all. Or was she trying to hold on to it all?

Either way, it wasn't helping her and it wasn't helping Mama.

Getting the yard in shape, that was a positive step toward the sale of the house and getting Mama situated. At least that's what she told herself even as she wrapped both hands around the thick, living cord of the kudzu vine. She'd make use of that Boatwright fellow to gather some free advice while he was here, and then she'd pitch in and do it all herself to save money. How hard could a little yard work be, after all?

She gave the surprisingly resilient plant a tug. One tiny piece of vine, thin as a spaghetti noodle, snapped. The rest seemed to coil itself tighter around the crumbling pedestal.

"Oh, so that's the way you want to play…" She repositioned her grip and planted her feet firm.

Calling forth all the penned up anger and frustration she'd tamped down this past month, she poured it all into her task. This outwardly innocent but actually cunning and invasive vine became all the things that stood in the shadows of her consciousness and clutched at her, ready to drag her into the darkness of depression and despair. The vine became her old friend Gayle's snobbery and Naomi's own loneliness, which was heightened by her return home and the quickening of emotion brought on by some stranger's kind eyes. It became letting go of Mama, one agonizing incident at a time.

She set her jaw. "Well, you are not going to best me, you hear that?" The vine bit into her palms. She gulped down an aching breath and heaved for all her worth. The vine slid in her hands, squeaked against her skin, then gave. The most delicate ripping sound filled the quiet of the afternoon, then Naomi staggered backward with nothing but a few plucked leaves in her hands.

The humid air hit the back of her open mouth, turning her

gasp into a strangled gurgle. Back and forth her flat-soled sandals flapped, unable to provide traction in the shaggy, dank lawn. Her arms, she could imagine in an oddly objective vision that sprang into her head, whirled front to back like someone doing the backstroke on dry land...in slow motion...all the while flinging bits of kudzu leaf like environmentally correct confetti to an unseen audience. It really seemed quite amusing and even, well, graceful, until, of course, she landed—*wham*—right on her backside, sending her head reeling backward to stick neat-as-you-please into the hydrangea bush.

"You're never going to get the job done that way, Ms. Beauchamp."

The voice shot through her with such a peculiar sense of familiarity that she should have been prepared. Yet it made her stomach fall like a rock sailing over a cliff when, still sprawled on the ground, she blinked up from what must have looked like an enormous Easter hat festooned with huge pink flowers—and saw *his* face.

Eight

Y ou?" She blinked and huffed away a downy petal clinging to her lips. "*You* are Taylor Boatwright?"

"Forgive me for not introducing myself the other day at the Cone and Coney King, ma'am. But I didn't realize then that you were going to be needing my assistance." He offered his hand.

She glared at it. "I am perfectly capable of getting out of this mess without your assistance, thank you."

"I meant with the prayer tree, Ms. Beauchamp."

"Oh." She swept her hand back through what she assumed would be her hair. Her fingers snagged in a fat, aromatic blossom. She yanked them free, causing a shower of pink petals to fall over her head and shoulders. Without giving him the satisfaction of acknowledging either blunder she said, "Oh, yes. Of course."

She pushed herself up to her knees and stopped to catch her breath—not that the slight exertion had winded her, but the humidity and the…situation did seem to have hampered her ability to take a good, deep breath. She used the back of her wrist to push away a snarl of hair scratching her cheek.

Before she could nimbly poke and tuck the stray strands back amongst the layers of her hair, Taylor Boatwright had knelt in front of her.

"There now, that's a nasty cut, Ms. Beauchamp." His face was level with hers. His knees, in faded but clean jeans, rested in the grass just inches from her own.

Despite the heat of the late afternoon, she could feel the

warmth of his body. He was that close. She could even hear the swish of his chambray work shirt when he reached to her.

Naomi braced herself but did not shy away. She did not think she could shy away from this man's touch, even though propriety and her own attitudes about men suggested she do just that. Instead, she waited, wondering how it would feel to have the man with the kindest eyes she'd ever seen lay his hand on her face.

The pads of his fingertips, which she expected to feel abrasive, stroked her stinging skin with supple tenderness, as though brushing something from an orchid petal, careful not to bruise.

"It's just a scrape, but it's going to smart for a while, I'd venture." He leaned in closer still, concern etched in his lined face. "Still, as a precaution, we really ought to get something on it."

"This is fine," she murmured, her gaze slipping deeper into those fathomless blue eyes as she put her hand to his, her light touch enough to keep his hand on her cheek.

"I meant something medicinal." He smiled that almost-smile she'd seen before. "Do you have any peroxide or iodine in the house?"

"In the…? Oh!" Suddenly the world came spinning right-side-up for her again, and she pulled away, blinking as if to adjust her focus.

The last thing on earth Naomi wanted was to go traipsing into Mama's house with Taylor Boatwright at her heels. Heaven only knew what kind of remark Mama might make about "gentlemen callers." Then she'd try to foist off on the poor, unsuspecting soul some of that frozen blackberry cobbler Naomi had refused to heat up for her business appointment.

He'd eat it, of course, and go on about how delicious it was, rivaling his own grandmother's recipe and so on. From a man raised in New Bethany, she could most assuredly count on that much. But Naomi didn't want this man to humor her mother, or to eat her blackberry cobbler, or to tell her to put iodine on an insignificant little scratch from a deranged hydrangea bush.

"I'm fine. Honest, I am." She stood, her legs wobbling only a second before she steadied herself. "I believe you came here to give me some pointers about caring for our group's prayer tree."

He straightened his long legs, slapping away the burrs and dried stems from his jeans as he did so. "Yes, well, don't really know what to tell you about that. See, there isn't much to do for it this time of year but check on it now and again, especially after a bad wind or summer storm, you know, to make sure it hasn't been damaged."

"What about watering and fertilizing and—"

"Not much call for that, ma'am. This is Tennessee, ground so fertile that you could start up a rock garden and get it to bloom and bear fruit." He glanced around, then aimed his gaze directly at her. "That's how the saying goes, anyway."

"Really? I've never heard any saying like that."

"Maybe that's 'cause I just made it up." He grinned, not a cocky grin or a smirky grin but more of a letting-her-in-on-the-joke grin.

She didn't want in on any of the man's jokes, or anything else he—or any man—had to offer her. "Oh? Is just making things up a personal fault or simply part and parcel of your business demeanor, Mr. Boatwright?"

Amusement sparkled in his eyes. "I *had* liked to think of it as one of my many, many charming eccentricities—"

"Well, maybe you've got some rethinking to do, then." Her delivery oozed refinement. "Now, tell me, were you 'just making it up' when you told me about Rose and the chocolate?"

"She liked the hot fudge well enough, didn't she?"

She had. But Naomi didn't see any point in carrying on about that to this man who had seen her embarrassed by her mother, flustered by a simple dessert order, and now wrestled to the ground by a hydrangea bush. "Well, then, were you just making it up when you said we needed to meet to discuss how to care for the prayer tree?"

"*You* asked to meet."

"And you could have told me by phone that there wasn't any taking care to do."

"Whoa, now, I never said there wasn't anything to do to care for that sapling. I did say you'd have to keep watch over it for storm damage through the summer. Then, come fall, there'll be mulching and in winter, protection from the frost and, of course, if it should begin to do poorly…But I don't see much chance of that."

"And why not?"

"That's one of our very best trees, ma'am." He crossed his arms and cocked his head. His thinning hair was dark brown and could do with a trim around the ears and collar. "Handpicked by me since only one of the best would do for this purpose."

"Oh?" Her stilted reaction relaxed a bit as she began to buy into his commitment to the little tree and the custom as a whole.

"Yes, I guess I always have had a special fondness for that grove and the tradition that built it."

She stiffed again. "Good for business, huh?"

"The Lord's business is good for everyone, I reckon."

"Oh. Oh, of course." She crushed one end of her scarf belt in her hand, feeling a smidgen of shame at her harsh judgment of the man. Maybe he did not belong lumped in with all the male losers she'd met throughout the years. Maybe, just maybe, she had met herself a good, godly man, with whom it might benefit her to pursue a relationship. "I saw you out at the dedication service. Your way of showing support, I suppose?"

"I do whatever I can, ma'am." He folded those large, capable-looking hands in front of him. "See, my mother served on one of the circles years ago as did both of my sisters later, so did my wife—"

Wife?

"Before she died—"

Oh.

"And I sincerely hope my daughter, when she's old enough, will choose to serve, as well."

"Oh? How old is your daughter?"

"Thirteen going on thirty-four."

Naomi smiled, though she did feel a twinge of sadness that the fine, old tradition, honored by so many generations of Boatwrights, would likely not be around long enough for Taylor's daughter to participate. She thought of mentioning that, but instead she said, "So, you're a widower?"

He nodded. "Four years now."

"Your daughter was terribly young to have lost a mother." Naomi fended off an inexplicable pang of sorrow on behalf of the child she had never laid eyes on.

"Yes, ma'am, it was hard on her for a fact. Hard on us all— my daughter, myself, and my son."

"Oh, so you have two children?"

"Wouldn't call my son a child, ma'am, least not to his face. He's twenty and has me bested by four inches in height and a good thirty pounds girth."

"So is mine! Twenty, that is, not bested, or, you know taller or…well, he is heavier, of course—than me, not you. Not that I

125

know what you weigh or was even, you know, meaning to size you up but…" So it wasn't nearly enough to flop around in front of the man and land tail-over-teacups in the hydrangea bush, she taunted herself, she had to perform a verbal pratfall as well. "Me, too. I have a twenty-year-old son. He's away at college this summer. At an Ivy League school."

"Brandon is at a state university, but it's a pretty good one."

"Oh." She widened her eyes at his droll response. "I hope I didn't sound pretentious."

"No, just proud. Like any mama would."

She nodded.

He nodded back.

Then they both just stood there, the heat pressing down on them. A mosquito did a bold dive-bombing maneuver past her ear, and she smacked the pest away.

The aroma of the hydrangea bush rose around them like fog swirling up from a low-lying pond, thick and heady one moment then nothing more than a wisp of a scent the next.

Naomi shifted her feet in the prickling grass.

He did the same.

They both started to speak at the same time, stopped themselves, then started again. Naomi, unable to squelch a girlish laugh that bubbled up from her throat, motioned for him to go ahead.

"Well, ma'am, I was just going to say that since there isn't anything for us to do about the tree right away, I guess I'll be going." He poked his fingers into his shirt pocket. "Let me give you my card in case you think of a question or need anything."

He held out a pristine white card with embossed green lettering spelling out all his pertinent information.

She took the textured card between her thumb and forefinger

and before he released it, looked up at him. "Actually, there is something."

"Yes?"

She bit her lower lip. "I hesitate to ask because I really don't have the money to—"

"Ask." He relinquished his hold on the card, but not on her concentration.

"It's this backyard." She stepped back and made a sweeping motion with both hands as if making a presentation of it to him.

"What about it?"

She huffed out a disdainful laugh. "Do you have to ask? The weeds, the trees, the maniacal hydrangea bush that looks—and acts—like some human-eating life-form straight out of a grade-B horror movie. It's just giving me fits."

"So I saw." He chuckled under his breath.

Being a lady—or, at least, having been brought up to know how one acts—Naomi chose to ignore his reference to her embarrassing moment. "And the kudzu."

"What about it?"

"Horrible stuff." She shuddered, but refrained from going into some lengthy philosophical monologue about what the dreadful vine represented to her as it literally consumed her beloved homeland and its old-fashioned ways. "It's creeping over the fence. It's like it has a mind of its own and it wants to swallow up Mama's birdbath, then the garden. I don't think the evil plant will be satisfied until it envelops the whole house, I tell you. And I won't have that."

"And you'd like Boatwright's Nursery to help you take care of the yard and treat the kudzu problem?"

"No. No, I could never afford that. But if you did have a few suggestions for things I could do myself—as long as they didn't cost too much and could be accomplished quickly. See, I'd like to get this house on the market as soon as possible."

"Is your mother moving?"

"Not to hear her tell it she's not but…" Naomi sighed. "You know, my sister is a realtor, Ms. Beauchamp."

"Oh, I'm not ready for a realtor yet." The suggestion startled her. Her stomach lurched as though the ground had fallen away from under her feet. She put her hand to her chest, surprised to find it clammy with sweat.

"I'm not trying to rush you into anything, ma'am. Don't get me wrong. I just thought if Kate could come by, she might could tell you what all you absolutely need to get done to have the house ready for the market. That way you won't waste your money doing things that won't make any difference."

A realtor? In Mama's house? In her *home?* Now? The idea hit Naomi like a gut punch, stealing her wind and confusing her senses.

"Like I said, I don't want to appear to rush you, I just—"

"Well, you *are* rushing me." She retreated a step. The emotions that she'd worked so hard to keep under wraps sprang to the surface. She felt awful—frightened and angry and lost—and she blamed this man, this Taylor Boatwright, for it. "Just because my mama's backyard is a shambles doesn't mean you have to run the sweet old woman out of her home. And for what? To get a hefty commission for your sister?"

"I never—"

"You—you're…you're as bad as that awful kudzu, you are. Insinuating yourself into all manner of places for your own benefit—"

"You're upset," he said quietly. "Maybe you just need some more time to deal with your feelings about this."

"I've had the time to deal with my emotions, thank you. I'm just not sure that's something I really want to do where losing my mother is concerned, because that's what this is about, Mr. Boatwright. Losing my mother and my home and my youth and a part of me that I'll never have again." The truth. How strange it felt to have it spoken out loud after so much time tap-dancing around it with Mama.

"I apologize for even bringing it up—"

"No." Naomi shook her head, her every conscious effort fixed on pushing the unpleasantness back down in its place. "No, I'm the one who should apologize. I was out of line. It's just that—"

The tears came like a burst from a lone gray thundercloud on a spring day—quick to start, hard and relentless, then ending almost as fast as they began. As she sniffed her last sniffle, Naomi realized that her injured cheek rested on something soft and cool: the chambray of Taylor's shirt. He had his arms around her.

"There, there. Watching your mother grow old and frail, even a little, is a very difficult thing. I've been there, I know." He patted her back.

"I'm so sorry. I'm usually more controlled than this." She lifted her face from his chest and looked up at him.

He did not let her go.

And she did not try to leave the shelter of his arms. "You're very kind, Mr. Boatwright."

"Taylor. Please, call me Taylor."

"Taylor," she complied, her voice a raw whisper. "I'm sorry I said you were like kudzu."

"I've been compared to worse, ma'am."

"Naomi."

"Naomi."

For one instant she thought he would kiss her. Her eyes drifted shut, her lips parted in anticipation. She felt him move nearer and then—

Thweeeep. Thweeeep. A shrill wail pierced the still, humid air.

"It's a smoke alarm," Taylor cried even as he bounded toward the back of the house.

"Precious Jesus," Naomi murmured in fervent prayer even as she ran into the house behind Taylor. "Please keep Mama safe in your infinite care. Please don't let her be hurt or suffer. Please…please…"

"I put the cobbler in and turned on the oven." Mama clutched at Naomi as Taylor rushed toward the smoke-filled kitchen. "But when I went to check on it, it was still cold. I laid my best pot holder on the stove top and fiddled with all the dials like I always do to get the thing to work and—"

"This is all it was." Taylor held the charred remains of Mama's "best" pot holder, the one Naomi had sewn herself and adorned with a crocheted edge in Brownies thirty years ago. He laid it in the stainless-steel sink. "No real fire, just a lot of smoke. Nothing opening a few windows can't help for now."

"Thank you," Mama said, her voice trembling. "Thank you very much, young man. I don't know what I would have done if you and Nomi hadn't been here."

Even through the milky white film of smoke between them, Naomi could see the look that Taylor gave her. It did not accuse or condemn, but it did hold a compassionate warning.

She coughed, her lungs and throat burning, but not from the smoke or the odor of the singed fabric.

"No, sir, I can't thank you enough, young man."

She tightened her grip around her mother's shoulders. "You know what, Mama? I can think of the perfect way to show Mr. Boatwright our proper thanks."

"How's that, Nomi?"

"Why don't we have him over for tea one afternoon as soon as he's free?"

The old wood squawked as Taylor heaved to push the nearest window open, then he turned his head to find Naomi's gaze over his shoulder.

Naomi brushed Mama's hair back but kept her gaze on Taylor. "And why don't we see if there is anyone he'd like to invite to join us? His sister, perhaps."

There was a somber recognition in his nod this time.

"Why, that sounds delightful, Nomi. Do tell us you'll come, Mr. Boatwright, and bring your dear sister, as well."

"Yes, ma'am. We'll be here. You just name the day."

"Is that the way you intend to spend your entire Sunday afternoon?" Lucy wiped her wet hands on the nubby terry cloth of her daisy print dish towel.

"What's wrong with you, gal?" The faux leather of her daddy's old recliner groaned then sighed as Ray Griggs settled himself more deeply into the chair. "You come home after getting all churched up for the week and you throw together as decent a meal as you can manage, given your limited abilities in that area."

Lucy dabbed the dish towel to the back of her neck and caught the lingering aroma of fried chicken and creamy pocket gravy.

"Gravy so thick you could carry it in your pocket," her granny, who taught her to make it, was fond of saying. Her granny had shared all her best recipes with Lucy, and Lucy guarded the secrets of them well. No matter how many times the church ladies would try to guess at the ingredients in her famous

chicken salad or her East Indian Delight casserole, Lucy would not tell.

According to just about everyone but Ray, Lucy was a good cook. Not a fancy one, mind you, just good old Southern basics and a few exotic casseroles culled from old junior league cookbooks and enhanced. Most of what Lucy cooked involved far too much bacon grease, salt, and sugar to be healthy for anyone.

So, on that account, she had to side with Ray about her cooking: she did have limited abilities in the kitchen. Still, it made her just the teensiest bit defensive to hear him put it that way.

"Once you get everything ready for the table, you give me a holler. Then I come over and choke down what I'm able—"

"You're lucky you *don't* choke as fast as you shovel it in," she muttered, surprising herself that she actually said it out loud.

But Ray must not have heard the contemptuous commentary, she decided, wringing the towel in her hands, since he didn't make a cutting reply. He just droned on, "Then you clean up while I come in here and park it in my favorite chair and watch my fishing shows on the TV."

As if to offer proof of his claim, he aimed the remote at her brand-new television and clicked down the power button. A quiet electrical pop came in ready response. Then a pair of good old boys could be heard, though not yet seen, discussing their latest catch. "Yup. Yup. Yes sir. She's a big'un, all right. Whooee. Hate to have lost that one."

"It's what we do every Sunday, ain't it?" Ray didn't even look at her, he just laid the remote in his lap and pushed the chair into full reclining position.

Lucy tapped her stockinged foot on the imitation tapestry rug that covered most of her living-room floor. "Well, since we do it every Sunday, it seems like it would be time for a change."

To that, Ray grunted, tipped back his head, and folded his arms over his chest.

"Well, we've done our part," one of the fishing experts' voices sliced into the ponderous silence between Lucy and Ray. "Hooked her and reeled her in. Nothing more for us to do but enjoy the bounty."

"That's it?" Lucy moved next to the chair. When Ray failed to even notice her nearness, she gave it a little nudge with her foot. "You're not even going to talk to me about doing something interesting today?"

"I'm doing what I'm interested in."

"Wouldja looky there," the fishing expert gave a whoop.

From the corner of her eye Lucy saw the fish slashing violently side to side as it dangled from the line in the man's hand. For some reason the sight made her angry. Very angry.

She kicked Ray's chair again. Kicked it, not just a gentle nudge this time.

"Whoo-eee. She's got some fight in her yet."

"Ray, sit up and at least listen to my ideas. I want to—"

Bing-bong. The doorbell sounded, like the bell at the end of a boxing round.

"Who could that be in the middle of a Sunday afternoon?" Lucy slung the towel onto her shoulder.

"Better not be your mother."

"And what if it is?" Lucy asked even though she'd shared the very same dread. She and Ray had trouble enough without her mother mixing in.

Bing-bong.

"Hold on, I'm—" Lucy paused to sweep back the white lace curtains that covered the multipaned window in her front door. "Why it's Nikki."

Even as she tugged the door open, Lucy heard the recliner bang into an upright position in the room behind her.

"Why, Nikki, what brings you by and on a Sunday?"

"Well, I…I…"

She looked nervous. But then Nikki always looked nervous, like some high-strung little dog that a rich lady might carry under her arm. The woman's huge eyes and pale hair caught up in a spout of a ponytail on the top of her head did not discourage that comparison.

"Well, that is, I have an itty-bitty problem." She pinched her thumb and forefinger together, her acrylic nails, which she'd had applied in a salon in Knoxville while visiting friends a few weeks ago, clattered together. "An eensy-weensie, tiny *puff* of a problem, to be truthful."

Here it comes. Lucy sighed. Another resignation from the day care. It was a crying shame, too, because Nikki had been one of her very best workers ever. Usually on time, always clean, courteous to the parents, and kind and loving toward the kids, she was a born caregiver even if her personal appearance might have made one suspect otherwise.

"Oh, Nikki," Lucy laced her fingers together and locked them in place at her waist. "Whatever it is, I'm sure I can help you work it out."

"Well, I don't need *your* help…exactly…Miss Lucy." She sucked in a breath through her pink glossy lips. Her dainty feet shuffled in a pair of strappy sandals on the porch. She smelled as if she'd doused herself in dime store eau de toilette, which, combined with her pink-and-white dress, made her seem younger than her thirty-three years. "You see, the thing is—"

134

"Hello there, Ms. Herndon, did I hear you say you have a problem?" Ray came up beside Lucy and put his arm over her shoulder.

Lucy flinched. Ray *never* put his arm around her in public. While she supposed it could be taken as a gesture of romantic possessiveness or even reassurance, in the presence of a physically more attractive woman, the effect to Lucy was, overall, downright creepy.

Ray squeezed Lucy's arm. "Is there something we can do to help you?"

"Well, as I was just telling Miss Lucy, it's not so much what *she* can do for me, but more a matter of, well, what *you*, Mr. Griggs, can do...for me."

"Me?" Ray thumped his chest like a first-rate ham in a third-rate melodrama. "Why, I don't know what I could do for you, but I'll sure try."

"It's my cable again."

"I thought you had that fixed." Lucy's tone was deadened, but her senses were keenly alert.

"I thought so, too." Nikki nodded, and her hair shimmied like a cheerleader's pom-poms. "But you remember I told you the cable man didn't have the right connector?"

Lucy started to answer, but Nikki rattled on like a runaway train on a greased track, hardly stopping to finish a thought much less allow a response from her listener.

"See, it turns out that that cable man used the wrong coupler or whatever it's called—Steve down at the Radio Shack told me what it looks like, but I don't recall the name. Anyway, even though he—the cable man, not Steve—said he'd gone and gotten the right one, he apparently didn't because now it's all come undone, the cable that is, come undone from the coupler or connector or whatever it is. So, what *I* need is for someone, Mr.

Griggs, I'm hoping, to crawl under the house and hook it all back together, and sort of…tape it…or something so Tiff and I can at least have some cable until the man can come again to see about it officially next week."

Ray, Lucy, and Nikki all exhaled at the same time as if the tirade had taken all their breaths away.

"Ray isn't exactly the mechanical type, you know, Nikki," Lucy finally said, because someone had to say something.

"Oh, he doesn't have to be mechanical. He just has to jab it all together and run some duct tape around it for the time being. I wouldn't ask you, on a Sunday and all, Mr. Griggs, but I didn't know who else to turn to.…"

"It just seems like something that could wait, Nikki," Lucy said.

"It *could.*" Ray nodded, his expression a bit too wise and concerned. "But why should it have to?"

"For starters because I thought you and I were going to—"

"Oh, if you two have plans…"

"Not at all." Ray released Lucy's shoulders to hitch up his white jeans, which he was usually content to let ride low and comfy just under the swell of his slight paunch.

Lucy did not want to jump to any conclusions about what was going on here, but Ray's behavior sort of prodded her thoughts toward definite suspicion.

"Nope, we didn't have no plans at all." Ray sniffed and rocked on his heels. "Matter of fact, we were just watching a rerun of bass fishing, nothing important. Don't see why I can't scoot over to your place and have a look-see."

Nikki squirmed with delight and beamed a thousand-watt smile at him. "How can I ever thank you, Mr. Griggs?"

It wasn't such a far-fetched notion that Nikki could actually find quite a few ways to thank Ray for his help—and that he'd have no trouble accepting that gratitude. *Just like Daddy,* Lucy thought, feeling ugly and insignificant. She'd worked so hard and come so far, or so she'd thought. She'd become a working woman with her own business as security against ending up like her mother, financially dependent on a man who was emotionally unreliable.

Lucy had heard the rumors. She knew Ray wasn't going to win any awards for attentiveness—at least not for attentiveness to her. But so far, she'd had no proof that he had ever strayed or broken the fragile understanding between them. Still, she knew what everyone said behind her back: Ray was just like her daddy.

But Lucy was *not* just one afternoon favor away from becoming her mother. Not yet she wasn't.

She pulled her spine erect and her lips upward in an impenetrable smile. "Then maybe I'll just tag along. I wanted to get out of the house this afternoon with you anyway, Ray. Why don't I come, too? I can hold the flashlight while you crawl under the house and jab everything together."

"Oh, no! No sense in you troubling yourself like that, Miss Lucy. I can hold the flashlight just fine."

Gee, you're pretty and talented, too. Lucy thought the sarcasm she could never in a million years bring herself to speak aloud.

"Besides," Ray chimed in, "Don't you have that sewing circle thing at four today?"

"Prayer circle." Luckily they were the kind of words that fit through tightly clenched teeth and caused enough hiss to sound out her displeasure with the man's slipshod memory. "And yes, I do have to go to that but you should be finished up long before then, shouldn't you? How long can it take to duct-tape together a cable connector?"

Ray started to argue, but Nikki stepped forward and cut him off.

"She's right, Mr. Griggs, it shouldn't take too long…unless there's complications."

Sounds like someone watches those popular medical dramas on TV, Lucy thought, again not rude enough to voice her disdain.

"And if Miss Lucy, here, really wants to be of some help—"

"I do."

Nikki dipped her head and her hair bounced one beat behind the movement. "Then I don't see why—oh! Oh! Goodness!" She put her glitter-flecked nails to her cheeks. "I just had a thought!"

Your first? This time she almost said it.

Lucy was no fool. She saw what was coming a mile away. She didn't know which insulted her more—that her boyfriend and her best employee would even consider betraying her or that they thought her so stupid that they could use such flimsy lies to lay their sordid plans right under her nose?

"You know, since it's at my house, I'll already be there anyway and Steve did tell me what to look for and all, so I really will be of more help holding the flashlight for Mr. Griggs. That does, however, present a problem for me, and if you're intent on being a help to me, Miss Lucy…"

"Tiffany?" She had to ask, not because she didn't already know but because it was her part.

"Why yes! How darling of you to offer."

Had she offered anything? She tugged at the big soft dress that suddenly felt like a circus tent draped wearily over her bulky body.

"Tiff just loves spending time with her Miss Lucy and if she stayed here, well, that would keep her out from underfoot."

Her and me both, Lucy thought, slumping, her hands stuffed deep in her pockets.

"She's in the car now and—"

"She's in the car?" Lucy straightened. "You left that baby out in the hot car?"

"The window is down and I've only been here a minute." Nikki's eyes grew huge and her lip trembled.

Lucy had no reason to suspect Nikki was anything but a good mother—a great mother if little Tiffany was the measure of her endeavors. The little girl was always clean and happy, quite advanced in her skills both socially and educationally.

It was her anger at Nikki and Ray and the fact that she had lost control of this situation that put a fierce edge on her tone. "Oh, just leave her with me. Just leave her. At least she'll be safe."

"The child *is* safe, Lucy." Ray grabbed at her arm, but Lucy pulled away and walked, stiff-legged, to the battered black car where Tiffany's blonde head could be seen above the lowered back window.

Lucy pulled the car door open with such force that the whole car rocked. Tiffany's tiny arms spread toward her as she worked to undo the buckles to the carseat. With near blind fury, she pulled the child out and hugged her close.

"Go, you two. Just go. Tiffany will be fine with me. I'll take care of her and you two can take care of—"

Each other, she thought, feeling humiliation and pain but not nearly as much as she might have expected. She lifted her chin, determined not to reveal her inner turmoil. What was so bad after all? So Ray found Nikki attractive, he'd be dead if he didn't. That didn't mean he had acted on his attraction, or that he would. She had no evidence that anything untoward was going to happen, and until she did it was vulgar to suspect it.

"You two take care of that cable. And remember, Ray, don't stay too long. I have to be at Rose Holcomb's house by four, Nikki, so don't be late picking up Tiffany."

"Course not," Nikki called out as Lucy slipped inside the house.

She shut the door firmly on the couple and the matter. Lucy simply would not allow herself to dwell on what might happen. She would, instead, hold good thoughts and hope for the best while Nikki and Ray were together—and by four o'clock that would all be over.

Nine

"Tell me y'all didn't start without me." Lucy floated into Rose's kitchen, her pulse thrumming like a jackrabbit's in her ears. She worked hard at keeping her expression pleasant and her demeanor light as she wove between the chair and the counter. In one hand she clutched Tiffany Crystal's sticky fingers, while in the other she struggled to manipulate her cumbersome bag and a backpack filled with toys to occupy the child. "I'm so sorry to be so late. Tiffany's mother didn't come to pick her up and so I drove past her house and they weren't there and—"

"They?" Gayle withdrew the long silver teaspoon from her tall glass and tapped it against the rim. "I thought your new day-care helper was a single mother, Lucy."

"Well, she is. She is." She tried to think of a lie. A good one.

Tiffany's father had recently returned—no, that would stir up a hornet's nest of questions that would only mean more lies and then more to cover those. Nikki had an old family friend visiting and had taken her out to show her the town—except that showing anyone all of New Bethany would not have caused anyone to be late. The whole tour, including a drive along Cemetery Road, a walk in the prayer-tree grove, *and* a cup of coffee at Dot and Daughter's Midday Cafe would not take more than a couple hours.

In the end all Lucy could think to do was to tell the truth. It was fast and efficient, not to mention the right thing to do. In a town this small she'd be found out for a liar within minutes of the meeting adjourning anyway. Mother always said, "It's not *what* you say that people remember, Lucy, it's *how* you present yourself."

Lucy guided Tiffany into the empty chair at the table and plunked her down, proud that, despite having no chance to use them in beauty pageants or society teas, Miss Trudi's strictly schooled lessons in charm had not been a total waste. She slid her bags to the floor, waved her hand as though flicking a lightly perfumed hanky, and spoke in soft tones.

"When I said *they*, I meant Tiffany's mother, Nikki, and Ray. He had gone over there earlier to help her with her…coupler." She ahemed into her fist to feign a genteel cough before resuming.

Rose coughed, too, but it was more of a gasping choke.

Gayle pounded Rose on the back to free her airways with all the delicacy of a farmhand.

Naomi actually muttered something that sounded, while not quite profane, quite descriptive, under her breath.

Then Lucy did something she did not learn in charm school, but at her mother's side all those many years. She put on a brave face and defended her man. "It's all quite innocent, I'm sure, ladies."

"Oh, Lucy…" one of them whispered.

"Ray and I have been together a long time." She lowered her gaze to meet each pair of eyes that fixed on hers with guileless defiance. "A long time."

"But—"

She did not look to see who had spoken, just went on. "I trust Ray, just as I'm sure he would trust me in a similar situation. Now, they said they would be done by four, but it's obvious by now that…" She looked up to the high, high ceiling and studied with vacant fascination the scrollwork around the kitchen light fixture. Not even her mother would have loved her delusions enough to be able to look anyone in the eye and finish by saying, "That is, it appears now that…complications have set in."

No one said another word.

Lucy walked around to stand between Rose and Tiffany and conjured up a smile. "I was hoping we could let little Tiffany sit at the table here and color. Maybe have a snack while we meet in another room? The—" she pictured the view of Ray's house from Rose's large front window—"the living room, perhaps?"

Gayle wasn't sure which impressed her more: Lucy's ability to ignore the obvious, or Rose's quick pick up on what was clearly a proffered change of subject. Barely a beat followed Lucy's request to move to the living room before Rose was standing and nodding.

"Why, of course, dear." Rose said, bending to twirl her fingers through Tiffany's pale hair. "I'll get this precious sweetie pie all fixed up with some milk and cookies while you all can make yourselves comfortable in the front room."

"I'll help you, Rose," Naomi volunteered.

Gayle suspected Naomi wanted a moment to decide whether to tell Lucy what she'd overheard at Ray's eatery, so she put her hand on Lucy's back to urge her toward the front room.

"We'll join y'all in a minute," Naomi assured them.

Lucy marched on ahead and Gayle paused only a moment to steal a look behind her. Rose had already begun pouring milk into a small plastic cup. Naomi was riffling through the backpack to pull out coloring books and colors for the little girl who sat, overwhelmed, on the kitchen chair with her toes pointed straight out and her hands folded in her lap.

Poor little thing, Gayle thought. Here among people she

didn't know, acting brave yet couched in such a fragile dignity that the wrong word or gesture might shatter it in an instant.

When Gayle strode into the living room, she found Mary Lucille sitting in the big wingback that had been Curry's favorite, looking just about as vulnerable as little Tiffany. But Lucy was not a child, and Gayle could not find it in herself to coddle her like one. She cared about the younger woman, and therefore would not feed her denial, just as Rose had refused to feed Cissy Jewell's almost thirty years earlier. Gayle could only pray her tact had better results than Rose's had.

"He's not there, Lucy." Gayle ducked her head and craned her neck, peering through a parting she created between Rose's gold-on-gold brocade portieres and the pristine ecru sheers.

"Who?" Lucy's small mouth pursed like some little old lady's.

Gayle looked down at the girl seated in the chair directly next to the picture window. Placing her hands on her hips, she sighed with genuine affection at the redoubtable demonstration. "Ray. Isn't that why you took this chair? Because you can see his house from here and tell when—or if—he comes home?"

"No." She gave a sort of sashay with her shoulders. "And he *will* come home, I know it."

"Oh, sweetie." She shook her head.

"I don't want to talk about this, Gayle." She froze Gayle out with a turn of her head.

"But, Lucy, you have to know—"

"Gayle…" Naomi's voice was hushed.

Gayle turned to see her old friend, one hand flattened against the arched doorway, backlit by the bright glow from the kitchen light. The dim living room put Naomi's features in shadow, but her intentions came through as clear as any earnest gaze ever could.

Gayle walked the length of the room feeling like someone relinquishing her turn sitting with the bereaved. When she got to the door, she twisted her head to speak to Naomi with her face in profile so that their gazes did not quite meet. "She's not ready, Naomi…"

"Then I won't say a word."

Gayle swallowed, she wanted to ask something more but she couldn't.

"Just trust me, wouldja?"

She could, Gayle realized. She could trust Naomi not to tell Lucy anything the girl was not ready to handle. She nodded and smiled, but not a happy smile. "Okay, but don't go thinking I'll make a habit of it."

"Oh, I knew you wouldn't let me off that easy." Naomi tossed her head back. "Because nothing with you, my old pal, is ever easy."

"I'm not sure I could say the same about you…pal."

"Was that a slam?"

Gayle just hummed and walked away. "You know, Rose, I believe I forgot to take my tea in with me."

"Was it?" Naomi, still standing between the kitchen and the living room, demanded.

"Oh, and while I'm here getting my own tea, why don't I get a glass for our Lucy as well?"

"Gayle?" Naomi looked over her shoulder.

"Now, I know Lucy takes lemon, but do you reckon she would like some mint, too, Rose?"

"Why won't you answer me?" There was no hostility in Naomi's tone.

In fact, Gayle got the idea she was enjoying the teasing lack of response, and to her surprise, Gayle was enjoying it as well. She scooped up the two tall glasses and two fruit-motif cocktail napkins and started toward the other room. "There now, I'll just take these both in then come back for the pitcher, Rose."

"I can get the pitcher, no problem." Naomi's skirt twirled as she started to do just that, but Gayle stopped her with a nudge of one forearm.

"Don't bother, Naomi, honey. I don't mind. Why don't you just go on in and sit down? You know, take it…easy?" Gayle winked at her.

"You are not one bit funny, Gayle Barrett," Naomi said, despite grinning broadly. "And furthermore, I'm telling Rose on you."

"Girl! Girls! None of that, now." Rose clapped her hands and laughed. "Go on in there and settle down, you hear? We've got work to do."

Gayle paused, stepped aside for Naomi, and nodded politely. "Age before beauty," she quipped.

Naomi's grin widened a bit. "Pearls before swine," she replied, and Gayle had to restrain a chuckle as she followed her into the living room.

Rose watched the two women walk into the other room and smiled. My, it had been a long time since she'd had to step into a quarrel between her girls, even one so obviously staged as the one between Gayle and Naomi had been. A long time since she'd uttered such chastisements as *"Girl! Girls! None of that, now."* It felt good to hear them again, especially in the context of light-hearted camaraderie, not frazzled motherly exasperation.

With a sigh, Rose turned to Tiffany. "Will you be all right in here, little one?" She stroked back the child's silky hair, then cupped her tiny chin in one hand.

The child just looked at her and nibbled on a cookie.

She looked so out of place, Rose thought, so tiny and insignificant in this old kitchen with a ceiling as high and rounded as some cavern and dark nooks and crannies in every direction. Curry had been wrong about this place, she decided just then. No house that made a child look insignificant was the proper place to invite grandchildren. Though she didn't have any yet, Rose made up her mind right then, that by the time she did have a grandchild, she'd be living somewhere more suitable.

Rose smiled kindly to the little girl and picked up a large silver tray to carry it to her other guests. She walked slowly to accommodate the glasses, pitcher, and a plate filled with flat, gooey cookies she'd sliced from a tube and baked earlier this afternoon.

In her younger years, when it was her turn to provide refreshments, she would have spent two days in preparation. She would have labored over heavily glazed petits fours with confectionary roses on top, then placed each on fluted pastel papers that cupped around their edges like a ballerina's frilly tutu. Or she might have served tomato sandwiches, an old Southern tradition for tea. With precise care, she'd have trimmed the bread to the perfect size with a biscuit cutter to better accommodate the Big Boy tomato, which she'd slice extra thin to make the sandwiches more delicate and less likely to drip juice onto an unsuspecting guest's lap. These she would alternate with cucumbers on crackers—the cucumber's deep green rind scored with a fork to give an appealing design to the presentation. Both would include homemade mayonnaise and a dill sprig on the silver tray for garnish.

"A delight for the eye and the palate," the society pages had always said about any of Mrs. J. Curran Holcolmb's repasts.

Rose set down the tray on the coffee table with an emphatic

thunk. She paused to inhale the sweet, promising scent of chocolate-chip cookies that had gone from freezer to table in a matter of minutes. She smiled to herself. How, she wondered, envisioning her younger self through what seemed a backward telescope, did anyone ever *stand* that Mrs. J. Curran Holcolmb?

Straightening, she commanded the attention of everyone in the room. "Well, ladies, I have some good news and some bad news to report to you today."

"Tell us the good news first." Gayle raised her hand like an old-time Southern Baptist giving her testimony to the congregation. "That way we'll all of us be in a better frame of mind when you have to hit us with the worst. I can't abide hearing the bad news first because no matter how good, the good news that comes after it just doesn't have the same shine that it ought to—that it would have—if we'd heard it first."

Apparently Naomi agreed with Rose's image of Gayle's reaction because she chimed in. "Preach it, Sister Barrett."

"Now who's not funny?" Gayle arched one of those spidery thin eyebrows at Naomi, who was ensconced at the opposite end of the sofa. But the remark lacked the bite of the exchanges these two had had during those first meetings. It seemed almost as if they were warming to each other. It looked like Naomi might have already found a friend in New Bethany, albeit not a bosom buddy.

"Is that a vote for good news first, Naomi?" Rose asked.

"It was," Gayle spoke for her, then flicked her hand impatiently toward Lucy, who sat glumly hunkered in Curry's wingback. "And Lucy thinks so, too."

Gayle scooted forward until she perched on the edge of the sofa, leaning forward, knees together—in fact everything about her was together tonight right down to her painted nails—unlike the last time Rose had noticed. Maybe she'd read too much into Gayle's marred appearance last time. That thought gave Rose some relief.

"As I've said I have good news and bad news. I will give the good news first as requested by—"

"Oh, go ahead and say it," Gayle urged.

"Come on already, Rose." Naomi laughed.

Lucy sighed and mumbled something that sounded like, "Go ahead, get it over with," but Rose couldn't be sure.

"The good news," she announced holding her hands out, "is that just by having y'all in my house this afternoon, I have made a discovery. Well, that is, I have given it some thought before and I'll confess that at the last meeting it did occur to me, but all of a sudden when I saw that sweet child in my kitchen looking so…puny…"

"Rose!" Gayle smacked her open hand to her thigh. "You're rambling!"

"Guess that makes her a—"

"Do not say it," Gayle warned Naomi with a lightning reflex.

Naomi played it all big-eyed and innocent, but the moment Gayle's back turned, she spoke from the side of her mouth "Rambling Rose."

"I did not hear that." Gayle put her palm toward the other woman. "What is it you've decided to do, Rose?"

"I am going to sell my house."

"No!" Gayle gaped at her.

"Really?" Naomi tipped her head thoughtfully to one side.

Even Lucy sat up and mouthed a "wow."

Rose smiled. "To be truthful, I never felt entirely at home in this house. It was always Curry's pride and joy and now that he's…" She tugged at the collar of her tailored shirt. "Well, with Stacey living in Atlanta and Kelley taking a job in Nashville, it is too much house for just me. I'm going to sell it."

"Good for you." Naomi gave her a look of self-satisfied amusement, held up one finger and added, "And when the time comes, I think I can suggest a realtor."

Rose began to ask whom above Gayle and Naomi's talking at once, but it was Lucy's quiet rasping voice that penetrated the undertones.

"B-but if you sell this house, where will our prayer meeting be held?" She cast a furtive glance out the picture window.

Raymond Grigg's house sat dark and quiet, Rose noted, and her heart went out to Lucy. "We'd still have it at my place, Mary Lucille. But it wouldn't be *this* place."

Lucy shook her head, her eyes unfocused. "B-bu...I...I thought..."

"Truth is, we're getting ahead of ourselves on that matter anyway," Rose said, the momentary headiness of her announcement giving way to the bleakness of the rest of her news.

"Because it will take you a long time to get this place in shape and then find a buyer, locate a new place, then pack and move and so on." Gayle said firmly what someone else might have posed as a question.

"Well, yes, that." Rose fished in her pocket for her hankie and, not encountering it, made do with rubbing her hand up the back of her neck. She was not perspiring, but needed something to do with her hands as she pressed down the cold, sickly feeling in the pit of her stomach and delivered her bad news. "But the main reason we may not have to worry about where we'll hold our prayer meetings is...that unless something changes immediately around here, there are not going to be any more prayer meetings to hold."

Ten

"Not one prayer request? Not one single prayer?" Ted leaned back in his chair and tossed his cloth napkin onto the table.

"Not a one." Gayle scraped the serving spoon over one everyday blue-and-gold china plate to push the dinner scraps onto a sauce-stained platter. "So you can see, I really do have my work cut out for me."

"You?" He handed her his own plate to empty onto the platter also. "Why do *you* have to do anything?"

She clanked his plate on top of hers a little too indelicately, which made her wince for the behavior as much as the wear on her dishes. "Well, if I don't help encourage some prayer requests, who will?"

"I don't know, Gayle, the ministers of the town's churches? They should be turning in prayer requests I'd think—or the hospital chaplain, the Sunday school teachers, the youth leaders. Those kinds of people. It's their responsibility, not yours." He splayed both hands over the white jacquard tablecloth and leaned in like a lion poised to pounce.

She braced herself, standing stock still at his side. "I made a commitment to this, Ted. It's not just another civic or social duty for me, it's a ministry."

"You made the commitment to do the *praying*, Gayle, not to beat the bushes to find people who need that ministry."

"Yes, that's well and good for you to sit there and say, but if we don't get any prayer requests, we cannot have a prayer circle." Just saying it made her breathing shallow, as if suffocated by the enormity of the consequences of allowing that to happen. When she spoke again she could only whisper. "For the first time in over fifty years, New Bethany will not have a prayer circle."

He looked up at her with sympathetic eyes. The late-day sunlight from the dining-room window skimmed across the brilliant white of his business shirt, making his back appear broader than possible and his hair gleam like gold. He sighed, and she knew he felt the weight of the passage of time—the loss of the things that gave their life a quiet dignity and a kind of intangible loveliness—as much as she did. Didn't he?

"You know, Gayle, it's a beautiful tradition, truly it is. Borne of a special bond that folks here have always shared—perhaps more in the past than they do now. But have you ever thought that perhaps it has outlived its purpose?"

She couldn't believe what she was hearing. He was talking about their town, the ways in which they were both raised, the things that made their lives…perfect.

"Noble as it is for you to want to try to save it, maybe it's time to just let this tradition…pass on." He reached for her hand.

Pass on? How could he say that? How could he suggest it? She jerked her hand away from his advance. "Nuh-uh. It may well be that the circles and the trees and everything they stood for—that they *stand* for—are no longer part of how we live today, but that does not make it without purpose. That does not mean we should just let it *pass on.*"

"Gayle, I—"

"Oh, it very well could be that this tradition will die off, that no one will want to take it on after our turn is over. The prayer circles may be silenced. But that will not happen while *I'm* serving. I will not *let* that happen—not on my watch. Nuh-uh, no sir."

"Let the music swell with passion, raise your fist in the air, and I'd swear you were Scarlett O'Hara come back to save Tara, my dear."

"If your voice hadn't simply dripped with husbandly pride just now, Mr. Ted Barrett, you can rest assured that I would have raised my fist indeed." She acquiesced to his good-natured ribbing with a tender smile.

He laughed, then his laugher changed to a groan. He rubbed his thumb and forefinger into the corners of his eyes and asked wearily, "Well, then, what about Rose?"

"What about her?"

"I thought she was y'all's secretary. I thought it was her job to collect the requests."

"She's willing to receive them, to make sure they get to the group, but she will not go out looking for them. She made that very clear."

Gayle slid their two plates on top of those laid out for, but unused by, two of her three children. She'd set the table before leaving the house that afternoon and had prepared the full meal so that all it would need was warming, just in case she was late returning. Dinner in the Barrett household was always at 7 P.M. Sharp. No exception. So, Ted and Lillith had already sat down to the meal when she'd arrived at a quarter past seven from her quarterly meeting of the Friends of the Library. Neither Nathan nor Mathina had joined them for dinner, and Lillith had scampered off as soon as she could to visit with the neighbor's new puppy.

Gayle would never allow her children to have a puppy. They were too messy—the animals, not the children. Her children, she thought, picturing them scrubbed and frilled and bright-eyed, understood the importance of tidiness in one's appearance and one's daily habits. Dogs, Gayle thought, ignoring the chunky clacking of the flatware as she gathered it in one hand, dogs were wild and smelly and all-together far too…upsetting to any reasonable household routine.

"But why?"

Gayle blinked. Had she been talking to herself and Ted overheard her? She cleared her throat and set the flatware down as gently as if it were delicate fragments of spun glass. "Why *what?*"

"Why won't Rose round up prayer requests?" he asked, slowly and far too loud.

She raised one finger at the man and lowered her voice in equal proportion. "Don't talk to me the way your mother does her gardener. I have a masterful grasp of the English language—and so, by the way, does he. He is a lovely man with an adorable family and an admirable way with the landscaping arts. And your mama makes a big ol' fool of herself shouting at him syllable-by-syllable like he was some kind of hearing-impaired mental deficient."

"So, she's a little politically incorrect—"

"She is politically incoherent!"

"Just leave my mama out of this," he muttered, then gave her a sly wink and added, *"Por favor."*

"I was just saying—"

"You were just saying why Rose won't round up…"

"Oh, that's right." She rolled her eyes, keenly aware of the white-on-white dining-room decor around them and all the work that awaited her if she hoped to keep the house looking neat and affable. She sighed. "But, Ted, honey that is a long story."

"Then sit." He pushed back the seat next to him with the toe of his wingtip. "I have time."

"But I—"

"Sit." It wasn't a suggestion. "I've hardly spent a moment alone with you since that meeting last Sunday. Catch me up."

"Oh, all right." She sank into the chair but remained poised on the edge, planning to capsulize everything and be back on her feet in three shakes of a lamb's tail. "All right. Rose won't solicit prayer requests because of something that happened when Curry was still alive."

"Is this going to be one of their fight stories?" Ted scooted his chair close to the table and leaned in over his folded arms. "I love those. They had glorious—*monumental*—fights. I never get tired of hearing about those."

"Ted! Listen to what you just said!" She slapped at his forearm. "That's horrid. Wanting to hear the cold, unhappy facts of someone else's marriage."

"Cold? Unhappy?" He laced his hands behind his head. "Curry and Rose? Their marriage was anything but."

"But the fights—"

"Don't you get it, Gayle?"

She shook her head, helpless to comprehend.

"Nobody could have fights like Curry and Rose did—flowers flying, high drama, the…the purity of it—nobody could have fights like that and still stay so obviously in love unless their marriage was filled with incredible passion." His eyes lit. Tension and intensity radiated, subtle but almost palpable, from his body.

It unnerved Gayle a bit and yet excited her. "Ted, I don't think yelling at one another and throwing things and stomping about is the mark of a healthy relationship."

"No, no, of course not. And you know they were never violent or abusive, just vocal and, well, enthusiastic." He rammed his fingers back through the shocks of his sandy brown hair.

"And that's not for everybody. No. It wouldn't do for us, of course."

"No."

He tapped his fist to the table and looked into the distance. "But sometimes, sweet thing, I wish…"

He cut himself off, and Gayle did not urge him to finish. He frightened her like this. It frightened her to hear him speak of arguments and…enthusiasm. That just was not like Ted, not like the man she married. And it certainly was not like her.

"Anyway," she said softly, rushing on to direct the conversation back to something that made her feel safe again, "Rose won't solicit prayers because she did not go to the prayer circles when Curry had that last heart surgery, and for very specific reasons. She had…lost faith…in the custom, felt it had strayed too far from it's roots, that kind of thing."

"And she thinks others may feel the same way and not want to be goaded?"

"No…well, yes, but that's not why she won't do it." Feeling calmer now, Gayle raised her gaze to the window and tried to get the story straight as Rose had told it. "It seems that when Curry took a turn for the worse she *did* break down and call the circles, and that set into motion something she is having a hard time forgiving. A deathwatch, she called it."

"A deathwatch?"

"Yes, it seems her call spurred a casserole baking frenzy— you know, to have something to bring to the house for after Curry died. The church ladies went on red alert, servers were rounded up and instructed to hold open their afternoons for the dinner in the church after the funeral—"

"Oh, I can imagine how well that set with Rose, especially given her falling out with her church at the time."

"It did not help things, no. Looking back, even Rose admits

though that it was probably just the work of a few overzealous organizational types. I can think of a couple past presidents of the Junior League who served that year." She narrowed the odds as she figured in her head who might have done it. "I would not put it past either one of them."

"Well, you know the Junior League's training is second only to war college in efficiency and organization—"

"Stop making jokes," she warned.

"You only think I'm joking. Don't forget, I've been on the front lines, *ex*-Madam President." As if his teasing hadn't nettled her sufficiently, he added a little salute.

She ignored him, but she could not ignore the uneasiness the comparison created in her.

"So, if Rose has such a problem with the prayer groups, why join one this year?"

"Well, she didn't let them pray for Curry and he...she lost him." Gayle hadn't really given it much thought until now, but as she did she felt her brow furrow. "Maybe she feels some measure of...contrition."

"You mean guilt."

"Ted!"

"What?"

"Guilt? It doesn't sound like a very honorable reason to volunteer to serve."

He laughed, but he did not appear one bit amused. "Maybe not, but Rose Holcolmb would hardly be the first woman to join the prayer circle for that very reason."

Her head snapped up. "What's that supposed to mean?"

"Nothing." He did not meet her gaze.

On another day she night have pursued it, but after the odd twists of this conversation, she lacked the curiosity to do so. "The point is, Ted, that Rose felt the ladies of those circles behaved like vultures, lurking around to prey on someone else's misfortunes. And to complicate things, Lucy Jewell agrees. She thinks asking people for prayer requests is the equivalent of prying into their personal business—"

"Oh, speaking of Lucy, you never told me, did her boyfriend ever show up back at his house?"

She blinked as if orienting herself to a sudden change in scenery. "Um, no. No. Not while we were there, at least. Of course, after Rose's pronouncement and our agreeing that if there were no more requests, we'd discuss it in depth next time, there didn't seem much reason to stick around."

She stood, hoping it didn't seem as if she felt the same way about this conversation. "If you'll excuse me, sweetheart, I have to get these dishes done up."

"That's the kid's job," he reminded her.

"Well, do you see any kids here to do it?" She held out her hands to emphasize the emptiness of the dining room.

"Maybe you should just leave it for them."

"I can't."

"Then maybe you should scale down the whole dinner event, make it more viable for the way we live now that the kids are older instead of clinging so much to—"

She struck down that suggestion with an icy glare.

The only sounds that followed were the clatter of silverware and the clink of china as she stacked and gathered them into her hands to take them to the kitchen. Walking so straight she could have balanced the plates on her head and never let them rattle—just as she learned with a teacup and saucer in charm school at age nine—she walked to the door. She felt Ted's eyes on her, felt something left unsaid or undone between them. What, she was not comfortable imagining. Yet something more needed to be said.

At the doorway, she turned. "Maybe I could just rinse these off and leave them for the children to finish. When did Nathan and Mathina say they'd be home?"

"Well, you know how things go on the nights Nathan mows your folks' grass. He comes home too late, too full, and too spoiled to be of much use to anyone around here."

Gayle smiled. She liked the fact that her son enjoyed his visits with her parents. "And Mathina? When will she be home?"

He shrugged quite deliberately. "Who knows? She and her friends were going to the movies. I just told her not to be too late."

"And did you bother to define 'too late'? Midnight? Two in the morning?"

"Calm down, Gayle. You know Max would never push her limits that far. She's a good kid, she can be trusted, and I think it's time you started treating her like it instead of like she was—"

The dishes felt like lead in her hands, her arms quivered as if they might not have the strength to hang on. "Instead of like she was what?"

"Instead of like she was Naomi Beauchamp. There, I said it. I finally said it."

"You've said it, but you haven't made me understand it. I didn't think you even knew Naomi."

"I didn't. I still don't. But I do know she was your friend when you were about Max's age. And I also know that since she's come back into town, that you've been…"

She clutched the plates until the rims pressed grooves into her palms.

"Different, somehow." His eyes held no accusation, no anger, no anxiety. He simply looked at her and, with his words, let her know he was struggling to see inside her as well. He cocked his head and concluded, "I just can't help but think there's some kind of connection, Gayle. Something about Naomi that has you…a little scared."

"Don't eat that," Naomi mouthed to Taylor before he could even settle the dolled-up Ritz cracker appetizer onto his fancy paper napkin.

He stuck his neck out a bit, his brow pleated down over those seriously mesmerizing eyes of his, as if to say "Come again?"

She glanced over her shoulder to ensure that Mama was still in the next room, rummaging through the buffet drawer for a photograph of the house in it's prime that Naomi had suggested they show their guests. When she knew Mama would not catch her at it, Naomi scrunched up her entire face in a distasteful display and stabbed her finger toward the tidbits they'd been offered with their coffee, which they'd told Mama they preferred to tea.

Taylor got the gist of it and nodded.

Naomi would have given him an apologetic smile in return but she had another, more immediate concern. Kate, Taylor's cheerful-faced younger sister, had lifted her cup and was on the verge of taking a sip of coffee.

Naomi sliced her hand through the air to stop the act. Then, laying her own hand atop her filled cup, she shook her head very slowly.

Kate's cup made a solemn little tap as she replaced it in its saucer.

Mama, oblivious to it all, waddled into the living room, the picture in her fist and lowered herself into her favorite chair. "How is everything?"

"You've outdone yourself, ma'am," Taylor said in that deep, lazy drawl of his.

Naomi noted how the man appeased her mother without telling an out-and-out lie. She liked that.

"Everything is lovely, Mrs. Beauchamp," Kate murmured.

"Oh, I am so glad you young people like it. You know, Naomi wanted to serve store-bought, but I wouldn't have it. Wouldn't let her do the fixin's, neither. I wouldn't hear of it. It's my home, don't you know, and I am still quite able to stir up some chicken salad."

Taylor set the napkin bearing the appetizer aside, as if he now understood it might be squirming with salmonella.

"And brew up a batch of coffee. It's instant but you can't taste the difference," Mama went on.

As if on cue, Kate and Taylor glanced down into their cups without moving their heads to give them away. Naomi wondered if they had as many coffee grounds, which Mama had mistaken for instant, floating in their cups as she did.

"I don't drink coffee, myself, of course." Mama sighed. "Nomi's daddy—now there was a coffee drinker."

Mama gazed off into space for one, two, maybe six seconds, as if she had totally disconnected from the moment. Then she looked at Taylor, then Kate. She smiled, her lips lifting up far more on one side than the other so that she looked almost in pain.

"We're having a bad day," Naomi whispered to Taylor, who was seated next to her.

"Nonsense." Mama waved the photograph in her hand. "Today is no worse than any other day."

Taylor and Kate gave Naomi a weighted glance.

"I hope preparing for our visit hasn't taxed you too much, Mrs. Beauchamp." Kate reached toward Mama.

Mama grasped at the young woman's fingers as one might catch one's self from falling on a slippery surface.

"Nonsense," Mama said. "Wasn't taxing at all. It's always pleasant, to my way of thinking, to have company come to pay a call, especially young people. It makes the day so…"

She trailed off again, not just in her voice but in her whole presence.

"Why don't you show us your picture, Mrs. Beauchamp?" Taylor urged, clearly trying to draw her back from wherever she had drifted.

"My—? Oh. Oh, yes, you wanted to see how we kept the yard and garden years ago, didn't you?" She gripped the arms of her chair and began to push herself up. "I have a picture—"

"Isn't this it?" Before Mama could heave herself upward, Taylor was on one knee in front of her chair, his hand on the photo. The effect of his swift action stilled Mama in her seat and so disarmed her by its charm that she actually admitted to him something she never would have said to Naomi.

"Thank you for getting the photograph for me, son. I don't know if I could have made the walk to the dining room to search for it. It seems I'm all done in today."

He smiled up at her. "Well, then maybe we'd better cut our visit short and let you go lay down awhile and rest up."

"Don't let me run you off." She patted the air above his shoulder, never quite making the contact she seemed to intend.

Taylor put his large, benevolent hand over her frail, trembling one and simply held it. "You aren't running us off. We'll stay and talk with Naomi awhile, and then we'll have a reason to come back again. To finish our visit with you."

"That's good." Mama nodded. "That's good."

Gently, so gently, Taylor helped her up from her seat. She took a step forward, clinging to his side, then wavered.

Naomi rushed to her, but Mama swatted away her outstretched hands.

"Leave it be, Nomi, leave it be. It's been a long, long while since I've walked on a handsome man's arm. Allow me this small indulgence."

Taylor grinned his somewhere-between-sly-and-shy grin and guided her mother forward with plodding patience.

Naomi hurried ahead to turn down the bedcovers and plump the pillows.

Taylor escorted Mama into the darkened room, the two of them looking like shadows as their huddled outline moved in front of the big oval mirror above the dressing table. Bending at the knees to accommodate her, Taylor lowered Mama until she sat on the edge of the bed. As he pulled away from her, a strand of her hair, wispy as cotton candy, was dragged out of place by the lapel of his black sport coat and left dangling along her nose. He paused to smooth the stray hair back against her temple where it belonged.

"You're a nice man." Mama patted him on the cheek. "A nice man. I like you."

"And I like you, too, Mrs. Beauchamp." He gave her hand a squeeze and straightened to move out of the way.

"I like him, Nomi."

"Yes, Mama." Naomi was thankful that the dimness of the room hid her schoolgirl blush from the man with the twinkle in his blue, blue eyes. She knelt and slipped the soft leather shoes from Mama's chilled little feet.

"You get a good rest now, Mrs. Beauchamp, you hear?" he told Mama as he waited, framed in the doorway.

"I will, I..." Mama curled her hands closed on top of the covers that Naomi had just pulled over her chest. "Goodness, I *do* like him. You like him, too, don't you Nomi?"

"He's..." She swallowed. She had no intention of declaring her growing interest and admiration for this man in such a disadvantaged situation. Her battered disposition toward members of the opposite sex simply would not let her be that vulnerable. "He's better than a creeping kudzu vine."

She heard him chuckle softly behind her.

"What's that?" Mama asked.

She leaned over her mother, much as she remembered her mother bending over her so many times, to place a kiss on her forehead. "I said he...he kind of grows on you."

"Take care of this one, Nomi."

"Mama, *please*," she whispered.

"You take care of her, too, young man."

"Mama, he's not in any position to make that kind of—"

"Yes, ma'am. I will."

The quiet conviction of his words and the fact that he did not shirk from the simple request surely made the old woman happy. As for the young woman, well, it made her hopeful. Naomi felt all warm inside and at the same time, she shivered as though buffeted by a cold wind.

"Mama, I can take care of myself," she protested, stroking her mother's brow and inhaling the scent of medicine, vapor rub, and day cologne. "I don't need a man to—"

"Promise me, young man," Mama warbled out to make herself heard over Naomi's claims.

"Mama, now stop that, he doesn't have to—"

"I promise."

Naomi looked into her mother's eyes. Years ago, a lecture, perhaps even a great show of flouncing about, head held high, would have answered her mother's interference. But the kindness in Taylor's voice coupled with the soft, pleading light in Mama's eyes staved that off. Mama only wanted Naomi to be happy. As a mother herself she understood that and she forgave her mother's meddling for what it was: the purest kind of love she'd ever known.

"Sleep tight, Mama." Naomi kissed her again. "I love you."

"I love you, too, Nomi." Mama's dry lips moved against Naomi's cheekbone. "I will always love you, no matter what, even when this tired old body isn't around anymore, I will love you, my baby."

Something about that alarmed Naomi even as it comforted her. She wanted to linger awhile, but Mama rallied from her sleepiness and pointed to the door.

"Now, you skedaddle, Nomi. Go take that young man of yours in there and feed him something and...be nice to him."

"Yes, ma'am," she murmured, smiling as she stood and walked away, glancing back just once before shutting the door.

"I don't need anyone to take care of me." Naomi could not look at the man as she brushed by him on the way back into the living room.

"I understand." Taylor followed at her heels.

"But I do appreciate—" She turned and found her nose inches from his chin. Recovering quickly from the shock of it, she tilted her head back. "I do appreciate your humoring my mama that way."

He nodded.

She hurried back to the end of the sofa where she'd been sitting before all this started.

Taylor took the other end of the Big Green Blob, as Naomi had often called the thing.

She felt his weight sinking into the sagging cushions, as if she needed anything to make her more aware of his nearness. She wanted to say something, to make some blithe, clever remark that would dispel the awkwardness tinged with the sad reality of what they had just experienced. Her lips would not move.

He must have sensed her unease because he became restless himself. He started to pick up his coffee cup, hesitated, then folded his hands and let them fall between his open knees.

Naomi thought of using Kate to get the conversation going again, and that's when she realized that Taylor's sister seemed nowhere to be found.

"I hope you don't mind—" a voice came from the kitchen just then—"but I took the liberty of making some real coffee and poking around the house a bit to get some idea of the lay-out and amenities."

Kate appeared in the doorway carrying a tray with three fresh, steaming cups of rich-smelling brew. She set the tray down between them and each prepared their coffee as they preferred it without saying a word.

Finally, Kate dropped into her seat, a shabby floral thing with a tea towel pinned in place over the back to hide its worst worn spot.

"I hope your mother gets to feeling better real soon," Kate said, just before she took a sip of her coffee.

Naomi tapped her nail against the rim of one of her mother's best china cups. "I wish I could say there's hope she will, but…her doctor says she's had a small stroke."

"Oh, no," Kate murmured.

Taylor shifted forward in his seat.

"I finally got her to go to see him this week, and that's what he said. She's had a small stroke. He doesn't know exactly when, but he does believe she'll have another…and then another. One of them will eventually end it all." Her voice sounded broken and childlike in her own ears. And that after she'd told Taylor she did not need anyone to take care of her.

Exhaling in a short, harsh huff at her immature behavior, she pushed down her fear and anxiety and tossed back her hair from her face with a confident shake of her head. "She'll need constant supervision, perhaps increased nursing care. Who knows what all to come. She has a tidy nest egg…for when she gets old she tells me." Naomi managed a smile at that. "But it won't be enough to pay for a rest home, not for long, not unless we sell the house. I'd like to be able to care for her at home, of course, but—"

"Don't you have family to come in and spell you?" Kate asked.

Naomi sighed. "I have a cousin in Louisville. His folks died when he was young and he came to live with us his senior year in high school. Mama is like a second mother to him but he's a very busy man. He can't put everything on hold to come down and help with this."

"And you or your mother, don't you have any friends who could…" Kate did not elaborate on what anyone could provide, but it didn't matter anyway.

Naomi shook her head. "Most of Mama's friends are in worse shape than she is. Up until a year ago she was the one taking care of them. Princess and Marguerite Johnson have volunteered, one or the other of them at a time, to sit with Mama while I go to the grocery store or if I have something I have to do outside the house. But that's only now and again, short term."

"What about you?" Taylor peered at her, studying. "Don't you have any old ties here?"

"Me? I haven't set foot in New Bethany for ten years. I used to bring Mama up to spend summers with me in my cottage in Maine, where it was cooler. She loved the ocean."

Naomi thought of Mama, bundled in a pastel-colored quilt,

sitting on the beach, savoring the smell of the water and wriggling her feet in the pale sand.

"And then we'd spend our Christmas holidays in Louisville at my cousin's big house. He'd come down and get Mama and I'd fly in with my son. We'd have a grand time, but it did keep me from coming back to New Bethany. I'm afraid any friendships I had have long ago evaporated."

"Funny thing about friendships," Taylor spoke into his coffee cup before lifting those serene eyes to focus solely on her. "Time doesn't seem to have anything to do with them. Sometimes someone you've just met can prove a truer friend than someone you've known forever. And sometimes those friendships that seem withered by neglect can come back full force with just a little attention and nurturing."

He spoke the truth, and it humbled Naomi a bit to hear it.

"Still…" She sank her teeth into her lower lip. "I'm convinced that the best thing for Mama, the safest thing, is for her to go into a nursing home where they can keep an eye on her round the clock."

"Have you looked at any places for her?" Kate asked.

"No, but I'm aware they cost a lot of money. I've done all right for myself as a local craftsperson selling folk-art pottery to tourists in my hometown in Maine, but right now I have a son in a very expensive college. That's a strain on any budget." Naomi stubbed the toe of her sandal into the braided rug at their feet. "So I'm afraid I'll have to put off choosing which home to place Mama in until I have some idea how much her house will bring in."

Kate gave a knowing nod. "Well, structurally the house is sound and the neighborhood is a nice one. In fact, it experienced a sort of rebirth a few years ago as a result of urban flight, the need to get back to simpler times."

"That's good, then?"

Kate winced a bit. "The thing is, it needs work. If you're desperate to sell, we could market it as a fixer-upper, take less money for it. But I'll be honest with you, I don't see how we can do anything with it until we get the yard squared away and maybe get a coat of paint on the house."

"I can help you with that in the evenings after I leave the nursery," Taylor volunteered. "In fact, I can get started on it tonight, just need to go home and change, see what Ashley—that's my daughter—has planned for the evening."

"Oh, that reminds me." Kate jumped up. "I met Taylor here so I could go pick Ashley up from school. I promised to take her to buy a new dress. For some reason she does not trust her daddy's fashion sense."

Taylor laughed, but Naomi got the idea he was a little hurt by the remark. He stood to tell his sister good-bye, so Naomi followed suit.

Kate gave her brother a hug as she passed by him, then, to Naomi's surprise, did the same to her. "I'll do some preliminary figures on the house for you tonight, Naomi, and give you a call tomorrow."

"Thank you, Kate, for everything," Naomi called after her.

And she was gone.

"Well, I guess I'd better git, too." Taylor seemed not to know what to do with his hands. "The faster I change into work clothes, the faster I can dig into the yard work. I can be back in half an hour or forty-five minutes."

Naomi twisted her fingers together, feeling put on the spot, her head swimming from everything that had just happened—and everything that *might* happen if Taylor Boatwright were to start coming around here every evening. "As much as I'd like to, I can't work on the yard tonight. We're having an emergency meeting of the prayer circle. Marguerite Johnson is coming by to sit with Mama for a couple hours so I can go."

"That's all right, I can get the work started without you. That is, if you trust my judgement in it."

"Oh, I couldn't let you…it's too much…I…."

"You don't have the luxury of *not* letting me, Nomi." He used the pet name like a child prodding a toad to see if it would jump.

She did not even bat an eyelash.

"I know you can't afford to hire it done," he went on. "And you don't have the time to do it piecemeal whenever you can slip away from caring for your mother."

"It's my problem, I don't need your—"

"I'll do it and I won't hear any more about it."

"Well, that's too bad because I have plenty more to say about it." Naomi planted her hands on her hips, fed up with his patronizing attitude. Who did he think he was, anyway? "Welcoming a little kindness toward my ailing mother is one thing, but to let you horn your way in and start telling me what to do with the yard and how I should let you start in on it right away? I don't think so."

"Then you've got another think coming, it seems." He didn't say it combatively, but more with resignation offered on her behalf. Then he turned and strode across the room, his pace clipped but not rushed or impatient.

When he opened the front door and stood with the afternoon sunlight streaming in around him, he fixed his eyes on hers and dipped his head as though tipping an unseen hat. "I am not doing this simply out of sympathy for a sweet old lady or just because it's the decent, neighborly thing to do, you know."

"Then just why are you doing it?" Challenge rankled in her tone. "I didn't ask—"

"Because I like your mama, Naomi." His soft-spoken accent somehow made it sound more honest, from the very heart of the man. "And—much as it seems to grate on your nerves—I like you, too. If it wouldn't stretch no one's imagination to hear me confess it, I like you a lot."

Not only did that shut her up, it silenced her anger and her indignation as well.

"And I'll tell you something else."

She blinked at him, trying to take it all in, unsure she really wanted to. "What?"

"I made a promise to your mother to take care of you. And I am not a man who takes his promises lightly."

He closed the door and left her alone.

Naomi's pulse thudded in her temples like hail on a tin roof. She had such a bad track record with men. Could she have finally found a good one? And even if she had, why did he have to come along when everything in her life was so...tumultuous?

Warm tears bathed her eyes but did not fall as she offered up this quick prayer, "In Jesus' name, dear Lord, show me what to do about Mama and Taylor, and give me the presence of mind and the grace to handle my delights as well as my disappointments. Amen."

She didn't know which one Taylor would provide—delight or disappointment—but the way things were going, she had a feeling it would not be too long before she found out.

Eleven

R ay? Raymond Griggs? Did you hear what I said?" Lucy
marched into the living room, soap bubbles still clinging to her dishwater-reddened hands.

Every Sunday for lunch, every Tuesday and Thursday night
for supper for the last three years, Ray had come to her house
to gobble up her cooking. Friday nights, "date night," he took
her out, though that usually meant grabbing foot-long coneys
at his store and eating in the office or the car. If he didn't cancel
the whole thing, of course. However, he never failed to show
on those nights when she prepared a home-cooked meal. So
even tonight, with the pressure of the important prayer meeting looming over her, not to mention her own growing misgivings about her relationship with this man, Lucy had thrown
together something hot and nutritious for him.

He'd lumbered in from work just as she'd put the food on
the table and proceeded to wolf it all down without hardly a
pause for pleasant conversation. He did ask her if she had lost
weight. When she'd demurred and said she thought maybe she
had, he'd told her she had more to go.

Then he'd quickly added, "Not too much now. I like you
plump enough you don't go drawing any other man's eye."

For Ray that was heady, sweet talk, and if it was meant to
take Lucy's mind off her suspicions it had worked—or, at least,
it had diverted her thoughts for a time. If Ray was jealous of
her, she decided as a flicker of confidence made her heart beat
faster, that meant he wanted to keep her. If he wanted to keep
her, then he wasn't going to run off with another woman. He

might stray from the path a bit, but he'd come back to her. Wouldn't he?

After all, Nikki was cute and slim and sweet in her own fashion, but Lucy wasn't a troll, exactly. Besides, she had three years invested in this man. And who knew how many meals.

She'd been a good girl through that time, too, not letting him take advantage physically. So she could understand if perhaps he felt tempted by a dalliance now and again, couldn't she? Everyone made mistakes, she'd told herself. Everyone needed a little forgiveness.

Besides, everything would change once she felt sure enough of him to keep him too…satisfied to stray. Once they were married. And Ray *would* marry her, Lucy determined. When his business was thriving and he was ready, it was Lucy and not Nikki that Ray would choose for a wife and—more to Lucy's concern—as the mother of his children.

Nikki had a child and she had other opportunities. She wasn't from New Bethany and she likely would not stay here for long. They never did. Folks moved here from bigger cities thinking they'd thrive on the simple small town life, only to find themselves bored and restless before a year was out. She'd seen it happen time and again.

Lucy and Ray weren't going anywhere. Their lives and their businesses were here. They couldn't survive elsewhere. They belonged here and they belonged together, it was—comfortable. And practical. And…

A sheer film of sweat dampened the back of Lucy's neck. She felt queasy and out of breath all at once and she could not kid herself any longer. Ray *had* to marry her, because where else would Lucy find a man who would want her?

She swallowed down a lump of what she suspected was her last bit of pride and moved toward the man. She could not afford the luxury of petulance right now, she had to find a more palatable way to shore up her lost ground with him.

"Ray, honey, did you hear what I asked you?" She stood over him where he was planted in his usual spot: in front of the TV, remote poised at the ready for channel surfing. "I wanted to know if you'd still be here when I get back from my meeting."

"I don't know. How long you gonna be?"

"No telling. But it's over at Rose Holcolmb's. I could stop by your house after if you're not going to stay here."

"No." He jabbed his thumb down on the channel button. "No, I'll stay."

She smiled and used a voice sweeter than honey dripped on sugar cakes. "Good, because there's something I wanted to talk to you about."

"Aw, Luce." Ray groaned. "Don't you know those are the four most dreaded words a man can hear—'we have to talk'?"

Her stomach went sour, but her smile remained unchanged. "But Ray, honey, that's what people in relationships do. Talk."

He grunted his response to that.

She poked her hands into her pockets and consoled herself with the fact that he hadn't said no outright or changed his mind about sticking around until she got home.

The light from the TV flickered across his sullen features as the channels whizzed by without stopping.

"We'll talk later then, Ray. Okay?"

The channels kept flicking past.

"Ray?"

"You know what you need, Lucy?" He did not take his dazed eyes from the screen.

She feared asking, but she had to. "What, Ray? What do I need?"

"One of them satellite hookups that pipes in five hundred channels. Now that would be sweet."

"Satellite? Five hundred—" She felt slapped. Not even slapped because that would imply deliberate intent to hurt her. She felt…mowed down. Thoughtlessly and irrevocably mowed down, as though she and her feelings were no more significant than a blade of grass.

Here she was trying to arrange a time for them to work on improving their relationship, and he could only think of finding more preoccupations—five-hundred of them—to eat into their time together. And he expected her to foot the bill for it as well. Her mind swam at the notion; her pulse throbbed in her temples. That was too much. Finally, it was too much.

She might have been willing to look the other way concerning Ray's indiscretions in order to eventually get what she wanted, but she would not be blindsided by his indifference to her feelings altogether. She knew the score, and as long as Ray knew that she knew it, he could not make a fool out of her. It might not stop him, but at least he'd know she wasn't some stupid ninny, too blinded by love to see the truth.

Lucy drew herself up, her jersey dress giving a shimmy over her tucked-in tummy. "Speaking of more channels, Ray, it might interest you to know that I got cable installed at the day care today."

"Cable? At the day care? What for?"

"It just so happens there is a lot of educational programming available. I wanted something more than indoor games and videos for rainy days or this winter."

The skin over her throat had grown hot and her jaw muscles coiled tight. She had decided, after her discussion with the cable man, not to confront Ray directly with what she had learned. It was too risky and it would probably only drive a wedge between them. She didn't need that right now. Still, that didn't mean that she wouldn't use her recently acquired knowledge to send Ray a subtle warning.

"You see, the thing is, I got to thinking about Nikki."

"Nikki? Huh? What are you talking about?"

"Just that I remembered Nikki saying she got cable on account of Tiffany. Well, I noticed how bright and advanced Tiffany is for her age, you know, since I've spent so much time with the little girl lately baby-sitting while Nikki…saw to personal things."

He squirmed in the chair, making the slick surface squawk.

"So, I made a call and today this very nice young man, Dwayne Cobb, came out—"

"Dwayne Cobb? Isn't that "Smooty" Cobb's son?"

Oh, you're not getting out of this that easily. She folded her arms. "I honestly didn't ask."

"Hmm. I think he is. Don't you remember him? He was a year or two behind you in high school. Beefy guy, played football—Dwayne, that is, not Smooty. What'd he play? Linebacker? Defensive end?"

"I don't care if Dwayne played football or footloose or even footsies with the Queen of England, for that matter. My point is, I had the cable installed today."

"Hey, you wanted to talk. I was talking."

About something sure to throw me off this track, she thought. But she wasn't falling for it. "Anyway, I got to talking to Dwayne and I asked him if there was any chance of us having the same kind of troubles Nikki had had with her cable. You know, with the installer bringing the wrong equipment and then the coupler going out and you, spending practically a whole Sunday duct-taping it back together…"

She feigned flighty unconcern, but she never took her gaze

off of Ray's flushed face. She watched his every minute reaction from the corner of her eyes. "I told Dwayne we didn't want a repeat of that kind of thing."

"That's not very likely," Ray muttered. He stared ahead. The channel did not change.

"Hmmm. That's exactly what Dwayne said." She tapped her cheek with her fingertip.

"Don't you have a meeting to go to?"

She did, and having gotten her message across, she could do just that. She gathered her bag and stole one last look at Ray in the mirror by the door. "I won't be late."

"Yeah."

She pulled open the door and started out.

"Hey, Luce?" The recliner creaked as he set it upright.

She froze, her voice nothing more than the whisper of a cool breeze over her lips. "What?"

"What made you mention that? About the cable?"

He knew. Getting her message across, she realized, also meant having to live with the consequences. She gripped the handle of her bag.

Outside her door, the sun shone down on hot pavement and deep, green grass, on the chrome of her neighbor's cars that gleamed so bright it stung her eyes. She could step out there. She could let the door bang shut. She could dissolve into the warmth of the evening and slip away without another word, without any peril to the relationship that hung so delicately in the balance right now.

"Luce?"

"I...nothing. Nothing made me mention it." *Forgive me, Lord, for the lie.* The sun still warmed one of her cheeks, but all her awareness was fixed on the man leaning forward with his hard gaze trained on her. "I was just making a…an observation."

He didn't say anything.

She moved out the door. But as she tugged it gently shut behind her, Ray's words came after her, his voice tight and softly tinged with unmistakable remorse and yet clear in his unrelenting intent. "Sometimes, Lucy, it can be a chancy thing to be too observant."

Lucy still shook with emotion as she swerved onto Rose's street. Why, oh, why had she tried to play that kind of game with Ray? What made her think she could out-maneuver a master of manipulation like that?

Well, she had tried it. Now Ray knew that she had not fallen for his little fraud concerning Nikki *and* that she'd been snooping around to try to confirm it. He also knew that she was capable of using what she'd learned to try to control his behavior, even if only by subtlety and shame. In short, she'd backed Ray into a corner, and if she ever brought it up again, it could not be as the devastated, wronged woman but only as his longtime girlfriend ready to issue an ultimatum. If she ever spoke of it again, it would have to be to tell him to choose her or Nikki.

The fine houses on the block blurred in her peripheral vision as she sped on, hoping for once not to arrive late to the meeting. Then she passed Ray's house and, in the driveway, Nikki's car!

The high-pitched squeal of brakes pierced through the blinding confusion of what she had seen. Her attention riveted to the looming side of a dark green minivan. Lucy churned the steering wheel violently to the right and stomped her foot down, all but standing on her own brakes. She felt her tires slide like a runner into home plate. She whispered a prayer—not because she feared for herself but because she could not afford the cost of any repairs.

Her compact car screeched to a halt facing Rose's house, parked next to Gayle's minivan just as neat as you please—except they were both in the middle of the street.

"Lucy, honey, are you all right?" Gayle rushed around the minivan, her heels clacking lightly on the street.

A peculiar, burnt-oil and scorched-rubber smell singed her nostrils as Lucy climbed from her seat, but the assault on her senses seemed the only damage. No scratches, no dents, no dings, except in her composure.

"Of course I'm not all right," she snapped, her hands trembling. "I'm…I'm…" *Dazed? Crushed? Resigned to the fact that I am going to have to share for a while the only man who ever really seemed to want me?* "I'm just a little unnerved, that's all. I guess I wasn't paying close enough attention."

Lucy saw how Gayle eyed the house across the way as she moved in to place her arm around Lucy's shoulders.

But Lucy was not in the mood for sympathy. She just wanted to get on with this obligation and get out of there. She stepped away from Gayle's intended comfort, her back straight, and turned away from the car in Ray's drive. "I was just trying, for once, to not be late to the meeting."

Gayle checked her elegant watch on her equally elegant wrist. "Well, if we hurry and pull into Rose's drive right now—one at a time, for a change—we can just about make it."

"Gayle! Lucy! We thought we heard tires squealing out there." A minute later, Rose stood at the back corner of her house and motioned for the two women coming up the walkway to the kitchen door to join her in the backyard. "Is everything all right?"

Lucy opened her mouth, but Gayle leapt in with a curt "Everything's fine."

She shot Rose a nonverbal warning that promised more detail later and moved onto the spacious brick patio to take a seat at the glass-and-iron table under an enormous floral umbrella.

Lucy sort of trudged along behind, not nearly so animated as in her usual entrances.

It had been Gayle's turn to supply the refreshments for the night. To Rose's delight, cheerful, young "Max" Barrett had delivered a Death By Chocolate cake earlier in the day—along with a bundle of fresh-cut flowers and the prettiest frosted pink dessert dishes and punch cups for serving. The trappings proved so enchanting that it gave Rose the notion to have the meeting outdoors, like a lady's summer tea. She'd made a light punch for the occasion and even polished up her wedding silver, complete with cake knife and server.

"It was so good to see your daughter today, Gayle. She is such a sweet girl." Rose handed Gayle one of her own delicate pink cups filled with a citrus juice and ginger ale potion. "What lovely manners she has and such a precious face!"

Gayle beamed in million-watt pride.

"You've done well with that one, sugar. She does so remind me of you when you were that age."

That pride dimmed. "I don't think so. She's…she's much more like her father." Gayle fussed with the napkin lying over her tightly crossed legs. "All my children are far more like Ted than they are like me. Everyone says so. I know it's true."

Rose felt thoroughly rebuked. "Yes, of course."

She quickly set about dipping up punch for Lucy, then

thrust a cup at her with a bit too much chipperness. "And my, don't you look nice today, Lucy."

"Me?" She pinched at the neck of one of her trademark baggy, sad, and sagging dresses. "Look good? I doubt it."

Rose set the cup down in front of the girl, assuring her, "Oh, of course you do. Don't talk like that. You look splendid. And Naomi—"

She turned her attention back to the woman who had arrived just ahead of the others. Enough ahead to give Rose the name of the realtor she recommended and to murmur something most intriguing about, of all people, Taylor Boatwright. Then Naomi had grown uncharacteristically quiet. She took the cup Rose offered.

"Thank you, Rose." Naomi gazed down into the pale liquid as though it were a crystal ball, or magic tea leaves, or some such place where someone who is very uncertain—and not ready to fully trust the Lord—might seek answers.

Rose took her seat, the tufted cotton pad not nearly as easy on the backside as it was on the eye. "So, Naomi, how is your Mama doing these days?"

Naomi sighed, shook her head, and continued staring bleakly into her cup.

No one said another word. The heat of the day had settled into a languid aura over the manicured backgrounds, and the fragrance from Rose's lavish garden drifted in close around them. Rose's once bright mood, though drained a bit by her guests' surliness and sulking, had not yet dissipated completely.

She did not have good news to share today, and nothing in the other's demeanor led her to think they did either, but that could not deter her. If they were going to hang on to this prayer group, if they were going to find a way to make it work despite the obvious disadvantage of having nothing to pray about, then they had to form a bond that would allow them to keep going.

She picked up the heavy cake knife and poked the tip into the evening's dessert. The blade sank down and down through the thick, rich layers, releasing the aroma of chocolate among the roses. The frosting, having melted just enough to glisten against the shining silver, swept into a creamy curl against the pad of her thumb as she withdrew the knife.

Instinctively, she licked the smooth, delectable sweetness away—and then it hit her. Chocolate. Bonding. At their first meeting, Naomi had mentioned how women tended to bond over chocolate.

Rose plunked a generous slice of the dark, layered cake onto an oval-shaped plate, her senses transfixed on the generous portion of chocolate temptation. If *this* cake didn't do the trick, nothing short of divine intervention would.

She raised up the piece for all to admire. "Who wants cake?"

"None for me, thank you," Lucy grumbled.

"I couldn't," Gayle muttered.

"Not hungry," Naomi mumbled.

"Oh, come *on*, ladies!" She waved the plate under Lucy's nose. "It looks fabulous."

"Yes, but we won't look fabulous if we eat it," Gayle reminded them.

"Is that what you're worried about?" Rose laughed. "A few calories? Don't you know?"

"Know what?" Lucy asked.

Rose brandished the cake and cocked one eyebrow with the same aplomb. "Calories consumed in the service of the Lord? Totally nullified. Rendered completely incapable of turning into fat on your body."

Naomi grinned. "Oh, yeah, sure. That would explain all those *pencil thin* people stuffing down doughnuts in the fellowship hall after church."

"Socializing in the fellowship hall is not technically service to the Lord," she reminded them, pleased that someone had joined in the jesting.

"Unless you are the minister's wife," Gayle added.

"Or the one pouring coffee," Lucy said, her head bent.

"Regardless, y'all, I do believe Rose has a point. How could our bodies turn against us to transform a bite of chocolate into a behind like cottage cheese? Not when we've come together to do the Lord's work." Naomi reached out to take the pink plate from Rose's grasp. "These are blessed calories."

Rose smiled at the way Naomi said bless-*ed*, using two syllables.

Naomi set the plate down and waved the fork in the air with a flourish. "Let us rejoice and be skinny!"

Gayle leaned over the table. "So says the brains behind the infamous Mustard, Zwieback, and Celery diet."

"The what?" Rose was as intrigued by the remark as she was pleased to have the conversation going.

"I was sixteen," Naomi said as if that explained everything. "And as I recall, Gayle Shorter Barrett, *you* stayed on it a whole week longer than I did."

"Nuh-uh. No, ma'am, I stayed on it *two* weeks longer. Allowing, of course, for the fact that you cheated on it from the git-go." Gayle pretended to be indignant, but her good humor shone.

Naomi fluffed her skirt and sat, looking skyward, all angelic and innocent.

"Just what did this diet involve?" Rose propped her forearms against the edge of the table, still holding the cake knife.

"You could eat anything you wanted." Gayle tipped her nose up to give herself an air of authority.

"Sounds like I'm already on that diet." Lucy looked longingly at the cake.

"I guess that means you'll have some cake with us, won't you, Lucy?" Rose nudged her. "I'll cut you a slice while Gayle explains this diet to us."

"Here, let me, Rose," Naomi offered, taking the knife from her hand. "I already know what Gayle is going to say about this diet."

As Naomi went to work cutting pieces for the others, Gayle expounded.

"As I said, you could eat anything you wanted—as long as you slathered it in mustard first."

"Oh, my!" Rose laughed.

"Yes, I know." Gayle feigned a shudder. "I still twitch uncontrollably at the sight of anything bright yellow."

Naomi smacked Lucy's slab of cake onto a plate.

Gayle reigned in a grin. "The idea being—Naomi's idea, let me hasten to remind you—that the mustard would act as aversion therapy. And if we did manage to choke down anything, the mustard would soon kill our taste buds so that we wouldn't be tempted to finish it."

"Well, there is a certain…logic in that," Rose admitted.

"Thank you, Rose." Naomi handed Lucy her plate.

"In most insanity there is a seed of logic." Gayle overplayed the drama, like some spoof of Nora Desmond in *Sunset Boulevard*.

"Too bad for you this one was a mustard seed," Lucy said, cake in hand.

Initially the three of them responded to Lucy's first attempt at humor and to really being a part of the group with stunned silence.

Then Gayle laughed. "So true, Mary Lucille, so true."

"Good one." Naomi gave the girl an encouraging wink.

Lucy lifted her head and scrunched her shoulders up like a five-year-old praised for a job well done.

"So, you put mustard on everything—" Rose prompted Gayle to keep the story going.

"Everything except celery and zwieback. Celery because Naomi read somewhere that you burned more calories chewing it than it actually contains."

"I've heard that." Rose nodded.

Naomi pointed toward the cake with the knife to ask Rose if she wanted a piece.

Rose nodded again.

"So, the Diva of Diets, here—" Gayle jerked her thumb toward Naomi—"convinces me that by consuming celery I would actually be ahead of the game."

"What about the zwieback?" Rose held an empty plate up for Naomi to place a "healthy" slice of cake on.

"Oh, the zwieback!" Gayle placed her fingers to the bridge of her nose and shut her eyes. "The mustard, as you've said Rose, has a certain logic, and the thinking on celery was a commonly held belief. But the zwieback!"

"C'mon! It wasn't that bad." Naomi put her hands on her hips.

"How would you know? You never ate any of it." Gayle's eyes sparked with laughter. "And there, Rose and Lucy, lies the rub. This woman—"

"Just sixteen years old then," Naomi reminded them.

"Had me eating the nastiest, driest, hardest food substance known to humankind."

"Tasted bad, huh?" Lucy poked at her cake with her fork.

"Taste wasn't even an issue—who could taste after two or three days living with mustard mouth anyway? The thing was these "cookies," as Naomi had so liberally labeled them to me, had a tendency to dissolve very slowly when they came into contact with saliva, which resulted in the slimiest, gooiest, cannot-get-if-off-your-hands-or-teeth-with-a-sandblaster mess you have ever seen."

"Eeewwww." Lucy's small nose crinkled up.

"Eeeewww is right. I went around our high school for two whole weeks with a yellow tongue, sucking celery string out from between my teeth, and with perpetually sticky fingers from handling those awful zwieback."

"How attractive." Rose grinned.

"Exactly. And the irony was we'd gone on this little regimen in order to be more captivating to the opposite sex."

"Well, you lost weight, didn't you?" Naomi pointed with the knife. "Cake?"

"I lost four measly pounds. And you—" She jabbed an accusing finger in the air—"you, Naomi, went off the diet after only five days and did not even tell me you did it. You just let me go right on gagging on mustard and slurping on zwieback. Now what have you got to say about that?"

"I was sixteen."

"Sixteen going on twenty-five! You always did things like that to me, Naomi. You always got me into things I would never have thought of on my own."

"Oh, Gayle, really! It's not like I made you get a tattoo or take up chain-smoking or cut class…oops."

"Thanks for reminding me, I'd completely forgotten about the time *I* got punished for skipping class, and *you* got off with a slap on the hand. Daddy made me work at the church for a month of Sundays—and I *mean* a month of Sundays—and what happened to you?" Gayle pushed her chair back and stood. "You had to spend two afternoons in detention staring at a handsome student teacher."

Naomi did show the good taste to look chagrined despite her smile. "Did you say you wanted cake, Gayle?"

"All of a sudden I'm not sure I should accept any cake from your hands, Naomi. Given our history, I have probably dropped an earring in the batter—you'll find the diamond and I'll choke on the post."

"I have a feeling this isn't just about diets and desserts anymore," Rose said through her teeth to Lucy, who responded with wide-eyed concern.

"Oh, don't be an old sour apple, Gayle. That was a long time ago. This is now. Why don't you have some cake?" Naomi started to cut a slice.

"Fine. I'll have cake, but not that much. I only want a sliver."

"Like this?" Naomi scootched the blade over a fraction.

"Less."

"This?" She adjusted the knife a hair over.

"Less."

"This?" She set off a piece as thin as toast.

Gayle heaved a sigh of exasperation. "For land's sake, Naomi, stop playing games and just give me some cake."

She thrust her open palm out toward her old friend.

"Okey-dokey, Gayle. Here's your cake."

Rose saw it coming and yet could not believe it would actually happen until she heard Gayle shriek when the moist, crumbling piece of cake filled her outstretched hand.

Lucy squealed in something between shock and delight.

Rose could not make any sound, but Naomi's reaction, well-deserved after weeks of Gayle's endless needling, inspired a laugh so silent and deep that it caused a stitch in Rose's side.

Naomi looked like the cat that ate the canary.

Gayle stared, gape-mouthed, for only a moment, before a glimmer of revenge flickered in her eyes and she began to nod her head. "Funny. Very funny, Naomi. Um, Naomi?"

"What Gayle?"

Gayle did not move to clean the cake away but simply stood there. "Do you remember when you said that chocolate could be a bonding experience for women?"

"Oh, no." Naomi took a step back. "No, Gayle, you wouldn't."

"Wouldn't I?" She lifted the remnants of cake now cupped in her hand. Dark crumbs dribbled through her fingers.

Whether she did or did not, Rose didn't get a chance to see for herself because just then the jarring jangle of the phone called her away.

When she returned to tell Naomi that Marguerite Johnson wanted to speak to her, a wad of cake lay in the grass and both Naomi and Gayle were wiping chocolate frosting from their fingers. Lucy had her arms folded over her middle, giggling uncontrollably.

"Is something wrong?" Naomi clutched at Rose's arm instead of taking the cordless phone she'd brought out to her.

"Marguerite didn't tell me anything, but she didn't sound alarmed, if that's what you're asking." Rose held the phone out, her hand over the mouthpiece.

Naomi bowed her head.

For an instant Rose suspected that the younger woman might just bolt and run. Then she took a sharp breath and accepted the phone, moving into the shadows by the kitchen door as Rose slipped back to the group to grant her privacy to talk.

"Is everything all right?" Gayle whispered, clasping at Rose's sleeve with her clean hand.

Rose met her gaze. "I can't tell. You know Marguerite, you can't get a reading from her voice. She's got such a beautiful faith—the peace that passeth understanding, they call it. With that, everything gives her cause to praise the Lord."

"Gosh." Lucy blinked. "That's something to admire."

"Daddy says that very few people in this town appreciate the spiritual debt we owe to Sister Marguerite and Sister Princess." Gayle sank slowly into her chair. "He says if they were white women, they'd have chapels or church libraries or awards named after them, complete with banquets and recognitions. He says he can't wait until he gets to heaven to see the glorious crowns the Lord will bestow on those two lovely souls."

"I can't wait to get to heaven to see the surprise on some of the faces of a handful of the pillars of the community when they find they're sharing eternity with people they wouldn't invite to supper."

They sat in silence for a moment, there being nothing to add to that sentiment.

Rose's thoughts flitted from the service of the Johnson sisters to her own contributions, thinking how hers fell short, especially these last few years. Since the new minister took over at Antioch Baptist, she hadn't done anything, really, to lend spiritual aid to others except her close friends and family and even that had waned—until she'd made up her mind to join the prayer circle. She pushed her plate away, suddenly not interested in the delicious-looking chocolate treat. "You know, girls, we don't have any prayer requests this time, either."

"Then maybe we should pray about *that*." Lucy folded her hands on top of the table.

"Pray for what, Lucy? That people start having troubles enough to turn to us? Simply to justify our turn at service?" Gayle's tone was tart.

Rose opened her mouth, but Lucy did not back down this time.

"Pray, Gayle, just like we did that day in the grove. Not for others to get in trouble, but for God to help *us* out of it. It worked before."

"Having the faith of a child is one thing, Lucy, but now you're acting like a child. Praying is not like ordering from some divine catalog, you know." Gayle touched one of her delicate pearl earrings, obviously unaware that she left a spot of chocolate on it. "It's one thing to pray for God's will and mercy and quite another to go to him with a personal wish list. The task of gathering prayer requests depends on us and our hard work, not on sitting here praying for everything to fall into place."

Rose could not have better illustrated the women's two diverse styles than this exchange. Lucy was the kind to wait and hope—and pray—for everything to work out. Gayle had to get out there and do what needed doing for everyone, no one else could seem to get it right except her. She and Naomi, from what Rose could tell of the other woman, existed somewhere in between. It was the perfect make-up for a prayer circle, the proper balance, if only they had the chance to use their strengths and weaknesses for that purpose. She started to say just that to the women, to put a positive spin on what felt like a terse, uncomfortable turn in their interaction, but Lucy rushed in to speak again.

"I think you're afraid, Gayle, that's what I think." Lucy started to bunch up her dress collar, then let her hand relax and smoothed it down instead. "Last time we prayed, we got Naomi, and that just didn't suit you very well. So you're afraid to try it again."

"Don't be ridiculous." Gayle smirked.

"I am not ridiculous and I am not acting like a child," Lucy countered. "I am, more than any of the rest of you, the person who knows best how it looks and sounds when someone is doing everything within their power to avoid looking the truth in the eye."

Lucy's face went blotchy red and her chin quivered. She sniffled but she did not break down.

In Gayle's expression, compassion for the girl warred with denial for her own behavior.

Neither seemed able or ready to speak.

Rose sighed. "Fact is, sweeties, that whether we go with Lucy's suggestion or Gayle's or both, unless we can fulfill our purpose—to provide prayer support for members of our community in an ongoing fashion—this group is going to flounder and fail. I don't want to see that happen. Now, I know there are people out there who have desperate needs, and here sits a group that is almost equally desperate to lift them up in prayer. We've just got to find—"

"If you're still looking for someone in need of this group's support, well, you've got it." Naomi stood at the edge of the shade, her hand, with the phone still in it, now limp at her side. "Mama just had a stroke."

Twelve

I never should have let her make that chicken salad." Naomi huddled in a hard chrome-and-vinyl seat in the emergency room while the doctors checked her mother over.

"What?" Taylor leaned in from the next seat, his shoulder touching hers.

Naomi fisted her hand in her lap just as a knot twisted its hard, cold grip in her stomach. "I knew Mama was having a bad day. I should have canceled everything and just let her rest."

"The doctor had already warned you that this was inevitable. If you had canceled and she still had the stroke, you'd be sitting here saying, 'Why didn't I let her do what she wanted to do?'"

"But, Taylor the stress of—"

"Was probably no less than the strain she'd have felt arguing with you over not coddling her and the anger she'd have at your taking away her independence in choosing when to have guests over."

Naomi huffed a tiny laugh. "It's like you really know her. And me."

He folded his hands between his knees and looked at the gray-white floor. "Just because I work with trees and shrubs and flowers doesn't mean I haven't learned a few things about people along the way."

"I'm glad you were there when…when it happened." She nudged him with her shoulder to get him to look at her. When he did, even though it was a sidelong glance, she fought back the urge to cry and whispered, "Thank you."

"I just did what anyone would have."

"Not everyone would have had the presence of mind to call the ambulance first, then call me. Marguerite said she wanted to call me first and have me come home to make the decision but you overrode her." She managed a bit of a smile. "Not many folks stand up to Sister Marguerite and win. You really do know how to handle people."

"It wasn't such a big thing."

"It wasn't a small thing, and more to the point, it was what proved best for Mama. The doctors say that with a stroke every minute counts. Whatever you did to convince Sister Marguerite to go your way, I'm glad you did it. How did you do it, anyway?"

"Well, I guess I'd better confess now and just hope you can forgive me for it." He gave a sheepish grin, still not looking directly at her. "I pulled rank on her."

He pulled rank? What did that mean? Only one sickening thought sprang to mind, that as a white man, Taylor had felt his opinion far outweighed Marguerite's and he'd pressed his will with that advantage. She did not want to believe that of this man, but then she was in the South now, and here many people still did hold those kinds of antiquated notions.

She batted her eyes and felt her head shake ever so slightly. "I don't think I understand. How did you pull rank, and why would I have to forgive you for it?"

"I'm afraid I—" He lifted his head and spoke in the direction of the full-color chart of the skeletal system hanging on the wall opposite them—"I told her I was your beau."

"My—"

"Actually, I think I said that we had feelings for one another." Now he turned to her. "In my defense, I don't think that was strictly a lie, and it certainly did elevate my status in her eyes."

Feelings for one another? She pressed her lips together to deny it, but then couldn't. Not while gazing into those eyes. Not while sitting next to a man who had promised her mother he'd take care of her. Not while feeling what she did.

"And in the end, it got the ambulance to your mama that much quicker," Taylor said.

"I...guess you're right," she whispered.

He waited for her to say more, and when she didn't he asked softly, "About what?"

Now it was Naomi's turn to study the graphic chart. Which she did for several weighted seconds before allowing herself to make a confession of her own. "All of it, I guess."

"*All* of it?"

She met his gaze and swallowed. This was neither the time nor place to begin a relationship discussion and she saw that he understood that, which freed her to smile weakly and nod. "All of it."

He sat back in his seat. His arm draped over the back of her chair.

She settled back herself, letting herself draw a bit of strength from his nearness and the feel of his arm around her.

They sat that way in silence as the clock ticked away minute after minute until Taylor finally said, "I suppose the ladies from your circle are still praying."

"Yes, I suppose."

Taylor had commanded her, through Marguerite, not to try to drive herself to the hospital or the house. As soon as the ambulance had left, he came by to collect her. Rose, Lucy, and Gayle had promised to stay and pray for a while—as well as pledging to continue praying on their own until they heard what else they could do for her and her mother.

When she and Taylor had arrived at the hospital, the doctors were with Mama, where they remained now, running tests. She'd urged Taylor to go on home, that there was nothing more for him to do and he had his daughter to think of. But he had insisted on calling Kate to watch his daughter so he could stay at least "until the doctors know something."

Now all they could do was wait, and she was very thankful for his presence. She snuggled against his side, and he curled his hand around her upper arm.

"Is there anyone we need to call?" he asked.

"No. Not yet. I'll want to call my cousin and my son but not until I have something specific to tell them."

They sat together, again in silence that wasn't really silent given the sounds of the hospital that came muffled and indistinct to her ears.

Taylor withdrew his arm and sat forward just enough to look back over his shoulder at her. "Naomi…do you…do you want to pray?"

"I have been. I've done nothing *but* pray since I got that awful call."

"I meant…I mean, with me." He held his open hand out to her.

She stared at the callused palm, then into the compassionate eyes. No man had ever offered to pray with her before. No man she'd cared about in all her years had ever even shared her beliefs enough to appreciate the necessity of it, she realized. Now that this man sat ready to acknowledge and go before the Lord with her in what was probably her most fervent time of need, she balked.

It seemed so intimate a gesture, beyond the romantic, beyond the physical, a uniting of spirits, in essence, before the Lord. Naomi wasn't sure she was ready to take that step.

"If you'd rather, I could do the praying and you could just hold my hand."

"Okay." Her voice sounded as meek as a child's.

"Okay."

She slipped her hand in his and felt it swallowed up by his masculine strength. She let the air slowly from her lungs and surrendered her spirit to the Lord as Taylor spoke firmly, yet softer than a lullaby.

"Dear Lord." He tapped the side of his hand against the inside of his leg. The cushions sighed as he readjusted his body. He splayed his hand on his thigh and braced himself, straight-armed. "Father, you know I don't do this as often as I should. I'm humbled to admit that here lately it seems I only make the time to come before you when I'm in serious trouble or when I want something."

Naomi could appreciate that more than she'd like to divulge, but she did divulge it to Taylor and the Lord when she closed her eyes and added in a hoarse whisper, "That's true for me, too, Lord."

"Fact is, humbled as we are, we're still not worthy to come before you at all except by the sacrifice of Christ the Savior."

She gave his hand a squeeze to both agree with and encourage him.

"But we don't come for ourselves now, Father. We come on behalf of your precious servant—"

"Ida Beauchamp," Naomi murmured.

"Ida Beauchamp. Father, you know the frailty of Ida's condition and you know what is right and best for her. Take her, Father, in your gentle hands and cradle her in your constant love."

The shifting of his shadow over her told Naomi that he had lifted his head and, even with her eyes still closed, she could feel his gaze fix on her as he began again. "Father, we entrust Ida to your wisdom and care and ask only that you be our strength and give us peace to accept your will with grace and thanksgiving. Amen."

"Amen." As much as she appreciated what he had said, she understood with dull, crippling heartache what he had left unsaid. She raised her head and blinked back the tears. When she looked into those calm blue eyes of his, she could only ask, "Why didn't you tell me?"

He took both of her hands in his. "Tell you what?"

"Just how truly devastating Mama's stroke was? That we haven't come here to wait for news, we've come here to wait for her to die."

"How'd your meeting go?"

Lucy let her purse slide from her shoulder to the ground. The weighty thunk of the fabric bag sounded just like she felt, heavy, abandoned, collapsed. The evening's events had emotionally drained her, and she simply did not have the resources to put on an act for Ray's sake. She sighed and said nothing.

"Luce?" The TV went mute. "What is it, hon? Is something wrong?"

Everything was wrong, but Lucy couldn't tackle *everything* right now. Overwhelmed, she had not even noticed when she drove away from Rose's house whether Nikki's car still sat in Ray's drive. She had *chosen* not to notice, she reminded herself, unwilling to succumb so easily to denial. She was still in control of her decisions, and this one she had made out of self-preservation. She could not have handled one more negative thought tonight.

"Mary Lucille?" The recliner clattered into its upright position. Ray pushed himself to his feet, the remote still in his hand. "What's the matter, girl? Is this…is this about us?"

She shook her head.

He tossed the remote into the seat and moved toward her, his big feet making a peculiar shuffling thunder over her old house's wooden floorboards. When he got to her, he laced his arms just above that comfy roll of a tummy of his and asked, "Then what is it?"

"Naomi's Mama had a real bad stroke," she answered. Then she told him the story of the cake fight and the phone call and the waiting and praying and waiting some more to hear how things were.

"So now let me get this straight in my mind, Lucy. The stroke did *not* kill Naomi's mama?"

"No, that is, not tonight. But the doctors say it's only a matter of time. Since the family has requested no heroic measures be taken, the doctor said he thinks she may linger on for two, three days at the most."

"I see." He scuffed at the floor with the toe of his shoe. "That's a shame, Luce. A real shame."

The faint odors of dinner hinted at a normalcy in her every day that she no longer fully recognized. Snarls of emotion entwined themselves throughout her being, choking her as she tried to speak, making her eyes burn and her lips numb.

"It's just that everything was fine. We were all laughing and Naomi was cutting up, acting all smart and sassy. Then the phone rang." Lucy looked up without seeing anything in particular. "And everything changed all at once."

"That's the way it happens, Lucy."

"Well, I don't like it. I don't." The tears came, their cool dampness almost soothing as they trickled down her hot cheeks. "Why do things have to change like that, Ray? Why can't things just stay the way they are—or at least change for the better?"

A flash of pain darted through his eyes. It was not grief for Naomi's mother but the naked acknowledgment that her question addressed something else entirely. He curled his lips against his teeth and his hands went into fists beneath his crossed arms. "I don't know what to say, Lucy. Things do change, and not always for the good. That's life."

"Well, sometimes—" she stopped to sniffle—"life stinks."

He smiled at that and opened his arms. He had not given her an encouraging answer, but then he had not rejected her outright. He was leaving all his options open. The man was a weasel. Some things, Lucy thought even as she took refuge in his arms and drew from him what little comfort he had to give, never changed.

"You awake?" Ted sat up in bed.

The crisp floral sheets rustled as Gayle rolled onto her back. "I can't get to sleep. I keep thinking about Naomi and her mother and wishing I could do something."

"Do you want to go to the hospital?"

She stared at the darkened ceiling and exhaled, then stole a peek at the glowing green numbers on the digital clock on Ted's nightstand. "It's after midnight."

"Only just."

"Still, it's too late to go traipsing down to the hospital."

"Not if that's where you think you need to be." He stroked one finger down the sensitive skin on the inside of her bare arm. "Do you think Naomi is still there?"

"I'm sure of it."

"So do you think you'd feel better if you went to sit with her?"

"Maybe I'd feel better, but I'm not sure she would." Or was it the other way around?

Naomi had been surprisingly gracious even in the face of Gayle's designed snippiness. Gayle, however, had never let her guard down, never relaxed enough to make a new connection or to speak to Naomi privately of the old one. She had wondered today as they had kidded around if she could finally allow herself to approach Naomi, not as a best friend but as someone with a shared history.

"Do you honestly think, Gayle, that Naomi wouldn't welcome the company right now? Especially from an old friend?"

"You just don't get it, Ted. Naomi and I may have been friends once, but that changed." Gayle's actions had changed it. She sat up and looped her arms over her raised knees, hugging them tight to her chest. "Naomi and I have really got a lot of baggage."

"I find that hard to believe."

Unassuming, sweet, trusting Ted, Gayle thought, pressing her cheek to her arm to get a better look at him in the dimness of their room. Of course he wouldn't understand. He had no idea how thoughtless and conniving the woman he'd married had been. And she could never confess it to him. That her actions so long ago would disappoint him, she had no doubt. But the secret she had kept—and the fact that she had kept it from him the entire length of their relationship—worried her most.

"How much baggage could you have?" He leaned in and nuzzled her temple. "Hey, I've traveled with you, the queen of efficient packing. You can get a week's wardrobe in a carry-on bag and still be the best dressed woman wherever we go."

"Ha, ha."

"If there's a way to rid yourself of anything extraneous and pare down to the necessities, you'll find it, Gayle."

She bent her neck to touch her forehead to his. "I was talking about emotional baggage, Ted, not luggage."

"Me, too."

If he only knew. She closed her eyes to keep from meeting the amused adoration in his gaze. "Oh, Ted, it's not that simple."

"Gayle, honey, the woman who was once like a sister to you is sitting in the hospital while her mother is dying. You can make it that simple."

She bowed her head. She gave her legs a squeeze and held her breath. She wished she could stay like that forever, just hide in a tight little ball in her bed and not deal with Naomi, the past, or dear Mrs. Beauchamp's passing.

Ted put his hand on her neck and began to rub the clenched muscles there. "How much baggage, emotional or otherwise, could you two have between you that you can't put it aside at a time like this?"

Gayle savored the warmth of his touch and the strength of his fingers as they sank into the obstinate flesh and began to knead away the tension. "Do you have any idea how annoying it is to live with someone who is always right?" she asked, chuckling.

"I know how it is to live with someone who is always perfect." He dropped a kiss onto the spot at the top of her backbone.

Despite the gentleness of his gesture and his ongoing massage, his kind affirmation made her stiffen.

He drew his hands away. "So, shall I drive you to the hospital?"

"No, thanks." She threw the covers back and swung her legs out. "I can drive myself."

hirteen

The doctors say you don't know me, Mama. They say you can hear me speak but you can't understand what I'm saying." Naomi stroked back her mother's downy, fine, white hair. The odors of the hospital made her nose tingle, and the contrast of the single unnatural light over the bed against the darkness of the room stung her eyes.

She was alone now with her mother. It was past midnight. And the precious time they had together was all too quickly slipping away.

"I say—" Naomi moved in close to help Mama's weakening eyes focus. She saw the glint of recognition; saw on Mama's thin, dry lips the feeble attempt at a smile. "I say the doctors don't know diddly."

Mama's frail hand lifted.

Naomi leaned over the bed and shut her eyes, relishing the feeling of being in her mother's embrace for what was probably the very last time.

"I love you, Mama."

Mama's grip became discernably stronger.

"And I know you love me." She planted a kiss on Mama's cheek. "There was never a day in my life when I ever doubted your love for me, Mama, although there were a few days when I don't think you liked me very much."

Another smile, another spark of recognition in her mother's eyes.

"I wish I could tell you everything that's going on in my head right now. I'm so afraid—" Naomi's voice cracked and she blew out a shuddering breath. "I'm afraid there's something left unsaid between us. But I've wracked my brain and I can't think what it could be, unless..."

She looked down at Mama all curled up on one side, physically helpless and yet still very strong in herself. The memory of seeing her son for the very first time overtook Naomi and she thought how very similar Mama now seemed to a tiny infant. Distilled to the essence of her spirit without guile or the pretense of habit, bearing, or the defenses learned through living.

Naomi thought of the day her son was born. Her mother had stood by her side that long, demanding day, encouraging, supporting, and comforting her. No matter how hard it got or how exhausting the labor, Mama's tender care and patience never wavered.

"You can do this, Nomi," she had whispered.

"I can't! It's too much. I can't!" Naomi had cried out in reply.

"You can do all things through Christ who strengthens you," Mama reminded her.

"I don't think that verse was about childbirth, Mama," Naomi had said through clenched teeth as another wave of pain hit her.

Through it she'd heard her mother chuckle and murmur, "It's about everything, honey. Turn it over to the Lord. Let him carry you the rest of the way."

Her son was born soon after that, but Mama's words stayed with her to this day. Those words had served Naomi well through many trials and frustrations, through pain and confusion. Tonight she thought of how they would help her through once again.

"I don't know what I have left unsaid, Mama, but on the chance that I never told you or I never made it understood, I want you to go now knowing how much I've valued you as a mother and friend." She bent at the knees to make sure that as she spoke their eyes remained fixed, their gazes one within the other. "You have been wise and kind, even when I didn't deserve either. You taught me to laugh, Mama, and to love the Lord. That in itself is an awesome legacy. So many people love you, Mama, and admire you, I hope you realized that."

Naomi glanced around the room, filled with plants and flowers from old friends and people whose lives her mother had touched.

"Your life, Mama—" Her voice broke. She swallowed and it only pushed down the lump there enough for her to continue. "Your life...has mattered."

Her mother's cheek twitched and her eyes grew wide and moist, as if she needed to find a way to show all the things she felt, to lay open her soul. The doctors would call it involuntary. Of no medical significance. They would urge Naomi not to read too much into it.

Naomi wondered if those doctors, who must have tended so many bedsides of those who lived on even though that physician had given them up for dead, ever looked into the eyes of their patients and saw what she saw now. If they did, they might have remembered the tenderness of the greatest healer of all, the healer of broken bodies and broken hearts and broken spirits.

"'The Spirit gives life; the flesh counts for nothing. The words I have spoken to you are spirit and are life,'" she quoted from the gospel according to John as she had read earlier in the day, seeking comfort as she waited. "This crumpled little body isn't life," she told her mother quietly. "But because we are the children of a loving God, life is here, now, and forevermore."

Naomi took her mother's hand in both of hers. "I can't imagine a person who had ever stood beside someone like you at a time like this who could not realize that, Mama. Do you…do you want to pray now?"

A faint squeeze came in answer.

"Okay." Naomi bowed her head, then—remembering how her mother used to crawl up on the bed beside her to read to her and say her prayers—Naomi climbed onto the bed. Gingerly, careful of the tubes that ran to Mama's arm, she lay down alongside her mother. She wrapped her arms around the small, curled-up body and lay her cheek against Mama's hair.

"Thank you, Lord, for this good life. Thank you for the love and time, fleeting as it seemed, we've had together. Thank for your grace and mercy on us poor, pitiful creatures who have tried to do your work, to follow you in love and goodness, and all too often failed and fell short. Thank you for the wonder of this world and the promise of the next. Thank you, Lord, for giving me my Mama and for taking her soon to be with you. Come Lord Jesus. In your name we say…Amen."

Mama made a small sound, or had Naomi imagined it? When she looked, Mama had shut her eyes. For one flicker of a moment, Naomi thought perhaps her mother had passed with peace into the Father's arms. Then she saw her chest rise and fall. Mama had fallen asleep. Naomi planted a kiss on her forehead and lay there, holding her mother, letting her rest.

Fifteen minutes later a timid tapping at the door roused Naomi, who had almost drifted off herself. Another nurse, no doubt, come to turn Mama or prod her or flick at her IV with her thumb and forefinger. Well, the nurse could try to do any of those things that disturbed Mama so, but she wasn't going to succeed. Why make the sweet woman's last day or so here trying and uncomfortable?

Naomi launched herself up off the hospital bed and took a

few silent but energetic steps to the door.

"Why can't you just leave things alone? Why do y'all insist on stirring everything up when it's better just left be?" Her hand reached the handle at the exact same time the door swung inward to reveal the visitor was not a nurse at all.

Gayle stood staring at Naomi, wondering for the hundredth time if she was doing the right thing.

"Gayle." Naomi's tone registered surprise.

"Hi."

"What are you doing here? It's so late."

"Not *too* late, I hope." The second she said it, Gayle realized she meant it on several levels. Not too late in the hour, not too late to tell Mrs. Beauchamp good-bye, not too late for her and Naomi to make some kind of amends, tenuous though they might be.

"No. Mama is asleep, though. I hate to disturb her."

"Well, could you use a break? A short one? We could get some coffee and visit."

"The hospital cafeteria is closed now, but they have a vending room down the hall. We could get a couple soda pops and sit in the third-floor waiting room across the way."

"Sounds perfect."

They did just that. Once they were both comfortable in the quiet lounge, which they had to themselves, Gayle popped the top of her soda can and stared at it as tiny brown droplets fizzed and crackled up through the opening. Water trickled down the side of the chilled can and an icy bead of it splashed onto her pants leg, making her flinch.

"Oh, your nice pants." Naomi made a motion as if to dab

up the water with the hem of her long skirt.

"Oh, it's only water. Heck, they're only pants, for that matter." She shrugged.

"Well, you look very nice, especially for coming down here in the middle of the night."

"Ah, well, it's my training. My mother's training that is. You know, dress appropriately for the place you are going, that sort of thing."

Naomi laughed. "I still recall being forbidden to wear shorts to the public library. I confess I was nearly grown before I realized that that was my mother's personal rule and not the decree of the powers that be on the library board."

"I'll never forget the look on my mother's face when you and I decided to wear painter's pants and velour T-shirts to school one day. I thought she'd faint." Gayle winced, thinking of her own reactions to her children's choices and how they might be poking fun at her one day, and rightly so. "'Course Daddy just laughed it off and that only made things worse. But at least my mother turned her indignation on him, allowing me to slip out the door, painter's pants in tact."

"I bet she blamed me for putting you up to that, too, didn't she?"

"No, don't be silly. She didn't blame you for *every* bit of nonsense I got into." Gayle took a sip of sweet yet harshly carbonated soda. "However, *I* did."

"Gayle!"

"Hey, it saved my hide more than once, especially—" She cut herself off, literally biting her lip to keep herself from bringing up that certain night, that certain incident. She exhaled and with a long, steady breath, released any emotion that might give away the depth of her shame and chagrin over their irretrievable past. "Anyway, I notice you look nice yourself. You didn't exactly change into your grubbies for the duration. A lot of people would these days."

"Old habits are hard to loose." Naomi fluffed the purple-and-blue print skirt, then ran her neatly trimmed nails up the embroidered edge of her long navy vest. "I was taught that it's a sign of respect for the staff and the patient and yourself to dress properly when you go to the hospital. I do feel sort of awkward about these shoes though."

Gayle glanced down to find Naomi tucking her feet under her chair. She was wearing that same pair of sandals she'd sported every time Gayle had seen her this spring and summer. Gayle frowned but really couldn't think why. The woman was traveling, she'd come a long distance to stay a short while. Why would she cart along different shoes for every occasion? And why did it matter one whit that she hadn't?

She smiled and cradled her soft drink can in both hands. "Oh, never you mind about that, Naomi. It's perfectly acceptable to wear sandals anywhere these days."

"I know. I know." Naomi took a long drink, then fixed her gaze out the rectangular-shaped window behind them. "Still, I hate the idea of wearing them to Mama's funeral, and the only other pair I brought are white ballerina flats. Those won't do with a mourning dress. Guess I'll have to do some shopping before the time comes."

And when might that be? Gayle might have asked if she'd have had the courage to hear the answer, to deal with the aftermath of it. Instead, she cleared her throat and looked down at her own feet. "You could always borrow something."

"Oh, I know. I even thought about wearing a pair of Mama's. We're the same size and all. But then I go over in my mind the kind of shoes she has in her closet and I have to tell you—there isn't a pair in there I'd be caught dead in."

"Oh, I see." Gayle set her drink down with a metallic clink, teasing humor in her tone as she said, "You wouldn't be caught dead in them, and yet you'd *bury* your own mother in a pair? A fine daughter you are."

Just as Gayle had hoped she would, Naomi stared at her, let the irony sink in, then burst into tension-relieving laughter.

Gayle joined her.

"I swear, Gayle, this is why I always liked being with you. When we were younger, my other friends could not fathom the relationship. They all said you had a pole up your spine."

"I'm sure that's *exactly* where they said it was," Gayle drawled.

Naomi cocked her head and mouthed a *well*…

Gayle rolled her eyes, still smiling.

"Anyway, I told them they just didn't know you like I did. They didn't know about your wicked sense of humor." She began to raise the cold can in her hand to her mouth, then stopped and settled it back into her open palm. Her sincere gaze zeroed in on Gayle. "They also didn't know about your tremendous capacity for kindness, your ability to put other's needs before your own. Just like you have tonight. I really, truly appreciate your coming down here to keep me company tonight, Gayle. It means so much to me."

"I'm proud to be able to do it, Naomi." She chose her words carefully. She didn't want to say she was happy to have had to come at a time such at this. "I sort of felt like you could use a friend."

"You mean you'd still count me as a friend?" Naomi sat forward slightly. "After all that's gone between us?"

"After all that's gone between us…" Gayle put her drink aside and folded her hands in her lap. "I'd think you are the one who'd have a hard time counting me as a friend, Naomi."

"Why?" Naomi laughed. It was a warm, generous laugh. "Because you didn't want me to serve on the prayer circle? Because you made a few snide remarks to me at our meetings?"

"I am sorry about that. I was out of line." Gayle meant it. She had been out of line, out of line and out of sorts, nearly out of her mind with worry this whole time that Naomi had been back. And what for?

Naomi was not Gayle's enemy. If Gayle let her, Naomi could become a confidant, an ally, a good and trusted friend. But fear had kept them apart. Gayle's fear. It wasn't who Naomi was or anything she'd done, but what she exposed in Gayle that made Gayle so distraught. None of that was Naomi's fault, and Gayle no longer had the strength to go on shoving her insecurities off onto her friend's shoulders. Especially now.

Gayle looked at her friend and thought of all she was bearing right now—the death of her mother, the handling of the estate, the loss and stress that lay ahead. The last thing Naomi needed was to have to carry the burden of Gayle's guilt as well.

"I never meant those things I said. I just said them to try to push you away because—"

"Because of what happened that weekend in Gatlinburg with my cousin?"

"Well, I was going to thank you for not having brought that up." Gayle folded her arms over her chest. She crossed her legs and looked away. "Of course, now that you have—"

"Now that I have, maybe we can just talk about it and get it out of the way so we can get back on the track to being friends again."

"Well, I can't think that's a good idea. The timing is all wrong, Naomi. How can we sit here and dredge up the past when your mother is so seriously ill?"

"What would you have me do, Gayle? Sit by her bedside and keen?"

Gayle said nothing.

"Well, I'm not going to do that. And I'm not going to sit here and make nice, safe conversation about nothing when we could resolve this and heal a lot of old wounds. Healing and friendship, that's what I need most now, Gayle. I thought when you showed up here tonight that maybe you understood that."

"I do," she admitted softly. "I do. It's just that it's not easy. You're asking me to speak of things I've kept secret a very long time."

"You mean Jackson?"

At the mention of Naomi's cousin, Gayle tensed like a steel cable pulled taut.

Jackson. Jackson McCovey. Dark hair. Dark eyes. In and out of trouble most of his adolescence—the mischievous kind of trouble that only poor boys ever seemed to get punished for. He came to live with Naomi and her mother when his parents died. He was intelligent but undisciplined, ethical but unreliable. He was not well liked at their school or around town, but that did not bother him. In fact, he seemed to revel in it.

That alone had been enough to draw Gayle to him.

Eyes like Elvis, charm by the bushel, a wild streak wide as the Chattahoochee, that was Jackson. Plus a little-boy-lost quality that cried out for that one woman to tame him, to love him, and to win his love in return.

In other words, Jackson McCovey was every naive, Southern good girl's fantasy. And the summer when he was eighteen and she was entering her senior year of high school, he had been hers. Not just her fantasy. Not just her mission. But hers, to love, honor, and obey, until life parted them. For one brief, wonderful, amazing, terrible weekend that summer, she had been another man's wife.

And in the process of the coming together and falling apart of that union, she had hurt and betrayed everyone that mattered to her, including Jackson and Naomi. How Naomi could even stand to be around Gayle now, much less want to mend their friendship, was incomprehensible.

Gayle got up from her seat and paced a few steps away. With her back to Naomi and some distance between them, it was easier to say, "Naomi, I can't talk about this. I can apologize. I can ask for your forgiveness. And I do both, gladly. But I can't sit here and talk about it like so much day-old gossip."

"I accept your apology, Gayle, not that I understand why you feel compelled to offer it. And I forgive you for whatever it is you think you've done. I won't bring it up again—to anyone. But if you ever want to talk about it, I'll listen."

"Thank you."

"Gayle?"

She turned to face her old friend.

"Honey, I can see this still troubles you, and I really wish I knew what to do to help you work it through. And, sweetie, you really have to find a way to work it through. Because Mama isn't going to live much longer, and that means that Jackson is going to be coming back to New Bethany for her funeral."

Sometime before dawn, Rose showed up at the hospital. The three of them sat, keeping vigil at Mama's bedside until the nurses came to check on things before the doctor's morning rounds. Gayle had left only long enough to call her house and give everyone his or her marching orders for the day.

The doctor came and *hmm*ed over Mama's chart, looking at the statistics of what she had become and never bothering to see who she had been—who she was yet. He said very little. What was there to say, really? Naomi could see that Mama was fading and she doubted her tiny body would last the day.

Shortly before noon Lucy showed up. Rose and Gayle seemed just as startled as Naomi when the younger woman, loaded down with her ponderous bag and the burden of her own unhappiness, just appeared at the door. Lucy sat with Mama while Naomi took a hurried lunch in the cafeteria, filling up on coffee more than food. Rose and Gayle had taken the opportunity to slip away from the hospital awhile, but by one o'clock they were all four there again.

By one-thirty Sister Princess and Sister Marguerite had arrived.

"I just felt the Lord calling me to come," Sister Marguerite told them as she came to Mama's bedside.

"Did the Lord call you to come, too, Sister Princess?" Naomi asked.

"No, he didn't. But my sister *did*." Princess bent to wrap Naomi in a big bear hug. "And, sugar, I am almost more afraid of disobeying her than I am the Lord."

They laughed at the much needed comic relief. Then all went quiet again as the two women took turns comforting Naomi and saying silent prayers over Mama's placid body.

Around two, a knock came at the door.

"Hi, Naomi?" Kate Boatwright craned her neck to peer inside.

"Kate?" Naomi blinked. "Um, come in."

Kate hesitated, then glanced around the room. "Taylor asked me if I'd stop in and see how you are. He would have come himself, but he couldn't because—" she tipped her head to one side and rolled her eyes—"because he's a man."

"Most of them are worse than helpless at times like these," Rose said.

"Amen!" intoned Sister Princess.

Kate came fully into the room. She moved to Mama's bed and put her hand on the rail. She said nothing for a moment, then smoothed down the soft blankets over Mama's legs.

"How is she doing?" she whispered as she moved toward Naomi.

"Quiet, mostly, but sometimes her breathing comes awfully hard and we think—" She didn't have to say what she thought.

"She does hang on, though," Marguerite said. "Don't you, Miss Ida?"

Marguerite's dark hand made a drastic contrast to Mama's pale cheek as she gave it a gentle caress.

"We don't expect to be here through the afternoon," Gayle whispered. "Her poor little body is just worn out."

"We've prayed for her to go on in peace," Lucy murmured.

Kate nodded. She moved around the room to Naomi, who sat in an olive green recliner by the head of Mama's bed. Kate bent to give Naomi a hug.

At another time, Naomi might have wondered at that, asking herself if Kate considered Naomi Taylor's girlfriend and was showing approval or what-have-you. Now she accepted the simple, compassionate gesture and returned it in kind.

"If you don't mind, I'd like to stay awhile." Kate straightened away and leaned against the bank of cabinets under the large window.

"Certainly." Naomi gave her hand a squeeze.

"Your mama was so sweet yesterday, having us over for tea and all. I'll admit, I have worried that our visit was too much for her."

"The doctor told us to prepare ourselves for it, Kate. He didn't think anything could prevent it, and he doubted that any one thing set it off."

"Still…" She let her voice trail off and it seemed like everyone's thoughts trailed off with it.

They stood and sat and leaned all around the small space, no one looking at the other, no one speaking for several minutes.

Then Kate said softly, "I do wish I'd gotten to know your Mama better, Naomi. Would it impose too much to ask you to tell us about her?"

"Why, no. It wouldn't impose at all." In fact, Naomi thought, marveling at the amount of insight Taylor's sister had shown, it was exactly what she wanted to do.

All the women around the room perked up a bit, their gazes now more alert and fixed on Naomi.

"Well, Mama was born right here in New Bethany—only not in the hospital. She was born in Sable Grayson's house, Sweet Haven. Did you know any of the Graysons, Sister Marguerite?"

"I remember stories of them, but not the family itself, no."

"Notice she asked you, sister, and not me," Sister Princess lifted her chin with almost regal bearing. "On account of you being so very much older."

Sister Marguerite scowled at her younger sister, her arms folding slowly one over the other as she narrowed one eye and said, "Do y'all know I almost drowned my baby sister once? Playing baptism in the rain barrel the spring that she was four." Marguerite arched one eyebrow and lowered her voice. "I *used* to feel badly about that incident."

Naomi savored a laugh at that.

"I knew the Graysons," Rose chimed when things quieted again. "Though Sable had passed on by the time I was big enough to remember, I have fond memories of that grand old house."

Everyone in the room stared at Rose, heads cocked, eyes blinking. While Sweet Haven had been lovely in it's day, even by the time Mama was born it had begun to show it's age. By the time Rose could have remembered it, the one-time mansion had been closed off so that the family lived only in a few rooms. Later still, it became a boarding house. Now the sole occupant rattled around in the huge place, the object of town gossip and curiosity. That someone of Rose's social standing in their small town would know a fallen family like the Graysons, much less appreciate their home, surprised Naomi.

"Really, Rose? You knew the Graysons?"

"Well, I wasn't *born* the town banker's wife, you know." She chuckled. "Actually, the Graysons are shirttail relations of mine. We share a distant cousin. When I was a young woman working as a secretary before I married Curry, I took up residence at the Grayson Boarding House."

"You are relation to the Grayson family?" Gayle's question smacked of innocent curiosity more than the snobbish disdain one might have expected.

"Honey, it's a small town." Rose smiled. "I'd wager that if we stopped to compare notes, we'd all of us—and I do mean *all* of us—" she put her hand on Marguerite's ample shoulder—"would find a few mutual forebears."

A few of them murmured, they all nodded, and in that moment they seemed to grow just a bit closer, as if a thin barrier that separated them by class and color and age and experiences had fallen away.

"Anyway, you were telling about your Mama," Rose said.

"Oh, yes." Naomi pinched at the skirt to arrange it on her leg. "Well, Mama was born at Sable Grayson's house, which is a funny story. Seems my grandma went to Sweet Haven so she'd have women around to attend to her when her time came, and she took Mama's older brother to stay with them as he was around four and would be too much underfoot on the farm with grandpa."

Lucy plopped her chin in her hand and leaned forward, looking like one of her charges sitting cross-legged on the floor.

"Well, it seems on the day Mama was born, they told my uncle that he couldn't see his mother because grandma was too sick, which made him mad—he had the McCovey stubborn-ness gene in triplicate, they say. Now, late that afternoon, there was a huge commotion, and my uncle realized that no one was paying any attention to what he was doing anymore. So, he slipped up to his mother's room intent on peeking inside and when he did he saw everyone gathered 'round the bed and the doctor holding up what he could only think was a skinned rabbit!"

"It was your Mama?" Rose asked.

"Yep. Just born. But my uncle didn't understand that and he had a fit, thinking all day long they'd told him grandma was sick when she'd really just been holed up in her room skinning rabbits! Right up until the day he died, he always called Mama 'Bunny.'"

At the mention of the old nickname Mama seemed to rouse. Naomi stood to lean over her mother. She waited, her breath caught in her chest, but Mama only lay still again.

"I think she hears us," Kate said, tenderly, as though she were speaking of a newborn.

"I hope so," Naomi said. "I can't think of anything more comforting, if only to me, than to know Mama's last little while was spent in the company of good women listening to stories of her life."

"Then why don't you tell us some more about your mother, sweetheart?" Rose put one hand on Lucy's shoulder and reached the other out to Marguerite, unifying them in her request.

Naomi did just that, telling them about Mama's life, from her childhood to snatches of incidents from her work life and the many volunteer roles she played. She saved the story of Mama's romance for the very last.

"Mama and Daddy never had an easy go of it, you know. They thought they never would have children, were married eighteen years before she got pregnant with me."

"My! And I thought that at twenty-eight, I'd gotten a late start on motherhood," Rose said.

"Well, she came to it late, but like you, Rose, she did a fine job of it," Gayle said. "Your mama was always so much fun, Naomi. I love my mother, y'all." Gayle gestured broadly as she spoke. "I loved our home. The discipline and faith my parents gave me have been all that's held me together some days. But I *never* had so much fun as when I was at your house, Naomi. Your mama was so lively—and creative, I swear!"

"Yes, she was creative, and that's one of the things I want to tell you about. In fact, that it's absolutely essential I tell you about it while Mama is still with us, while I feel she can still comprehend—on whatever level—that this story is being told."

ourteen

I know you've all heard the stories of how the prayer-tree tradition came into existence, probably every one of you can tell your own version and there's no sense in us debating which one is more or less accurate than the other," Naomi began.

"Except that whopper about Mary Lou Masterson coordinating the whole thing from the git-go." Rose held up one hand. "I want to go on the record as saying that was a bunch of political propaganda perpetrated by her husband to get him reelected mayor time and again."

"Nothing quite so 'grass roots' as standing in that grove, talking God and country, family and community, and laying claim to the town's most revered and cherished custom, now is there?" Naomi smiled as she said it.

"No kidding." Gayle scoffed.

"I think we all know better than to believe that hogwash, Miss Rose," Princess said in affirmation.

"So, while we agree that's not how it started, we may not agree how it *did* begin. I make that disclaimer so no one is offended when I share Mama's story of how it all came into being."

Heads around her nodded, and once Naomi felt she had the consensus of the group, she went on.

"In New Bethany, just like all over the country, Pearl Harbor galvanized emotions on the war and sent our town's young men flocking to volunteer. My own daddy, who was about twenty-two at the time, signed up immediately. He and Mama were married at Christmas of '41, and he reported for duty after the first of the year, leaving Mama behind in town, of course."

Naomi looked down on her mother and placed one hand on her withered arm, needing to feel physically connected as she told the tale she'd so often heard.

"Everyone wanted to do their part in the war effort, the young men to enlist, the older men to hold drives and sell bonds and do whatever they were able to contribute," she went on. "The women were no different. They wanted to help, too."

"My mother ran the Red Cross for a time," Rose said, pride singing in her voice.

"My grandmother held society teas to raise money for various causes," Lucy said softly.

"Ted's grandmother was in on that, as well." Gayle sighed a "We love her despite that obvious shortcoming" sort of sound, like a person who just admitted she had an artist or a...a...*Yankee* in the family.

Naomi chuckled, then grew serious. "Now, let's not beat around the bush here. This is the South, we've all grown up here and we know how things are. And if we don't have first-hand knowledge, we can imagine how things *were*." She smiled at Lucy who's solemn face told Naomi she fully understood. "Only a few certain people, especially among the women, were actually allowed to head committees and lay claim to the organizations centering on home front service." Naomi gave an apologetic look to Princess and Marguerite who smiled back in return.

"Oh, we had our charities and war support groups," Marguerite said.

"Of course." Naomi shifted her feet. Mama's bed rattled quietly, but Mama did not stir. "However, there were a lot of people who felt excluded and my mother was one of them. She'd taken a job formerly held by a man. On a dairy farm of all things."

"I recall getting milk and fresh cream from that place." Rose's expression seemed faraway for a moment, then she turned to the others. "They sold that farm to the city in the fifties to set aside for the prayer grove. Before that I think they just let people plant trees out there for—wait a minute! Naomi, are you saying your mama was one of the founders of the prayer tradition? Did she get that dairy farmer to donate some land for the trees?"

"Now, it wasn't just her." Naomi grinned. "She and a group of young women met for picnics that spring in the place we now think of as the grove. They were poor, most of 'em, away from their families, raising small children, their husbands and sweethearts gone off to war. They couldn't afford fancy Sunday dinners, so after church they'd meet there and pool their resources for a meal. Later, they'd sing songs and talk about the men they missed and how wonderful it would be when they were together again."

"I wonder now if Miss Ida is thinking how wonderful it will be to see your daddy again, and her brother? And all of her folks?" Marguerite asked. "I bet she'll get quite a fine welcome home."

Naomi patted back Mama's hair and tried not to choke up as she spoke again. "Mama told me one of their favorite songs to sing at these picnics was a popular tune of the time, 'Apple Blossom Time.'"

"Oh, I do like that song." Rose hummed the opening.

"I think I've heard that," Lucy said. "It's about getting married isn't it?"

"It's very sentimental," Rose said. "I think it evoked much more than just the idea of getting married."

"Mama explained to me that it touched the mood of the young women, the hope of things being all right in time, the promise of spring and of a tree that will someday bear fruit, of being together again in joy. That's why they chose to each plant an apple tree for their fellows and to pray together each Sunday around the trees."

"Wow," Lucy whispered.

"That's lovely," Kate said, hugging her arms around her raised knees.

"That's the song they sang when they planted the first trees," Naomi said softly, her eyes on Mama's serene face.

"You mean they didn't sing a hymn?" Lucy blinked in disbelief.

"If you were a young woman whose sweetheart or husband was off at war and you didn't know if you'd ever see him again and you were all full of emotion and romance, anxiety, and pent-up energy, would you have picked a *hymn*?" Gayle arched her perfectly plucked eyebrows at the young woman. "Honestly?"

"I guess not," Lucy conceded.

"Besides, the way Mama explained it was that back then things weren't all separated out like that. Your faith and the trappings, hymns and such, weren't relegated to Sunday and church, they were an ordinary part of every day. They didn't think they had to make a special designation to sing a hymn, they sang hymns all the time. She was just as likely to sing 'The Old Rugged Cross' while doing the dishes as she was a popular tune."

"I still am," Marguerite said.

"Of course, what she doesn't tell you is the last *popular* tune this one learned was in the days of platform shoes and disco music."

They all joined in the levity and when that faded, they

turned their attention back to Naomi once again.

"Anyway, Mama said that through the years she came to think of that old song as a kind of hymn. The references to the blossoms were like the hope of the Resurrection, the marriage like the promise of Christ to his bride." Naomi stroked Mama's cool cheek and watched her labored but quiet breathing.

They were all silent for a while, each watching as Mama struggled more and more with each breath.

A nurse poked her head in, wanting to know if she could do anything. She took Mama's pulse, then bent down to lift Mama's eyelids—to check her pupils, Naomi assumed. As she straightened, Naomi gave her a guarded look and asked so quietly she scarcely heard it herself, "Will it be much longer?"

The nurse shook her head and to Naomi's wonderment, she saw tears rim the woman's eyes. "We're all surprised she's still hanging on." She leaned down again and put her hand on Mama's shoulder, saying loudly, "You are so lucky to have so many good friends with you, Miss Ida. You must feel very loved."

The nurse turned and walked to the door. She opened it, then turned again to face them all. Her voice was raw, but her expression clear and kind. "You know, surrounded by all this love, maybe it's just too hard for her to leave. Maybe you should think about telling her it's okay to go on, to let go—if you think you're all, Miss Ida included—ready for that." She left then.

Naomi drew a shuddering breath and bent down to kiss Mama's cheek. Then she whispered the very thing her mother had said to her when Naomi's son was born, "Turn it over to the Lord. Let him carry you the rest of the way, Mama."

"It's time, Miss Ida," Marguerite said.

"It's time," Princess echoed.

"It's all right," Gayle said, her voice strained as though by the effort to keep from sobbing. "You can let go. You can finally just let it all go."

Fat tears trickled down Lucy's round cheeks and she said nothing.

Kate sniffled and looked out the window.

Naomi, torn between hanging on to her mother for dear life and allowing her to pass on, finally released her mother's hand and stepped back.

No one said a word for what seemed the longest time. Mama continued to grapple for every breath.

Naomi thought to call the nurse to ask for a pain reliever, to let her mother go swathed in some manner of comfort, but comfort came in another form.

From Rose, the almost inaudible words of "Apple Blossom Time" began. After a moment, Naomi then Marguerite joined in as much as their voices would let them, the others hummed or sat in silence.

And not long after the last words had been sung, Mama was gone.

"It was quite the inspiration to come out to the grove like this and have dinner on the grounds, as it were, after your mother's funeral." William Taylor Boatwright, a Southern gentleman of the old school, with a tanned face and hair the color of freshly bleached cotton, patted Naomi on the back. "Don't you agree, Miz Holcolmb?"

Rose smiled and nodded. "Indeed, I do, Mr. Boatwright." She glanced at Naomi, watching the younger woman carefully. For all that it had been a difficult day, Rose could tell Naomi was handling things well.

"Well," Naomi said as she fussed with her short hair and gave a weary smile to Will's son, Taylor, who stood at her side, "it only seemed appropriate. I just couldn't stomach the idea of being closed up in some fellowship hall, with a gaggle of church ladies gliding silently around us, refilling tea glasses and offering to bring seconds on ham or creamed green beans with fried onion topping, or worse yet, five-can casserole."

The invocation of the classic Southern funeral foods made everyone smile. The last two days had been a roller coaster of smiles and tears brightened by an occasional downright belly laugh. Naomi had borne it well, Rose thought, much better than one would have expected, given the suddenness of the loss. Faith played a big part in that, of course, as did the new relationship blossoming with Taylor. And, to some extent, the support of the other members of the prayer group.

Still, it troubled Rose a bit that Naomi seemed so calm, so immediately accepting of her mother's death. Having just lost her husband a little over a year ago, Rose knew the way grief sneaks up on a person, the depths to which it can bring them, the confusion, denial, and anger that are its outgrowths. She wondered how long Naomi would hold together before the reality of it all got to her and she had to confront her feelings and work through the pain instead of whisking it aside.

Gayle's youngest daughter, Lillith, went sweeping past them, an empty paper plate in her hands. "I'm going to get me some more before they put it all away," she called out to her father, brother, and sister, who were seated at a long table not too far away.

Naomi watched the girl run past, then turned back to say, "This seems more friendly. Happier. Mama would have liked that. And I have Rose Holcolmb and Gayle Barrett to thank for arranging all of it."

Rose took Naomi's offered hand and gave it a squeeze. It warmed her heart to know she could help her new friend at this trying time. "I only wish I could do more."

"You being there was enough, but then to have you organize all this," Naomi said, "it's more than I know how to thank you for."

"You're very sweet, but Gayle did most of the real work." Rose looked around for the other woman, but she was nowhere to be seen. Probably carving ham and dishing up desserts and the like, Rose decided. "I just made some phone calls and got some folks motivated."

"Well, you did a splendid job, I do say." Will beamed at her.

Everyone in their small after-the-meal social klatch—Taylor, Naomi, Kate, and Will—looked at Rose, but only Will's gaze made her feel uncomfortable. In the best of ways.

She smiled back at him. "Why, thank you. You're too kind." Rose hesitated, not sure whether to call him by his first name or not.

"Rose?" Naomi took Rose's arm. "You do know Mr. Boatwright, don't you? I'm sorry if I overlooked any introductions—"

"Oh, pa-shaw, darling." Will gave a rasping but hearty chuckle. "Rose and I have known one another since before Methuselah took his first step. Isn't that right, Rose?"

"Well, I won't admit it's been that long, William Boatwright," she teased, feeling slightly giddy and hoping no one else could tell. "But it has been a while."

Yes, she thought, and in all that time why hadn't she noticed before what a fine, handsome man Will was? Probably because up until this very moment, she'd been too busy being Curry's wife—then Curry's widow—and Kelley and Stacey's mother. She hadn't thought about a man or looked at one "in that way" since before she was married. That had been a long time ago. All her romantic instincts had probably gone stale and rusty.

It was a good thing they had, too, because, if she had even an inkling of an idea in that vein, the pure fear of making a big old donkey's hind part out of herself would prevent her from following up on any attraction. She'd just gotten herself used to the idea of downsizing her home, of reordering her life, of trying to get herself spiritually and emotionally grounded again. The last thing Rose needed in her life now was the distraction of a man.

"Well, I'm so glad you know one another, then," Naomi said absently.

"Daddy, Rose is thinking of putting her house up on the market." Kate squinted in the brilliant afternoon sun, which made the smile she gave Rose seem childlike and even more endearing.

There has to be something inherently decent about a man who has raised his children to be such lovely adults. Rose sighed and covered the telltale sign of her admiration with a quick remark. "Well, it's just too much house for me now."

"Rose!" Will shook his head, his cheeks rounded on either side of a broad grin. "This is the South. And you're a fine, resourceful Southern belle. Too much house? That's like saying too much food or too much jewelry—or too much hairspray. There *is* no such thing."

"Now, that's true, Rose." Naomi's genuine laugh rang out. "Mama always used to say, 'In this part of the country, too much of anything is just about enough.'"

Rose laughed, too, then admitted something out loud she never thought she would: "Truth is, y'all, I hate that house. It was always Curry's treasure, not mine."

"Really?" Naomi batted her eyes while the others murmured similar sentiments of surprise.

"Now, don't go telling that all around, Rose," Kate warned, her eyes shining with mischief. "Elsewise someone might get the idea they can slip that prime piece of property out from under you for a song."

"It'd have to be a pretty *good* song." Rose folded her arms. "I'd have to get all the royalties and rights to it, too."

"Don't never you worry, Katie-doll," Will said, snagging his daughter and giving her a boisterous hug around the shoulders. "Not anyone with any sense at all's going to try to pull any funny business on Miss Rose Tancy Holcolmb. She is one woman that it is wise to take seriously or just leave alone."

Rose wasn't sure if that was a compliment or an insult. She studied his warm expression only a moment before she made up her mind. "Why, thank you, Will."

He nodded.

That awkward silence followed—that minute or so when nobody quite knows what to say or do. Though some folks seize the opportunity to make their excuses and extricate themselves, most others merely stand there and fumble with their cups or clothes while their minds race to find a new topic of conversation. They, however, didn't have to search long, for before any of them could speak, Lillith came charging through, her small plate piled with a veritable mountain of potato chips.

One crisp chip fluttered off the child's bountiful reserves and landed on Naomi's black pump, looking as delicate as a butterfly there. She bent to pick it up.

"Well, you can be for sure that Gayle isn't anywhere to be found. She'd never allow that child to fill up on these if she were." Naomi tipped the paper-thin chip back and forth between her fingers.

"Just where is Gayle, anyway?" Rose asked. "She's not with her family, and it appears she's not at the serving table. I wonder where she could have gotten herself to?"

Naomi flung the chip out for the birds to feast on. "I can't say where she might be, but she's a big girl, she can take care of herself."

Rose nodded absently, thinking that Naomi's choice of words was a bit odd—but not nearly so odd as the fact that she sounded very much as if she knew exactly where Gayle was and why she was there.

"Gayle Shorter, you haven't changed a bit since you were seventeen years old."

"It's Barrett now, Jackson. Gayle Barrett." Gayle paused among the whispering leaves of a secluded snatch of trees far enough from the crowd for privacy but not so far as to cause talk. She wound her arms over her chest and raised her chin. "And I could say the same for you. You haven't changed one bit, Jackson McCovey. You are still one strong, handsome, congenial, and flawless…liar."

He laughed that deep, rolling, thrilling laugh that had only grown richer with age.

Gayle shut her eyes in defense against the image before her. Jackson McCovey, in the flesh. Older, yes, but no less striking, especially now with a man's broad shoulders and lean build, and with silver shot through his black hair at the temples. He was not, in the strictest sense, more aesthetically appealing than Ted. Certainly not more charming. Still…there was something about the man that captivated her, just as the younger Jackson had captivated her all those years ago.

That scared her. It scared the living daylights out of her.

"That response was pure Gayle, which proves my point. You haven't changed." His black suit rustled as he shifted his weight. He tugged at the burgundy-patterned tie knotted against his throat until it hung just loose enough for him to undo the top button of his shirt. He glanced away, then brought that dark gaze of his fully to bear on Gayle's face. "I can't tell you how often I've thought of you all these years, Gayle."

"Then don't." She inhaled the scent of the food and the trees, hoping the familiarity of it all would brace her against the compelling trepidation Jackson represented.

"All right then. May I at least say it's good to see you again?"

She dipped her head in consent, but did not return the sentiment. She couldn't. It was not good to see him again. She had tried to prepare herself for this moment and whatever catastrophic fallout might come from it. However, standing here now, so close to Jackson she could see his cheek twitch and smell his dry citrus cologne, she realized nothing could have readied her for the rush of emotions the man—and her own long-held secret—inspired.

"Was that your family sitting with you in the pew at the funeral?" Jackson looked off toward the gathering of people milling about in the clearing nearby.

"Yes." Her voice cracked. She fiddled with the golden button on her black suit jacket, then tried it again with more conviction. "Yes. That was my husband, Ted, and our three children."

"Three?" He stuffed his hands in his pockets. "That's nice. Very nice."

"We think so." The muffled chatter from the people, the sound of food being taken up and paper table coverings tearing in the effort to get things tidied, blurred with the dull throb of Gayle's heartbeat in her ears. She bowed her head and squeezed her eyes shut.

The dinner was winding down. People were kissing Naomi good-bye. They were telling how much they loved her Mama and commanding her to holler if there was anything they could do for her. Of course, that would always be followed with the admonishment, "And I *mean* that, too, now."

Somewhere in that crowd Gayle's husband and children had surely begun to wonder where she'd gone. Ted was probably looking here and there for her, making casual social remarks to others as he did. "Yes, a lovely service," he'd agree with someone. "What a stunning hat," he'd say to some elderly lady in her funeral finery. "I'll pass along to Gayle how much you enjoyed the lemon bars," he'd assure some woman she'd served with in the Junior League. Eventually he'd tire of small talk and begin to ask outright, "Where's my wife?" and "Have you seen Gayle hereabouts?" Or worse yet, "Well, who was she with last?"

Gayle's stomach lurched, her back muscles clenched, and her cheeks burned, anticipating her mortification at being found out. She really must get back, she realized, before that question got asked—or more pointedly, *answered.*

She whipped her head up to make her excuses to Jackson—but found herself arranging her expression in her sweetest smile and asking instead, "What about you? Don't you have a family?"

"I never married." His gaze bore through her cheery facade like a hot poker through tissue paper. "Except the once."

She tossed her head back, defying the sudden weakness in her knees and the depths of her shame over her selfish and foolhardy behavior so long ago.

"Why didn't you just slap me, Jackson? It would have been more direct, and probably more satisfying for both of us."

"Because I don't want to slap you, Gayle. In fact, given half a chance, I'd just as soon kiss you."

"Well, you'll never get that chance, Jackson." She retreated a step, her eyes still on him. "What happened between us was childish and foolish and—"

"Wonderful."

"Meaningless," she substituted, though his description exploded through her mind and body like a shower of glittering sparks. Wonderful. Despite how badly she had treated him, how terribly she had hurt him, he still looked back on their time together as wonderful.

"C'mon, Gayle, don't tell me you never think about me— about then?" He took a step toward her. "Don't tell me you're not curious? Was it all just adolescence and hormones or was there something more between us?"

"I'm married." This time she did not retreat.

"So were we…once." He moved closer.

She straightened her back, but this only made him feel closer still. "*Happily* married."

"We never got a chance at that." The grass beneath his feet swished with each tight, controlled step.

"Jackson." He was so near now she had to tip her head back to keep her gaze on his.

"What?" He placed his finger under her chin.

"I can't." The air around them went still. Time fell away. After all she had done, all that had done her in all these years, she felt young again—if just for a fleeting moment. She felt bright and sure and fearless, just as she had so long ago with him.

"You *can't?*" he whispered.

"I won't." Her heart pounded in her chest—pounded like she'd run a hundred miles and yet, she was still here, still looking into Jackson's deep, discerning eyes.

He said nothing, but she felt him question her resolve as

clearly as if he'd murmured intimately into her ear.

"I won't." Her repeated words were so dry they could have crumbled and blown away like dust.

"Then you'd better go now, because if you stay any longer, I don't know if I can stop myself."

Gayle ducked and slipped away from him. She wanted to run but knew that would only draw attention to her. And because she did not run, she was afforded a split second of afterthought—and she acted on it.

She turned to face him. "I'm sorry about what happened when we were young, Jackson. I know I hurt you. If it's any consolation, I hurt myself, too."

Cast in shadow, he nodded, not looking at her.

"In fact, I hurt a lot of people and I will never, as long as I live, ever, do something that impetuous and self-serving again. Do you understand?"

With his face still in profile to her, he said, "I'll be back in New Bethany at Thanksgiving, if Naomi is still living here. Can we…do you think we could see one another then?"

"No," she murmured.

"Not even to talk? Just talk?"

Her breath stopped in the back of her throat. Her thoughts felt thick and jumbled and like they were all coming at her too fast. She knew the right thing to say. She knew what God expected and what Ted would ask of her. She knew she dared not take this risk.

Images of her youth flashed through her head. Fragments of memories washed over her of free and fun and reckless times. And Jackson. Then her family came to mind…first her parents who trusted her to represent them well in all areas of her life, then Ted with all his demands on her heart and her body, then the children who treated her like a cross between a personal assistant and an antiquated, dotty woman that they'd prefer remain locked in a closet when not needed.

She thought of how many people relied on her to run things and organize things and be places and go places and do things. She thought how her hair, which had once been long and flowing, now looked like something sculpted out of plastic, and how her panty hose bit in too much at the waist, and how she loathed high heels.

For one instant she saw the young girl she had been standing beside the woman she had become and could not for the life of her say how it had happened so fast. Then her mind clicked off and she just *felt*...empty and yearning and frightened. Only one question echoed through her being: How would it feel to be that free again?

"What do you say, Gayle? I'm not making any assumptions here. I just want to talk to you again. Tell me that I can talk to you again."

She turned away from him to stare from the covering of the lush row of prayer trees into the glaring sunlight and she whispered, her voice strangled and hoarse, "We'll see."

Fifteen

The biting, smoky October air tweaked at Rose's nostrils as she dragged the metal teeth of her large fan rake over the resilient grass in her front yard. She repositioned her gloved hands on the worn wooden handle to better flick the small cluster of leaves into a bigger pile. She had a gardener who did this type of thing for her, but he didn't come until Tuesday and she needed the grounds looking shipshape in time for the open house this afternoon and the prayer circle meeting after that.

Besides, she had extra energy this crisp Sunday morning. She leaned the rake against the For Sale sign in her front yard and wiped the blue jersey cuff of her work glove over her brow. Kate would be here in a couple hours to host the open house for prospective buyers—and more than a few gawkers, Rose ventured.

The house was spotless, and as soon as she finished here in the front yard, Rose would go in and clean herself up. Then, while Kate entertained guests in this old house, Rose would herself be entertained—by none other than Will Boatwright.

Just thinking of the man and the afternoon ahead made Rose's spirit's soar. They were just friends, of course. Just friends. Rose still was not ready to face the complications of a man who wanted more than amicable companionship. And Will accepted that.

Or he said he accepted it. Some days when he fawned a bit too much over her cooking, or noticed too sweetly how her new hairstyle flattered her eyes, she wondered. Then there was the time he took her arm at the town's Labor Day picnic. He said he meant only to help her across a soggy low spot in the ground, but if that was so, why didn't he let go of her when they reached the picnic pavilion?

The memories of the last few weeks warmed her despite her misgivings. Rose was on the right path. She'd get out from under the burden of this house, and, with one daughter settled in a good job and her youngest confidently poised on the brink of her own life's adventure, Rose could forge on ahead. For the first time in a long time she knew where she was going and she was happy about it.

Now, if she could just keep her focus, and not let herself be sidetracked by self-doubt and concern over things she couldn't change, she might still find her way again in this life. Of course, she'd have to keep her feelings for Will in check. That was not going to be easy if he didn't stop being so charming and funny and...persistent. She put her fingers to her cheek, remembering how he had pressed his advantage in arranging time to see her again and again. More than once Rose had wondered if she'd taken up with a...a fast mover.

Like father, like son, one might argue, she told herself as thoughts of Naomi and Taylor's blossoming attraction came to mind. She pictured the two of them, Taylor so chivalrous and attentive and Naomi with her bright eyes and engaging smile— and the new aura of fragility about her.

Rose worried about Naomi. Oh, she was glad she had the care and support of the Boatwright clan—Taylor most especially—but Rose still worried. The romance seemed to be going so fast, getting serious so suddenly. All at a time when Naomi seemed unable or unwilling to deal with her own problems, much less tackle those created by a relationship involving not only a new man but his young daughter.

Rose folded both hands over the end of her rake and leaned her chin against them. Summer had swept over their beautiful Tennessee town and fall had begun. The warm nights twinkling with stars up above and lightning bugs all around had given way to an exhilarating chill and yellow-and-orange leaves swirling in sudden updrafts before blanketing the ground with their short-lived bursts of glory.

Still, Naomi had made no move to sell her mother's house or to pack up her things and return to her life in Maine. Neither had she made a move toward putting down permanent roots here in New Bethany. Naomi just sort of drifted along. She went on dates with Taylor and to church with him on Sundays. She told Rose about the letters she wrote to her son and sometimes read aloud the answers she received in return, neither of which gave any insight into her true thoughts and emotions. She never once scolded her son for not coming to his grandmother's funeral or gave any indication when they would see one another again.

She showed up at the prayer meetings, prompt and amiable, but with a sort of wistfulness that made everyone want to coddle her, which she permitted. All that seemed very much at odds with the woman who had stepped up and insinuated herself into the group that first day—the one who stood up to Gayle and who agreed to do what she must to preserve Lucy's dignity when Naomi had found out about Ray's cheating ways. Yes, Rose worried about Naomi.

But then, she also worried about Gayle, even though she couldn't think why. There was just something not quite...*Gayle* about her these days.

Rose scratched the bridge of her nose with one finger, thinking of how Gayle was late to the last prayer meeting. And when she had arrived, she'd had to excuse herself three times to take calls concerning things she'd forgotten to do, from reserving the room for the Friends of the Library to not noting in their personal register the amounts of the last half dozen checks she'd written. Nothing earth-shattering. Nothing Rose could really point to and say, "See, there's the difficulty." So, without knowing exactly why, she did worry about Gayle, too.

On the other hand, Rose knew exactly why she worried about Miss Mary Lucille. She raised her head and narrowed her eyes at the house Ray Griggs had inherited from his family a few years back. It had once been a stately place, no rival for the Holcolmb home, but grand in an understated, traditional way and well kept. That could no longer be said of it.

That lazy Ray had let the shutters go unpainted until they had chipped and faded and the wood splintered along the edges. He'd let all the carefully landscaped plants and flowers die off slowly, as if one by one they simply gave up the fight, shriveled up, and disappeared only to be replaced by cheap mulch that choked the air with a sour stink on rainy days. When the front porch steps had cracked, Ray did not bother to repair them but simply stretched a piece of twine across the entrance and hung a sign that said Please use back door.

The place was not completely an eyesore and would do little if anything to bring down her own property value, but it troubled Rose. If she were perfectly honest, she'd admit it was not the general shoddiness of the house that distressed her, it was the lack of integrity and kindness and plain ol' human decency dwelling within that had her hackles up. Not to mention that black car.

Rose narrowed her eyes at the battered black car that sat so boldly in Ray's drive every night of the week that he wasn't with Lucy—and a few of them when he was. Rose would have told Lucy that, too, if the younger woman had ever asked. But clearly this was something Lucy did not want to know about, though they could all see in her eyes and her carriage that she did know—and all too well.

Rose sighed and shook her head. She bent to scoop the small pile of leaves into a bushel basket so her gardener could add them later to the compost heap behind the garage. As she balanced that light basket on her hip and turned to walk away, she glared once last time at Nikki Herndon's black car.

"Oh, Lucy," she murmured. "If you don't stop closing your eyes in hopes of protecting your future with this man, he's going to keep stealing your present right out from under you until he's taken everything—your youth, your self-respect, your dignity, and any hope you ever had of becoming a mother."

"Lucy, I'm going to be a father."

"A fath…" She couldn't even complete the word much less make herself grasp what Ray could mean in using it. "What?"

"Nikki is pregnant."

A stark calm fell over Lucy that made her recall the war stories of generations past and the tales of brave deeds done by mortally wounded men who, because they never felt the bullet that pierced their flesh, fought on. She plucked up a tomato to cut it up into the salad for their usual after-church meal.

"Lucy?"

Chop, chop, chop. The blade fell against the cutting board.

"Lucy, did you hear me?" Ray edged toward her, his thick fingers fumbling together above his rounded belly.

You never hear the bullet that strikes you down, Lucy thought, recalling the words of her grandfather extolling the courage of some gray-suited lad who'd given his life in the cause of the South. *"You only know you're done for,"* her grandfather had warned, *"when you see the blood, the scarlet evidence of your life force draining slowly away until you can no longer go on."*

Lucy flicked the tomato bits into the bed of crisp lettuce and stared at the red juice dripping from the sharp steel edge.

"Lucy?" Ray peered at her, his eyes just slits. "Lucy, what are you thinking?"

"What a flowery-talking, old fool my grandfather was," she muttered. Then she put the knife aside and sat. Right there on the kitchen floor. Just placed her back to the counter and slid herself down to sit, crossed-legged on the cold, bare floor, with her lavender jersey dress all pooled in her lap.

Ray squatted down beside her. "Lucy, hon, are you all right? You're not talking sense."

"Sense?" The pain had started now. Deep, throbbing pain buried way down in her chest. "You said what you said and now you want me to talk sense?"

He hung his head like the dog that he was.

"Ray, how could you let this happen? I always thought that I—" Tears welled up in her eyes. "That we—"

"I didn't plan this, Lucy, if that's of any consolation."

She huffed out a humorless "ha."

"Why, yes, Ray. Knowing that this was just an act of callous disregard is like a pure healing salve to my wounded heart."

"Your grandpa ain't the only flowery-talking fool in your family," he grumbled under his breath.

His scorn slashed through the fog of her hurt and disbelief and burned hot and low in her belly.

"The only thing that keeps me from slapping your face right now, Ray, is that you're speaking the truth. I *have* been a fool." She made herself take a deep breath. A tear dripped from her cheek to her collarbone and she didn't lift a finger to wipe it, or any that followed, away. "Where you're concerned, yes, I've been a fool for a very long time."

"I intend to do the right thing by her, Lucy." The floorboards creaked as he shifted his weight in several little jiggling bounces. "I intend to marry Nikki."

She could not look at him. "Of course you do."

"Soon. Real soon."

She nodded. "Can I ask you one thing?"

"I guess."

"If I hadn't…or if I had…how can I put this so it's not too flowery and yet doesn't make me feel stupid and petty?" She shut her eyes, the muscles in her jaw pulled taut and her eyes and nose stung like she'd taken a dose of smelling salts. "If I hadn't held to my moral conviction regarding sex outside of marriage, if it'd been me that ended up pregnant, would you have married me?"

"Of course I would have." He even had the brass to sound insulted that she'd think otherwise.

She laughed, though she didn't find it one bit funny. The one thing she'd refused to surrender in hopes it would make him treasure her was the one thing that, if given, might have made him hers. "*Now* you tell me."

"Huh?"

"Never mind, Ray. Never mind." He wouldn't appreciate the irony. Irony, like most things subtle and steeped in truth, was lost on a man like Ray. "Can I ask you one more thing? Will you be totally truthful?"

"No point in being otherwise—now."

His last word hit hard. Still, she strangled out her question. "If we had married, had a baby, maybe even more than one, would that have been enough to keep you from falling to temptation with Nikki Herndon?"

He scuffed the toe of his shoe on the floor. "Probably not."

No, it wouldn't have been. She looked down at the ample curves of her body, feeling dumpy and stupid and unworthy.

"But you'll be faithful to her," she whispered. "She's nice enough and pretty and a good mother, and she must really care about you—you'd never risk that by straying."

He didn't answer and that pretty much said it all.

Lucy looked up. She'd known what a jerk Ray could be, but for all these years she'd blamed herself for it. If she had only been slimmer or prettier or smarter or kinder he'd have straightened up. He was only treating her as she'd deserved to be treated, or so she thought. Now, in this one split second, she realized none of that was true. Nothing she could have done—ever—could have made him treat her better. It simply wasn't within him. It wasn't who he was.

It isn't often, she thought, that she actually got to see so clearly and in a single instant how following God's plan had worked out for the best in her life. But now she did. Now she knew that following God's guidelines and not bowing to her own judgement or Ray's desires had saved her from a lifetime of misery, and of repeating the life her own mother and father had so sadly lived.

She slumped back against the cabinet. "I suppose I should tell you now that I hate you, Raymond Griggs, you and Nikki, too. But try as I might, the most I can muster up for you both is pity."

He growled out something he didn't learn in Sunday school and stood. His eyes grew cold, his mouth ugly in his ruddy face. "Well, Miss Holier-than-thou, if that's the way you feel, then maybe you should start praying for us in that old biddies circle of yours."

If she hadn't already realized he'd never understand the irony, she'd remark that the suggestion, clearly made in contempt, was precisely what they all needed. Instead, she called out as she watched him storm out the backdoor, "That's exactly what we'll do, Ray. And we'll start tonight—because I don't think the Lord can get to your cause soon enough."

"Well? Did you get any interesting offers?" Naomi came gliding in through Rose's backdoor, left open as a traditional sign that someone was home and that guests were welcome. Even though it was late October and early evening, it was not too cool out to warrant shutting the door, so Naomi left it be.

Rose stood at the countertop arranging a long-stemmed fall bouquet in a tall crystal vase. She sighed, her fingertips brushing the velvety petals of the yellow roses and rust-colored mums among the orange-and-brown sprays of leaves. "Kate said she had plenty of people come through the house but no serious buyers yet."

"Who was talking about the *house?*" Naomi gave her friend an overplayed wink and a quick elbow nudge. "When I asked if you'd had any interesting offers, I had more in mind your afternoon with Will."

"Oh, Naomi! Really!"

"Really." Naomi wriggled her eyebrows.

"Now you know that Will and I are nothing but good friends." She sat the vase down with a decisive thunk. "All we did today was take a drive to soak in the fall color, then stop for coffee and conversation. That's it and that's all. We are friends. And if anyone goes 'round saying otherwise, I'll personally slap whiskers on them and call them a weasel."

Naomi laughed. Not many things made her laugh these past few weeks, but she could count on Rose to lighten her mood. In fact, she'd come to count on Rose for quite a lot since

Mama died. The older woman had become on some days her life support and others, her sounding board.

That's why Naomi had come early today to the meeting, to talk to Rose—and she'd had to time things just right to do that. She'd wanted to arrive long enough before the others to allow for a few private moments, but she didn't want to show up so much in advance that she took the chance of running into Kate.

Not that Naomi didn't like Kate. She liked her a lot. She liked Kate as a friend. She liked Kate as Taylor's sister. But here lately she couldn't seem to be around the vivacious woman without thinking of Kate, the real estate agent.

Naomi slumped into a chair and placed her purse on the kitchen table. She fingered the gold-toned clasp and tried to reason away the swell of guilt within her. The first time she'd ever met Kate was because Naomi had summoned her to help with the sale of Mama's house. Now just seeing Taylor's sister made Naomi cringe with the fear that that very topic would come up again.

She was not ready. Naomi had returned to New Bethany with a plan—to take as much as a year settling Mama into a new home and dealing with any business that required. That God and Mama had other plans did not change things. She still had plenty of time to sort through and organize and make decisions. In fact, with Mama gone, she had more time than ever and she was going to use it.

Why rush things? The rest of her life was whizzing past like a line of fast cars on an unpatrolled stretch of rural highway. It moved so fast it sometimes seemed a blur to her. So, why should she hustle through the one aspect in her life over which she felt she still had some control? Why should she hurry to rid herself of her only reminder of Mama and of a gentler, happy time? Why should she let go of the only thing she seemed capable of hanging on to anymore?

"I got a letter from Justin, yesterday." Naomi snapped open her pocketbook.

"Oh, good, this means we're done discussing me and my fictitious love life." Rose held up a pitcher of tea in offering.

Naomi shook her head to say "No, thank you."

Rose brought her own filled glass around and took a chair opposite Naomi. "So, what does that brilliant, Ivy-League son of yours have to say for himself these days?"

"Nothing much." She reached in and withdrew the single thin page from her purse. "Weather's lovely. The fall scenery, breathtaking. He hasn't gotten a haircut but neither has he gotten a tattoo or a nose ring, so he urges me to count my blessings."

Rose gave the perfunctory smile expected at that.

Naomi returned it in kind, then scanned down the compact, angular printing on the milky white paper. "Oh, and he's dropped some courses."

"Oh?" Rose set her glass down and hiked up one eyebrow. "How many?"

Naomi forced her gaze to stay on the page and her tone to remain matter-of-fact. "All of them."

"He's dropped out?"

"Apparently so."

"Well, you certainly are taking this calmly. If I'd paid out the kind of money you have to keep a child in a prestigious school only to have him tell me in a note—a note, not a phone call or a very long, very contrite letter—that he's dropping out—"

Naomi didn't have to look at Rose to know her temper was hot and there was a fire in her cheeks to prove it.

"If my child did that, Naomi, I'd be giving them two choices about now—hightail it back to class or say hello to Jesus when you pass by heaven, child, because that's how high I'm booting your behind."

Naomi smiled. She'd needed that. "Well, you do notice I have on my sturdy boots today."

Naomi stuck her leg out to show off her practical, heavy hiking footwear.

Rose took a gander, then broke into a soft chuckle.

"But he's twenty-one now, Rose, there's nothing I can do."

"Well, maybe nothing you can do but there are quite a few things you can *say*." She tapped one finger adamantly on the tabletop.

"Oh, he must be quite aware of how much I'd like to say on the subject." Naomi crossed her legs again at the ankle. "That's probably why he also told me he's not coming home for Thanksgiving."

"Not...?" Rose reached out to give her wrist a squeeze. "Oh, darling."

"It's not really a surprise, Rose." She patted her friend's hand.

"Oh? May I ask, has this been brewing awhile? That is, is that the reason he didn't come to your mother's funeral? Because things were bad in school and he couldn't face you with it?"

"I wish." Naomi folded her son's letter in half and pressed her thumbnail along the crease.

"What do you mean?"

A lump as hard and cold as a stone in ice weighed in the pit of her stomach. She fumbled with the paper, then quickly tucked it away inside a hidden pocket in her purse.

"Justin said he didn't come because he'd just seen Mama at Christmas and he wanted to keep those happy memories. I was all right with that, after all, he was good to Mama and he has a right to grieve in his own way."

"But?" Rose sat back to give Naomi time to answer.

The ice in Rose's glass cracked then clinked as it settled downward in the rich, dark liquid.

Naomi wet her lips. She'd come here to share this, hadn't she? She had to tell someone and clearly Taylor was not the person, and her friendship with Gayle, though progressing, was still too new and tentative and this subject too sensitive for them to broach. Rose was the only person she could trust with this.

Naomi drew a deep breath, pulled her shoulders up, and just let it out. "It seems on the day Justin was ready to drive out to Mama's funeral someone he'd been trying to contact just showed up on his doorstep. And, since he had not seen that person since roughly…his early childhood…Justin decided to stay and try to get to know…that person."

"No." Rose closed her eyes as if that could blot out the possibility even as she spoke it aloud. "Your ex-husband has turned up again?"

"Turned up being the operative term in as much as that's how one usually finds a worm, by turning it up from under a rock." She felt the soothing warmth of tears in her burning eyes but sniffled and looked upward to quell their flow. She'd cried enough on Rose's shoulder these last months, she wasn't going to start blubbering again now. "Justin waited until now to tell me about it because he thought I might overreact and he didn't want to add to my sorrow over losing Mama. But mostly the overreacting thing, I suspect."

"Naomi, darling, what are you going to do?"

"What can I do? Justin is an adult, he can see whomever he wants to see, listen to whomever he wants to listen to. I just hope he's wise enough not to take whatever he hears at face value."

"Do you think your ex could be telling Justin ugly lies about you?"

Naomi gave the briefest shake of her head. "Justin wouldn't tolerate that. I am concerned, though, that Wade, that's my ex-husband, might be filling our son's head with half-truths about what ended our marriage."

"Those half-truths are sometimes the hardest thing to fight. Once you've heard them you can never quite get them out of the back of your mind. You always wonder."

"I know." Naomi scrunched her eyes together, determined not to give in to her emotions. "And if I wasn't a Christian I suppose I wouldn't care, Rose. But I carry a lot of guilt about my divorce as it is, about what it did to my child and knowing that divorce is so unpleasing to the Lord."

"Even after all these years, you still regret it?"

"Oh, I never regretted it—not once I realized it was my only recourse. I mean, Wade had up and disappeared and I hadn't seen him for almost a year when I finally knew I had to make the break and move on."

"Abandonment is a biblical reason for divorce, especially in a marriage with partners so unevenly matched as you two must have been."

"Still, I didn't take it lightly. I didn't take my marriage lightly either, and I'm hurt and angry and just plain old scared of Wade coming back in after all this time and telling my son otherwise, or worse yet—influencing Justin in other ways."

"Do you think he played a part in Justin dropping out this semester?"

"Justin says not, but—" her voice cracked, she shut her eyes and sniffled.

"Here, let me get you a tissue." Rose started to rise.

"Oh, sit. I'm fine, really I am." She forced a smile to prove it. "This will all work out. I raised my son right, it will all smooth over soon enough. I'm just feeling sorry for myself because this will be my first Thanksgiving ever without Mama and now without Justin."

"Well, don't you fret about that, sweetie, you come and have Thanksgiving here. It'll just be me and Kelley this year. Stacey can't get away, and even Kelley has to leave Thursday afternoon to be back for work Friday. But that just means you and I can kick off our shoes, prop up our feet, and gorge ourselves on pumpkin pie and whipped cream later."

"Tempting as that sounds, I'll have to pass. My cousin Jackson is coming down for that long weekend and we've been invited to the Boatwrights for the official family Thanksgiving meal. I believe you and Kelley could get invited there, too, Miss Rose, if you played your cards right."

"Naomi Beauchamp, I am a Baptist. I don't play cards."

"Oh, I see, you don't play cards but you *do* play hard to get." She grinned, her tears abated.

"I don't *play* hard to get, young lady, I *am* hard to get." Rose held up her head regally, her eyes twinkling. "All things of quality really are."

Naomi laughed again. "Oh, you do my heart good, Rose. You know maybe I *will* stop by after dinner with the Boatwrights. I have the feeling I'll need a laugh after enduring an afternoon under the microscope—especially from the scrutiny of a certain thirteen-year-old."

"Taylor's daughter still not quite sure what to think of you, huh?"

"Yes, and that's the good news."

"What's the bad news?"

"I have a feeling that's what I'm going to find out when she makes up her mind."

"Oh, she'll love you. They'll all love you. And if they do or if they don't, you come on over here Thanksgiving night and tell Rose all about it."

"Who's coming where Thanksgiving night?" Lucy cupped her hands on both sides of her face, her nose pressed to the dull gray mesh of the screen.

"Get yourself in here, Mary Lucille," Rose scolded through a smile. "Hasn't anyone ever told you it's impolite to eavesdrop?"

Lucy ducked her head and shuffled inside.

"I think you'd know by now that where we're concerned, it's best to just charge right in and don't stop asking questions until you've heard *all* the details."

A small grin worked over Lucy's pale face.

Rose stood to fetch the pitcher of tea and a glass as Lucy sat herself down at the table.

There was something different about the younger woman today, Naomi noted, but she couldn't quite put her finger on it. "Rose was just inviting me to stop in Thanksgiving evening and have some pie and girl talk."

"Sounds perfect." Lucy cocked her head.

It wasn't her hair that was different, Naomi decided.

"It does?" Rose and Naomi swapped glances, then Rose said, "I don't suppose that means you'd like to—"

"What time?" Lucy placed both hands flat on the table.

That assertiveness, an almost palpable sense of clarity and purpose, that was definitely new, Naomi thought. Of course, Naomi hadn't caught on to that until this moment. No, it was something else.

"Um, well, I don't know what time we'll get together." Rose

served Lucy her tea, then sat down. "I'd say anytime after about four, wouldn't you Naomi?"

"Hmm?" Naomi blinked, still trying to pinpoint what exactly she found altered about Lucy. "Oh. Four? Yes, that's about right. Is that all right for you, Lucy?"

"Perfect." She gave out a long sigh, but not one of those sad, old, weary sighs that usually punctuated a conversation with Lucy. This was more the sound of someone no longer carrying a heavy burden, it sounded strong and satisfied. "In fact, more than perfect. I imagine that by four o'clock on Thanksgiving day I will be in desperate need of a place to hide-out from my mother and my relatives and just lick my wounds."

"Oh, now, Lucy it can't be that bad," Rose chided.

"Actually, it's not that it's usually that bad—except they taunt me about when am I getting married and going to start having babies, that kind of thing. But this year I'm going to finally have some kind of answer for them—and after they hear it, I won't know a moment's peace about it from a one of them." She paused to look across the room and Naomi got the impression she was conducting an inner debate.

"Lucy, does this mean that Ray has finally made some kind of decision?" Rose asked.

Ray. The man's name made Naomi want to shudder but she held it in for civility's sake.

"Yes," Lucy said. "And let me tell you, it's going to give my family fits."

Lucy's expression and demeanor gave no indication as to what about Ray would give her family fits. Naomi could think of a few things on her own, but she wondered what it was Lucy meant. For all Naomi knew, Lucy could be about to announce her engagement to the two-timing cur.

Naomi braced herself and followed the younger woman's line of vision, hoping it would clue her in to what went on in Lucy's mind. The cheerful Proverbs For Daily Living Two-Year Calendar caught Naomi's eye.

"The pleasantness of one's friend springs from his earnest counsel." Naomi read and suddenly she found herself in her own inner debate.

She'd kept silent for so long now about Ray's infidelity and what she knew of it. Every time they met here and she saw Lucy steal a peek out Rose's front window toward that snake's house, a stab of shame had cut through Naomi. She knew they'd agreed not to talk about it, not to throw it in Lucy's face or force the issue unless Lucy wanted to know. But today the fresh pain of her son having kept something from her—her ex-husband's reappearance—for her own good, coupled with the verse from Proverbs and her fear that Lucy may be thinking of marrying that lout Ray made Naomi reconsider.

This new Lucy that sat before her, this Lucy that was somehow changed from the mousy girl who usually slumped in her chair and mumbled responses mostly when spoken to, this Lucy might just be ready to hear that earnest counsel from a friend.

"About Ray, Lucy," Naomi said quietly, glancing at Rose who returned a scalding glare. Naomi wet her lips and went on despite Rose's silent warning. "Um, about Ray—"

"He's getting married."

Naomi's jaw dropped.

"He's getting married?" Rose plopped into her chair. "To…?"

"Nikki. Nikki Herndon, my assistant at the day care." Lucy tipped her finger inside the edge of her glass. "You know. Tiffany Crystal's mother?"

"I can't believe this." Rose fanned her face but it did not fool any of them into thinking she was flustered or upset or, heaven knew, about to have a fainting spell. It was pretty clear to all of them she was trying to cool her famous temper. "Why that—"

"I can certainly see why your family might be disturbed," Naomi said, forgoing her instinct to add that she, however, was so delighted she could do handsprings. "But you seem to be handling it very well yourself, Lucy."

"Funny, isn't it?" She rattled her ice back and forth in her glass. "Maybe you'll understand better how wildly my family will react and why I'm at peace with this when you hear the rest."

"Well, don't say a word about it until I get in there!" They heard Gayle call out before they saw her face at the door.

"Another eavesdropper." Rose slapped her hand against the table. "Have I not taught you girls *anything*?"

Gayle came in, looking softer in appearance if not in form.

"Sorry, I'm late. I promised my folks I'd help plan the church harvest party they are having in place of Halloween. *And* I'm having to make a costume for Lillith that is appropriate to the fall season but decidedly not for the celebration of that no longer acceptable holiday, so I was shopping for fabric....Do you like this pattern?" She held up an envelope with a colorful array of children's costumes on it for about a millisecond, then stuffed it back in the bag.

"Nice."

"Very cute."

"Uh-huh," they all muttered to appease her.

None of their responses seemed to register with Gayle anyway as she placed her things down, continuing to talk the whole time. "My whole schedule got off when I went wild at a hair appointment this morning and let the stylist do highlights instead of my usual streaking. He said it would look less…severe. After I got over the shock of learning I'd been walking around all this time looking *severe*, I let him do it."

She touched the undercurve of her meticulously arranged hairdo.

Rose blinked. "You know, I believe he's right. It does look less—"

Gayle frowned.

"It really brightens your face up," Rose concluded.

"Why, thank you." She bobbed her head, then turned. "Oh, my, Lucy!"

"What?" Lucy started.

Rose and Naomi waited, edging forward in their seats to see what Gayle would say.

Gayle blessed her with a dazzling smile. "You're not wearing one of those tired, old baggy dresses you usually live in."

"That's what's different about her." Naomi snapped her fingers.

"You look radiant, sugar." Gayle gave Lucy an unexpected hug around the shoulders. "I hope we're going to see you in pretty sweaters and things like this from now on."

"I think maybe you will, Gayle. In fact, I think maybe you'll see a lot of different things about me from now on and I have Raymond Griggs to thank for it."

"Ray?" Gayle shook back her hair and slid into a chair. "What on earth has he done now?"

"He's proposed to Nikki Herndon," Lucy said calmly, catching Gayle up on the facts. She angled up her chin, folded her hands, together, and announced to them all, "*And* they're going to have a baby. Now, before anyone says another word—"

Tongues were bitten at that table just then, for sure. Every one of them wanted like their next breath to say "another word," but they each honored Lucy's request.

"Before anyone says another word about this," Lucy said again. "I want you all to know that I am all right with this and furthermore, I want very much to add Ray and Lucy and their marriage to our list of people who need prayer."

That night when they bowed their heads to begin their prayers and petitions, Naomi noticed that Lucy put her open hand in the hands offered her instead of pinching her fingers to theirs. That was an improvement, she thought, a definite improvement. Maybe this breakup with Ray, despite its painful overtones, would prove a very positive thing—in the long run.

As Gayle began to intercede on behalf of Ray and Nikki, Lucy let out a shuddering sigh and sniffled.

The very long run, Naomi added.

She shut her eyes and joined her heart to those of the women around her. Even as they stood before God asking his mercy and guidance for others, Naomi silently asked it for each of them as well.

Individually, they'd gone through so much these past five months. Now, as it finally seemed their group was beginning to have a sense of unity, she felt compelled to pray in earnest for the rest of their year together. What they'd come to mean to one another was still so fragile, and each of the women was at a point in her life when she was especially vulnerable. If ever a group needed God's mercy and guidance, Naomi thought, holding tight to the hands in hers, this was it.

Rose must have been thinking the same thing because after Gayle finished her prayer Rose spoke up.

"Father, I know we don't often ask things for ourselves, but I just want to ask you to prepare us as we go into the hectic holiday season. Prepare our hearts and minds and spirits to cope with the stress, the joys, and the…*surprises* that lay ahead."

Sixteen

"Ashley, sweetie, you'll be able to reheat that turkey later in the microwave so much easier if you'd pop it into one of these plastic bowls instead of wrapping it up in tinfoil like that." Naomi held up the perfect size container.

Thirteen-year-old Ashley Boatwright narrowed her eyes at Naomi, pressed her lips together so tightly they went white, and ripped an arm's length of foil from it's box. The tiny metal teeth growled against the silvery wrap, and the extended sheet grumbled like warning thunder across a great distance.

Naomi plastered on as phony a smile as she had ever given anyone. "On second thought, why don't you do as you see fit, then."

Fit being the operative word, Naomi thought, since the girl had been having one prolonged temper tantrum starting the moment Naomi had showed up at the door shortly before noon. It was after three now, the turkey had been praised and prayed over, the various traditional dishes declared delicious, and the men had retired to the den to watch football on TV, leaving the women to clean up. It wasn't so much work, and Kate had done the bulk of it before she had excused herself to put her youngest child down for his nap, but it did require that Naomi and Ashley finally spend a few minutes alone together to finish up.

"I know you are not happy about having me here, Ashley."

The girl did not argue.

"You've made it quite clear that you see me as some kind of intruder in your family's celebration."

Ashley crumpled the excess foil with a vengeance around the turkey platter piled high with leftovers.

"I want you to know how very sorry I am that you feel that way." Naomi meant it. She'd have given almost anything if Taylor's daughter could have made the effort to just be civil to her. Naomi had no idea where her relationship with Taylor was headed—or, for that matter, if it was *headed* anywhere at all. For all she knew it was simply drifting without purpose in the river of time that ended when she picked up her life and headed back to Maine. If she ever did head back to Maine.

Naomi was beginning to think that one word from Taylor could alter her plans completely, though she had hesitated to let him know that. Life had taught her that letting a man know he could have that kind of effect was like giving the keys to your kingdom to the enemy. Though she no longer believed Taylor was the enemy, nor that he was the kind of man to use her emotions against her, Naomi's tender heart could not suffer the risk. Not just yet.

Besides, there was the matter of Ashley to consider. If Naomi could not find a way to reach the girl, to form some kind of bond, then she could not pursue anything more serious with Taylor. Period.

Committed relationships were enough work without the added burden of holding a child's happiness and well-being in the balance. As someone who had held on to a bad marriage for her son's sake, even after the marriage vows had been shattered and she and her son abandoned, Naomi understood this. She would not do that to herself, or to Taylor and Ashley. Either Ashley learned to accept Naomi, or Naomi would have to accept that she and Taylor had no future.

She turned to look at the budding young lady sharing William Boatwright's cheery, warm kitchen with her.

"Oh, no, hon. Don't throw all the bones away just yet. We haven't saved the wishbone yet." The leather-soled loafers she'd bought just for the Tennessee fall, a season not long-lived enough for such an indulgence in Maine, slapped against the faux brick flooring. "Let's save it out and let it dry, then you can make a wish on it. Or hang it up above your doorway."

Naomi reached down into the bulging black garbage bag to retrieve the turkey carcass.

"Why would I want to do that?" Ashley demanded.

Butter and turkey fat dripped onto Naomi's fingers. The coffee grounds from the after-meal pot clung to her wrists and filled her nostrils with the pungent odor of fervent brew. "Which, make a wish or hang it above your door?"

"The second thing." Ashley stood so close by that Naomi could feel the rigidness in the girl's thin body. "I already have a pretty good idea why I'd want to make a wish. And what I'd wish for."

I'll bet you do. If Naomi had any doubt what the girl would wish for, the glower in Ashley's eyes made it abundantly clear. "I see. So, how about before you break the wishbone and I have to start worrying that at any moment the ground beneath my feet will open up and swallow me whole, you try the old Southern tradition my Mama taught me? Hang the wishbone above the door." Naomi wrestled with the picked-over bones, hoping not to send the greasy remains shooting out of her hands and across the floor. The way her luck was going today, the picked-clean bird would take flight and seek freedom through a closed window, breaking the glass and the strained silence in the room with one stomach-churning splat and crack. Putting the picture from her mind, she went on. "My Mama said that if a girl hangs the wishbone of a turkey she's cooked above her door, the first man who walks in will be her future husband."

Ashley flicked her hair off her shoulder. "I didn't cook the turkey."

Naomi swiped at her own forehead to sweep away a pesky lock. "But you helped."

Ashley's sweater rasped as she folded her arms, winding one beneath the other so that neither of her hands showed. "No, *you* helped. Aunt Kate was supposed to do most of it but she got busy with the kids and grandpa and you did most of it."

The girl had a point. "Still, it's just a silly tradition, done in fun. Don't you want to try it?"

"No."

Naomi got her fingers securely around the wishbone and held her breath, if she could just…

Snap. Too bad the tiny, brittle sound was just the bone coming out and not the breaking of the tension in the room, which lingered on, making Naomi unsure of what to say next. She lifted up the perfectly curved bone joined in one flat tip. "So, what shall it be, door or wish?"

"Do whatever you want. Why even ask me?"

Naomi got the feeling the girl wasn't talking about the wishbone anymore.

"I ask because I care about your opinion." Two could play at "hide the agenda." Naomi seized the chance to open any line of communication between herself and Taylor's daughter.

"You care what I think about a dirty old turkey bone?" Ashley scoffed. "I doubt it."

"Okay, so the turkey bone is not the issue here. But I do care about your feelings and opinions, Ashley. I really do." She reached toward the girl, whose demeanor seemed to soften just a tad, then caught herself. Naomi paused to rub her food-muddied hand on the white apron she had tied around her waist. "I wouldn't do anything—*anything*—that would make you purposefully unhappy. I know you don't like the idea of me seeing your daddy, and if you can't find it in your heart to accept me, then I'll stop dating him."

"Really?"

She forced her voice not to waver. "Yes."

"Hang it."

Naomi blinked. "What?"

"Hang the turkey bone over the door." The girl made an overplayed shrug. "Has to dry somewhere, doesn't it?"

"Yes, it does." Naomi's spirit buoyed. It wasn't a vote of confidence, but then it wasn't the old heave-ho, either.

The rubber-capped legs of the chrome-and-black step stool squawked against the floor as Naomi dragged it behind her toward the doorway. She set the stool in place with a firm clunk, then climbed up the three steps that would enable her to prop the wishbone up on the door frame.

"Now, how's that?" Naomi asked, leaning back to admire her handiwork.

"Okay, I guess."

She twisted her head to give the girl a reassuring smile. "And now, the first man who comes through—"

"Would you *really* do that?" Ashley cocked her hip.

"It's just a silly superstition, Ashley. It doesn't mean anything. I certainly wouldn't marry a man based on the whim of a wishbone and a swinging door." Naomi rapped her knuckles on the wood of the closed kitchen door. "In fact, I only did this because it's something my mother taught me and I'm missing her especially today. Besides, I thought it might give you and I a fun secret to share and that might help—"

"Then do it."

"I beg your pardon?"

"Do what you said you would." Ashley's straight hair fell

forward like a curtain closing over her darkened features. "Stop dating my daddy."

"How are my girls doing in here?"

Naomi didn't know which threw her more, Ashley's request or the fact that the first man she'd really, fully trusted and cared for since her divorce had just passed under the turkey bone.

If Mama's old wives' tale was true, then Ashley had just demanded Naomi stop seeing the man destined to be her husband.

"Don't tell your grandmother. It'll kill her, Mary Lucille. It will just kill her."

Lucy cringed at the mention of her grandmother. It had been hard enough to tell her mother about Ray and Nikki, to endure the questions and to let her mother offer comfort when Lucy really felt no need of it. Now, she faced all her father's relatives with the news they'd probably expected to greet them each and every year, that she had been rejected, thrown over for someone prettier and thinner.

"What am I supposed to do, Mother? Lie to everyone?" Lucy scraped a solid glob of stuffing from a china bowl into a disposable tin pan so she could heat it up. She slid that into the oven and switched on the knob. Then she nabbed up a butter tub with a faded label. She dumped the contents, a quivering mass of congealed gravy, on top of a cold mountain of mashed potatoes in a microwaveable bowl.

Lucy jabbed at the proper buttons, then a few beeps and boops later the rest of the food was warming.

Leftovers, she thought, her chest tight. Ever since her father had died, they'd become the Jewell family Thanksgiving tradition. That hadn't always been so.

When Lucy was a child, her mother had put on a big feast at her father's insistence. A big show. Both sides of the family came. Even after there were no relatives from her mother's side around anymore, they kept up the facade of the huge family gathering. Lucy had loved Thanksgiving because it meant her whole family would be together—and by whole family she meant herself and her parents. She could have cared less about the others. She just wanted one whole day when she had her father's full attention, and not in a negative way. No remarks about her weight or lack of beauty, no digs at her awkwardness or ineptitude. And he stayed all day and all night. He did not rush off to work or sneak off to see another woman. With all the aunts and uncles around he was on his best behavior—for one day out of the entire year.

In recent years, she and her mother had had her father's family over late Thanksgiving day and they each brought whatever they hadn't eaten during their personal family meals. It seemed quite appropriate, she decided, that on the one day a year she saw his relatives, they would come bearing leftovers from their family banquets. Hadn't she gotten by all her life on her father's emotional leftovers?

Lucy watched the potatoes gently revolving on the turntable inside the lighted microwave. She felt all turned around herself, not really angry or sad but not happy either. In fact, the more she thought of walking in and facing the folks in the next room, the less happy she became.

She planted her feet and pushed aside her ill-defined emotions. "I am not going to lie to these people, Mother."

"Oh, fiddlesticks, sweetheart, I'm not asking you to lie. I'm asking you…not to tell the truth." Mother checked her tightly permed curls in her reflection in the window over the sink.

Lucy frowned at her over her shoulder.

"I mean, don't tell them anything." Mother inched her nose up in the air just enough to seem regal and removed from it all. "If they ask you directly, just smile and pass the sweet potatoes and say nothing."

"Neither sweet potatoes nor sweet nothings will satisfy these people, Mother, and you know it. They'll want to know why Ray isn't here, and I can just imagine what they'll say when they hear the reason."

"Now, Lucy—"

"Don't ask me to pretend with Grandma or any of them, Mother. I won't do it." The conviction in her voice surprised even Lucy, not that she didn't feel it. She'd felt stronger and stronger each day since Ray had walked out of her life permanently. "I won't compromise my self-esteem or my sense of right and wrong for anyone again. And most especially not for people who all they ever do is pick at me."

"Oh, sweetheart." Mother plucked a tuft of white lint from Lucy's black sweater vest. "No one picks at you."

Lucy clenched her teeth.

Mother brushed her hand down Lucy's brand new outfit, then stepped back and sighed.

For once Lucy could not hold her mother's critical nature against her. The older woman was under the microscope and under extreme pressure. Mother would not only be held liable for her own behavior and appearance but for Lucy's as well. And with Lucy's announcement, scrutiny would rise to an all-time high. Lucy gave her mother a quick hug—a quick, stiff hug—then straightened Mother's dress collar and said, "You look great. Everything will work out just fine, you'll see."

"Thank you, Mary Lucille, I'm sure you're right." Mother returned the straightening gesture, tugging Lucy's sweater one way then yanking it back to exactly the same place it was before. She scowled. "You are going to change before we sit down to eat with the family, aren't you?"

That was it—the feelings, the new convictions, the stress of this and many Thanksgivings past welled up within her. She couldn't stay and put up with this, not from her mother or her father's family. Suddenly, she thought of Rose and her invitation to come by this afternoon. "No, Mother, I am not going to change. Not my clothes or myself. I am fine just as I am, and if you or Daddy's family can't appreciate that, then I think I'll just go someplace where they can."

"You've done it, Gayle, another Thanksgiving done to absolute perfection." Ted came up from behind her as she stood at the kitchen sink.

"Tell that to this sad little reject." Gayle held up a milky orange-colored mousse molded in a Bundt cake pan to give the illusion of a pumpkin and decorated with chocolate-dipped leaves and yellow and red sugar crystals. A culinary triumph scarred by a half-moon scoop mark on top and three deep gouges made by children poking fingers into it, trying to make it wiggle like Jell-O.

She picked up one leaf with most of the chocolate licked off. "I feel guilty throwing food out, but I have no idea how to save this or if it will even keep without getting all weepy and gooey."

"Speaking of weepy and gooey, your sister was in classic form today." Ted swiped his finger along the edge of the mousse to steal a taste.

Gayle stiffened. "Very funny."

"Sorry, but it's the same every year As she heads out the door it's a bunch of moaning and groaning about how this may be the last year we're all together as a family." Ted scrunched up his nose and smacked his tongue against the roof of his mouth, then ran the finger he'd used to test the mousse under cold tap water. "I just wonder, does your sister know something we don't?"

She fluttered her hand in the air. The overhead light gleamed in the wide gold of her wedding band. The heavy rock of a diamond on her finger flashed. "She just has a flare for the dramatic and you know it."

"A flare?" Ted chuckled, wiping his hand on Gayle's hand-embroidered apron. "She has a flamethrower."

Gayle raised an eyebrow. "She's eccentric."

"She's a nut." He wound his arms around her and laid his cheek to hers.

From the dining room the rich, full tones of Kenny G's saxophone radiated a slow, almost sensuous holiday tune around them. Gayle shut her eyes and inhaled the mingled aromas of the day and the familiar scent of Ted's hair and skin. She held the breath inside her, wishing she could lose herself in her husband's arms now, wishing for once she could be with him the girl she'd been with...someone else.

Gayle pulled away.

Ted's arms fell to his sides, his crisp cotton shirt barely whispering with his tightly controlled movements. He took one step backward, away from her.

She'd hurt him, she knew. But then she always knew she would, if not in one way, then in another. If she let him get close to her again, close as they had once been before everything got all stirred up—if she let *herself* get close to him again—it would only prove all the more devastating when he found out the truth about her. And it would not be long now before that happened.

"So, my sister is a nut, huh?" She lifted the plate full of desert, hoping for a light-hearted diversion. "Nuh-uh. I don't think that's what you meant to say at all. Because, Ted Barrett, you should know better than to make unkind remarks about a person's family. Especially when said person is holding an expendable, messy, and obviously nasty-tasting food item in her hands."

"You saying if I don't eat some humble pie right quick I'll be wearing pumpkin mousse?" He leaned back, and a twinkle came to his eyes, then faded. He sighed, something akin to disappointment in his tone and demeanor. "You'd never do it. It'd be too...unseemly."

He said it like an accusation, a sneering quality to what, on the surface, should have rung of admiration.

Gayle's stomach lurched like she'd just stepped from the edge of a cliff. She got the feeling that if she broke down this once and did the thing Ted thought she'd never do, it might burst the dam that held their marriage and family life in such calm and predictable restraint. It might break through to a new way of dealing with one another, it might bring spontaneity and flexibility to things that had so long held her life rigidly—and safely—in place.

Gayle set the plate on the countertop.

Ted's jaw set in a grim, solemn expression while his eyes seemed incredibly sad, but without judgment or contempt.

She had to look away. She did not deserve this man, and he did not deserve her cold treatment—yet she couldn't find anything else within herself to give him. "I've just about finished filling the dishwasher, Ted. Why don't you make one last round of the house to see if there are any stray glasses around."

"Sure. Goodness knows we can't have anything out of place in this house," he muttered.

She watched his broad back as he walked away, her chin trembling with the desire to call him back but her mouth unwilling to form the words. She blinked, and tears turned the dining room into a muted mosaic of the glow of the candles and a fall-toned centerpiece set against the pristine white of the room.

It had been a lovely holiday, a kind of Norman Rockwell meets Martha Stewart affair—with just a hint of Hollywood, courtesy of her sister's theatrics. The pies had been baked to delicate perfection, the turkey a succulent, golden brown, and the china and silver shimmering by candlelight on her great-grandmother's fine lace tablecloth. The conversation had been lively but cordial, and her twelve-year-old son had not even complained once about not getting to sit at the "big people's table."

All in all, Gayle thought, it had been an absolutely miserable experience.

Why did everyone in this family have to be so nice? So good? Why couldn't they sometimes do something ugly or common or let go just a little? If they had, she might not feel like such a heel for what *she* had done…for what she had been contemplating doing all day.

She leaned her hip against the kitchen counter and picked up the mousse, with one hard clatter of the serving piece against the plate, she launched the day's one unsalvageable disaster into the sink toward the garbage disposal. "Correction," she muttered under her breath. "One of the day's *two* unsalvageable disasters. The other one being me."

She reached out to flip on the disposal, but before she could, the phone rang and she snatched it up, knowing full well who would be on the other end.

"Well, what do you think?"

Rose gulped down her gut response and just stared at the diamond chip set in the thin gold circle around the third finger of her daughter's left hand.

"Why, Kelley, it's—" She moved Kelley's hand to make the diminutive stone wink in the late-afternoon sunlight streaming in the living-room window. "It's…it's just…precious."

"Precious? Rommie, what a thing to say." Kelley withdrew her hand. "Tiny little girls in their first dance-recital costumes are *just precious*. Tiny little tea sets and oil paintings and chandeliers for doll houses are *just precious*. Even those tiny little rat-sized dogs with big old bows tying back a snatch of hair from out of their eyes are *just precious*."

"And so is this." Rose patted her daughter's knee as if the girl were a child again. And why not, she defended to the part of herself who knew it was a petty thing to do, Kelley certainly was acting childish.

"Oh, Rommie! This is my engagement ring." She stuck her lower lip out in the kind of pout that had always secured her father around her little finger—and now probably had the same effect on her fiancé. "I think you could come up with something better than the way you'd describe those tiny, little—" Her eyes grew wide. "That's not it, is it? You're not bothered because it's so small, are you?"

"Listen here Miss Kelley-co," Rose invoked the nickname Curry had given his youngest child to imply this message bore his stamp as well as her own. "We may have money and status around this small town, but we are not the type of people who judge others by material things. You know better than that. No, ma'am, the size of your ring doesn't matter one bit compared to the size of your love for this fellow—"

"Oh, Rommie, I knew you'd understand." Kelley threw her arms around Rose and laughed.

Rose placed a kiss on her daughter's temple. "But that's just it, sweetheart, I *don't* understand. When you called me this spring to say you had big plans, I thought you were going to take a promising job in Nashville."

"I have a job."

"Part-time, doing bookkeeping for an auto-repair shop. Now, that's good honest work, and if it was all you could find or just a temporary thing, I'd never even bring it up, but—" Rose stood and faced the window looking out on the quiet, leaf-strewn street. How many times had she lost herself in that peaceful view, pondering the future, hers and her daughters'. Somehow it had seemed so different in her mind. "Kelley, what about a career?"

"I don't need a career. Jeffrey says—"

"I don't care what Jeffrey says," Rose snapped. How had this young man who had only known her child a year usurped her place in Kelley's regard? Had Jeffrey gotten this girl through chicken pox and algebra and her father's funeral? Did Jeffrey care that Kelley had been sheltered and protected and desperately needed the seasoning that life on her own, making her own way, could bring? "This Jeffrey has his own agenda, Kelley. He isn't putting your best interest first. Not in the long run."

"How can you say that?"

"How can I not?" Rose dipped into her pocket to retrieve her hankie, which she then proceeded to wring with both hands as she spoke between full, tightly-curbed breaths. "How can I let you rush into something like this and not say *something*, sweetheart? How can I sit by and watch you surrender your unique, individual identity before you even have a chance to explore what that is?"

"I know who I am."

"Of course, you think you do. But there's no way you can compare the way you think of yourself now, when everything from your rent to your clothes to your education has been provided for you. When you pay your own way, chart your own course and, most of all, keep yourself company for a time, that's when you really begin to learn who you are." Rose released the strangled coil of handkerchief in her hands. "Please, Kelley, listen to someone who was out on her own for a while before she got married and who—"

"Yes, I've heard all about how you used to live in a boarding house and you worked as a secretary until you met Daddy and blah, blah, blah."

"Kelley!"

"Well, Rommie, that's all about the past. If you think finding your identity is in taking care of yourself, then why don't *you* get a job and pay your own way instead of living off Daddy's pension and plans?"

"That's not the point." It was a good point, she conceded silently, but not the point that concerned her daughter. "Kelley, I'm only thinking of what's best for you."

"So am I. So is Jeffrey."

Though it was not yet four o'clock, Rose watched a porch light go on across the street. She saw Nikki Herndon-Griggs's face peek out from the white sheer curtain over the window in her disused front door. Ray's car was not in the drive—and the light told Rose that Nikki expected him to be gone into the night. A wisp of melancholy enveloped Rose's heart as much for Nikki as for Kelley—and most probably for herself, as well. "Oh, Kelley, you just seem so young."

"I'm twenty-three years old. I know a lot of girls my age who already have husbands *and* babies."

Babies? Rose clutched at the custom-tailored portieres. "Kelley, you're not…?"

"Oh, Rommie, of course not! How could you even think that? Jeffrey is a good Christian man. He never pushed me to go further than I was willing. He and I have certainly never done the…well, you know." She made a face, then broke into a gleeful smile. "But just wait 'til our honeymoon—"

"Enough!" Rose cut off the song. "I don't care to hear the details, not on a holiday."

A peel of laughter rose from Kelley's lips. "On a *holiday?* What does that have to do with *anything?* Are we reviving some old Puritan tradition?"

"Just the one where the mother says something stupid in order to try to keep from perceiving her little girl as a grown woman." Rose went to Kelley. "Of course, that isn't strictly a Puritan tradition. Mothers have been practicing that custom all over the world since the first young lady announced her plans to marry before the mother thought she was fully ready."

"Before who was ready, the mother or the daughter?"

"Take your pick."

"Oh, Rommie." She hugged her mother around the neck. "I'd think you'd be pleased that I'd saved myself for my marriage."

"I am, sweetheart." She drew Kelley into an embrace and rocked side to side, burying her face in her daughter's long, soft hair as she patted her back and murmured to herself, "Now I just have to figure out how we are going to save you *from* your marriage."

Seventeen

A job? Rose you can't be serious!" Naomi drew up one knee to tuck her foot beneath her on the kitchen chair. "Why would you suddenly want to get a job?"

"Why wouldn't I want a job?" Rose's silver pie server glided through the creamy pumpkin filling of a fresh-from-the-oven pie. "I'm still vibrant and healthy and capable. Why shouldn't I do something more constructive with my time than just putter around this old place all day?"

"You do a lot more than just putter around, Rose. Why you…you…" Naomi gave a frustrated sigh then leaned over to jab Lucy in the ribs. "Say something Lucy."

"Nikki left a job opening at the day care."

"Nikki left a…? That's not what I meant, Mary Lucille. Say something to convince Rose of what a ludicrous idea this is."

"I don't think it's ludicrous. In fact, I think it's a wonderful idea." Lucy sat tall in her seat, her cupid-bow lips drawn into a smug show of satisfaction. "Furthermore, I think you're only against it, Naomi, because if Rose is at work during the day, you won't have anyone to go to lunch with or call up when you want to shy away from working on fixing up your mama's house to sell."

"Thank you, Lucy." Rose set the first piece of piping hot pie in front of the cherub-faced younger woman.

The moist aroma of spices and feather-light, flaky crust tweaked at Naomi's nose as effectively as Lucy's observations pricked at her sensibilities. She knew it was un-Christian of her, but for one fleeting moment, Naomi did long for the old, mousy little Lucy she'd met that first day, the one who would never have dared challenge her much less peg her selfishness and shortcomings so handily.

Of course, she justified, her little run-in with Taylor's daughter did have her feeling vulnerable. That and the notion of Rose being unavailable to talk about it....or about Naomi's son or to give advice on what she should do about selling the house and going back to Maine...well, it terrified her.

"All right, I'll admit it," Naomi said. "I'm a horrible, self-serving, lunch-gobbling, work-postponing monster who was putting my own needs above my dear friend's."

"Don't worry, sweetie." Rose patted Naomi on the back and placed a big old wedge of pie in front of her. "We won't hold it against you."

Naomi leaned back in her chair and spoke to Rose's back-side as the other woman reached inside the icebox to retrieve the whipped cream. "You were supposed to say, 'Oh, no you're not dear. Yours was a perfectly normal and considered observation, which I am taking to heart.'"

"Is that what I was supposed to say?" Rose cradled the bowl in one arm while she used a huge spoon to fluff up the thick cloud of cream. The utensil clinked against the bottom of the mixing bowl, scraped the length of it and up one side, then Rose turned the mixture over making a full-bodied plopping sound. "Hmm. I guess that's two things I've done today that don't fit with your expectations, isn't it?"

Lucy giggled.

Naomi sulked. She didn't want Rose to go to work. It was immature of her, she knew, but that did not make her feelings of loss any less real.

Clink. Scrape. Plop.

This time the plop fell on Lucy's pie, making a flawless

276

swirly-topped dollop in the center of the ample triangle.

"Oh, don't worry, Naomi, hon, I'm only going to work, not to the ends of the earth."

"But you don't *need* to," Naomi argued.

"Actually, I think I do. I think I need to work to give my life some purpose and focus again. Work has a way of doing that, you know."

Naomi jerked her head up. "Are you saying my life lacks purpose and focus?"

"Actually I was only speaking for myself." *Clink. Scrape.* "But if the remark has you feeling this defensive, maybe it's something you should think about." *Splat.*

The scoopful of cream landed off center on Naomi's pie and began to ooze over the edge of her plate to drip onto Rose's simple checkered tablecloth.

Naomi shut her eyes and fought against the wave of jumbled emotions threatening to overtake her. "You're right, Rose, you're right. My life has lost focus."

"That's not uncommon in a period of mourning, sweetie." Rose handed her a napkin and, when she took it, the older woman placed a hand to Naomi's cheek. "Losing your mama, it's not like any other loss in the world. It's not an easy thing to just take in stride, especially coming so unexpectedly as it did for you."

"On a spiritual level I'm honestly all right with this, but when it comes to dealing with it day to day…" She shook her head. "It's so hard, not to hear her voice, not to smell her day cologne and to know I never will again. And then when something happens like—"

She cut herself off. She'd almost blurted out that she'd wished she'd had her mother to turn to for advice regarding young Ashley and her request that Naomi break off things with

Taylor. It didn't feel right to tell her friends that yet, not before she had a chance to tell the man himself that they had no future.

How she wished she had her mother to comfort and guide her through this awful patch. Mama would know what to do. She would have known just the thing to make it all better, to stop the hurt and confusion and to put things right—or if not right, at least to put them in perspective. But Mama wasn't here. And Taylor wouldn't be around much longer. And now Rose was going to work.

The graying of the afternoon sky outside Rose's kitchen door aptly matched Naomi's mood.

"I haven't handled losing Mama as well as I thought I would," Naomi whispered. "In fact, I'm not sure I've handled it at all. If it wasn't for this group…" She couldn't finish the thought, but then she didn't have to. Rose gave her shoulders a hug, and Lucy lightly brushed one hand against Naomi's forearm.

Naomi drew in a deep breath and with it a sense of strength to go on. She dabbed the napkin at the messy glob on Rose's table. "The money from Mama's estate has afforded me the luxury of not having to go back to work for even longer than I'd planned. And Lucy is right, too, I have used lunching with you and spending time with Taylor as an excuse not to face the things I really should be tending to. It's just hard to face that that's all going to change."

And all at once, too. She didn't add that part. "Anyway." She found a smile she didn't feel and placed her napkin in her lap. "Maybe your taking a job at the day care will be just the thing for all of us. It will help Lucy, of course, and it may just make me crawl out of my blue mood and get back on track again."

"That's right." Rose settled at the table with her own piece of pie. "That's the kind of attitude to have. I'll admit I wasn't very happy about the notion when Kelley first threw it up to me, but after she drove off back to Nashville, I chewed on the idea a bit and it really took hold. And Lucy's job offer—I especially like the idea of working with children."

"You'll be wonderful at it, too, Rose." Lucy hurried to swallow down a mouthful as if she felt she had to speak now or miss out on getting back into the conversation. "I think most of my babies could really use a—if you'll pardon the expression—grandmotherly role model."

"I'll pardon the expression and it's funny you should use the term because that's exactly—"

"Rose! You're not going to be a grandmother!" Naomi's hand froze halfway to her mouth with a forkful of pie.

"Not yet, thank you. The wedding isn't even until spring!" Rose laughed. "The term I was referring to was role model—that's why I'm going back to work, to be a role model to my daughter. You see, for all my big talk of self-sufficiency, she's never seen me put it into practice. It was a classic case of do as I say not as I do—well, it's high time I stopped saying so much and started *doing*."

"When can you start?" Lucy grinned.

"When do you need me?"

"Well, let's see. Nikki quit when she and Ray got married the end of last month. *That's* when I needed you to start."

"Will Monday be soon enough?"

"Do you think you can get your references in order by then?"

Rose laughed.

"I'm serious, Rose." Lucy laid down her fork. "I will have to have some kind of written references on file in case any of the parents ask to see them."

"Oh." She put her hands to her cheeks, then dropped them to the table. She folded them in front of her, then fiddled with the rim of her dessert plate. "Well, I suppose I could gather quite a few references from my years teaching Sunday school?"

"That would be fine." Lucy nodded, just like a professional job interviewer.

Naomi took another bite of scrumptious pie, then noticed someone coming at a brisk pace up Rose's back sidewalk.

Rose pushed her plate away and leaned her elbows on the table. "Let's see, I guess I do still know quite a few people over at the Antioch Baptist Church, I suppose I should start there."

"Well, speak of the devil." Naomi caught herself and cleared her throat. "That is, I mean, the preacher."

"What?" Rose cocked her head.

Lucy craned her neck to inspect the view outside the small window in the kitchen door.

"The preacher from the Antioch Baptist Church is standing outside your kitchen door, Rose."

Four rapid thumps against the glass confirmed it.

"Wow." Lucy looked as amazed as a child on Christmas morning. "What are the odds of *that* happening?"

"Actually, pretty good," Rose said as she pushed her chair back and got to her feet. "The church canvases the whole town every year on Thanksgiving night to invite people to come to some services during the Christmas holiday season. Every year the church board draws straws to see who gets to…minister to me. Guess the preacher drew the short one this time."

"Maybe we should excuse ourselves and hide out.…I mean, wait in the front room while you two have your visit," Naomi suggested, her chair legs already scooting over the floor as she backed up to stand.

"No." Rose held up one hand and placed the other on the

doorknob. "What I have to say to this man is something I want both of you to hear."

"Oh, no! She's trying to make us accomplices to her dastardly deed," Naomi muttered behind her hand to Lucy but not so quietly that Rose didn't hear her.

"This could get messy," Lucy singsonged back.

"I just hope I remember how to dial 911." Naomi jabbed one finger in the air as if punching numbers on a phone, her tongue poked out from between her teeth to show the level of intense concentration required.

"You two behave!" Rose admonished as she squared her shoulders and churned the doorknob to the right. "Brother Paul! Come in, come in!" She swung the door inward with such enthusiasm that the ruddy-faced pastor leapt backward in an involuntary display of surprise.

"Why, Miss Rose, what a pleasure to find you at home this Thanksgiving afternoon."

"Oh, yeah," Naomi murmured, obviously secure in the knowledge that Rose wouldn't light into her with the Baptist minister at the door. "A *pleasure* that surely ranks right up there with having a root canal."

"Won't you come in, Brother Paul?" Rose stepped aside, nailing the two women at her table with her best knock-it-off-or-prepare-to-meet-your-maker Sunday school teacher glare.

"Uh, well, now, I see you've got company. I'd hate to intrude."

"It's no intrusion."

"Would she lie to a preacher?" Naomi batted her eyes, acting the image of sweet innocence. "Besides, don't think of us as company—"

"Think of us as potential witnesses for the prosecution," Lucy threw in.

Naomi snickered behind her hand.

Rose put one finger to her lips as she wound through the kitchen toward the counter where the pumpkin pie sat. "Brother Paul, I believe you've met the ladies in my prayer circle."

"Yes, ladies." He nodded and they returned in kind. "I didn't realize you'd be meeting tonight."

"Oh, this isn't an official meeting," Rose said not realizing how true her remarks were until she gave them voice. "We're together tonight because...because we're friends."

"I see." He nodded again, probably because he didn't know what else to do.

Rose pivoted toward the counter again and began to slice into the pumpkin pie to serve up a piece for the latest arrival.

"Well, you know why *I'm* here, Rose," Brother Paul began.

"Every year, just like clockwork—or should that be calendar work?" Rose wondered, dishing on the topping.

"Yes, that's right."

She heard the shuffling footsteps as Brother Paul moved through the room towards her. "I've just dropped by to invite you back to church."

Rose turned toward him.

"You know, to extend the hand of Christian—"

"Pie?" She didn't have to glance down to realize that Brother Paul's entire palm had mashed into the whipped cream-topped dessert she'd thrust toward him just as he'd reached out in a conciliatory gesture.

Lucy gasped.

Naomi stifled an indistinct sound.

"I am *so* sorry." Rose pulled the plate away. The pie wedge fell back onto it from Brother Paul's hand. Bits of crust went bouncing into his pants cuffs and whipped cream dribbled onto his shoes.

Rose set the plate aside. "I'm so..."

"Well, I never saw *that* coming," Naomi murmured.

"Yeah, I figured she'd go for the face," Lucy added. "But I did tell you it could get messy."

"Would you two *hush?*" Rose hissed.

"It's all right, Rose. I'm not the first preacher to get caught with his fingers in the pie." He chuckled. "Now, may I have a...a napkin, dear? I'd wipe this gunk on my tie but I'm color blind and I have no idea if it would clash or not."

"Oooh, color blind, that explains a lot." Naomi put her hand over her lips too late to hold the quip in.

Brother Paul laughed outright. "It does, doesn't it?"

Rose handed him a fresh napkin.

He wiped the mess from his hands, his expression quite jolly given the circumstances. From the looks on Naomi's and Lucy's faces, that came as a bit of a shock. Rose, though, wasn't surprised. Her difficulties with this man had never been personal, nor about doctrine or practice. The man knew the Bible, and beneath that synthetic tie from the local discount department store he had a heart after God.

Though Rose did think he could come off sounding patronizing at times, she knew he did not mean things the way they sounded. This was more the result of his being the kind who enjoyed a good laugh but had not been blessed with the talent to engender one in others. Hard as he might try, Brother Paul was rarely funny and a lot of people mistook his fumbled attempts at it for put-downs.

No, Rose had no problem with the man himself. Their falling out sprang from an all-together different source, one she only now could admit was her own fault.

Brother Paul finished cleaning the last bits of pumpkin and cream from between his fingers, then folded the napkin in four neat quarters. "I'd ask you where I should put his, Rose, but I have a feeling that might inspire some eyebrow raising comments from the choir section here."

He had a way of grinning and admonishing someone at the same time so that they could laugh at themselves but still know they had not gotten away with a thing. He turned that gift on Naomi and Lucy, who had the graciousness to appear taken to task, but pleasantly so.

"Here, let me take that for you." Rose accepted the napkin, which she draped over the edge of the sink. "Now, tell me, please, is there anything I can get for you? Tea or coffee or…more pie?"

"I think I've had enough pie, thank you." His plump face squished into deep wrinkles that all but hid his eyes when he smiled. "No, Rose, there's nothing you can *get* for me. But there is something you can *give* me."

"What's that?"

"Your promise that you'll think about coming back to the church again. We'd love to have you."

Rose glanced down at the floor. "I'd love…I'd love to come back, Brother Paul."

"You would?" He blinked at her like a startled hoot owl.

"You *would?*" echoed Naomi and Lucy in unison.

Rose folded her hands in front of herself, raised her chin, and squared her shoulders. "Yes I would. And furthermore, right here, in front of my friends, I'd like to make a long overdue apology to you, Brother Paul, for the way I acted these past few years, ever since…well, ever since you came to our church."

"I've heard of Christmas miracles, but this is my first-ever Thanksgiving miracle," he teased, his eyes glittering with excitement and delight. He held out his hand to her. "Apology accepted, if, indeed, there was even a need for one."

"You and I both know there is." She put her hand in his. "I acted horribly. I was petty and small and, quite frankly, terrified."

"Terrified?" Naomi shifted in her seat. "Rose, of what?"

"The truth." Rose leaned back against the counter and braced herself with both hands. "That's what this whole falling out business was about after all. Brother Paul came to our church and had the nerve to change things that needed changing and to stand up to people whom no one had ever stood up to before."

"Like you." Lucy said it to Rose, she didn't ask it of her.

"Not *like* me, Lucy, *me* in particular." She softened her tone to make sure no one would mistake her words for chiding, and remembered to dip her head in deference as she spoke to complete the effect. "This new minister, fresh in from a big, fancy church in Memphis, had the backbone to stand up to me and tell me to my face right there in the foyer of the church I'd gone to all my life...that I was bossy!"

"Imagine that!" Naomi laughed.

"Now, Rose, I don't think I used that exact word. I believe I said you were confident in your leadership abilities—"

"You said *abundantly* confident," she reminded him. "In fact, the whole term you used was 'abundantly confident almost to the point of being strident.'"

"I did." He grimaced at the other women.

"And you pointed out that this made others reluctant to challenge my way of doing things. Which is, in the final analysis, just preacher-talk for bossy." She narrowed her eyes at him, just daring him to deny it. When he didn't she went on. "And furthermore, he had the audacity to tell me that twenty-five years of teaching Sunday school was enough. Time to step down and let someone else take a whirl at it."

"Is this still a part of the apology? Because I have to admit, I think it's drifting from it's original intent." He smoothed down his polyester lapel.

Rose smiled and put one hand on his sleeve. "The fact is, you were right, Brother Paul. I was—I can *be*—bossy. And opinionated. And stubborn probably long past the point of being strident."

"Now, don't be too harsh on yourself," he said.

"Oh, I'm not, and if Curry were alive today he'd be shouting amen to that." She lifted one hand like someone offering testimony. "To top it off, your telling me to step aside from the Sunday school terrified me, and that did not improve my reaction. I saw giving up my church duties as the beginning of the loss of the identity I'd come to value a bit too much, that of Rose, the good wife and mother and pillar of the Antioch Baptist Church." She cast her gaze down, then cleared her throat and went on. "That's why I walked out of the church that day and never came back. I will say that decision has cost me quite a bit over the ensuing years. I don't think I realized how much until I volunteered to serve in this prayer circle. Being around and interacting with these women has made me realize there is more to me than that role I'd tried so hard to cling to."

Rose gave Naomi's arm a squeeze, then reached out to stroke Lucy's fine, silky hair. "I'm going to be all right, Brother Paul. I think I'm finding my way again and part of that means coming back to church."

"Well, praise the Lord, Rose, we're more than happy to have you!" He took her hand and gave it a firm shake.

Rose hadn't felt this good, this *right* about something in so long she couldn't remember. "Praise the Lord, indeed. Funny how we sometimes think the Lord is only at work in us in the big things, the crisis, the times of great fear and sorrow. But he is always there, always willing to guide us, just like the Good Shepherd, if we'll just follow him. I've seen his handiwork in this prayer group and in my everyday life—and in you showing up on my doorstep today, Brother Paul."

"Will we see you in services Sunday?" He turned to make his way toward the door.

"Count on it." Rose followed to show him out. As she did the phone rang, and Naomi offered to get it for her, to which Rose nodded a thank you.

She could hear Naomi murmuring in the background as she told the minister good-bye and assured him again that she'd see him on Sunday. When she closed the door behind him, she stood there for a moment, needing to soak it all in.

The dimming sky of evening made a vivid contrast to the warm glow of her kitchen's light. It made a lovely metaphor, the inner luminescence holding the darkness at bay, the thought of Christ within untouched by the darkness that surrounded them. She thought of the light in her windows shining out against the deepening dusk and took the imagery to heart. From now on she would try more often to let the Lord's inner light shine through her so that others could see him. That was, after all, the most important identity she had. Being a Christian superseded any temporary role she might step into—and out of—here on earth.

"That was Ted Barrett on the phone."

The concern in the other woman's tone made Rose turn toward Naomi, one hand still resting on the doorknob by her hip.

"He wanted to talk to Gayle."

"Gayle?" Lucy pushed her empty plate away.

"Yes, he said she'd left more than an hour ago to come have coffee with us."

"Really?" Rose had a bad feeling about this.

"Yeah, he said he called because he needed her to bring some dishwasher detergent home with her when she came."

"So, what did you tell him?" Rose asked, gripping the knob tighter.

"What *could* I tell him?" Naomi shagged her fingers back through her hair, her expression about as tranquil as a deer caught in the headlights. "I told him I'd make sure she did just that."

"You lied to him?" Lucy said it far too loud, or maybe Rose's sense of impending bad news only made it seem so.

"I didn't lie, I just said the first thing that popped into my head," Naomi defended. "I…I just couldn't tell him she wasn't here."

"Why not?" Lucy demanded. "What if she's been in an accident? The sooner he knows she's not here the sooner he could—"

"I don't think she's been in any accident," Naomi cut Lucy off, her gaze fixed on Rose. "I think she may have gone off to meet with my cousin, Jackson McCovey. You see, he made a phone call tonight and then rushed out. You may not know this, but he and Gayle were in love once a very long time ago."

Lucy gave a gasp like a schoolgirl shocked out of her knee socks. "And you covered up for them!"

"I did not cover up for anyone, okay?" Naomi slapped her hand on the table. The forks jumped on the china pie plates with a nerve-rattling clatter. "I just…I don't want to be in the middle of this and I was afraid if I said anything more to Ted, my own suspicions would have somehow leaked out. Until we know otherwise it's wrong of us to assume that just because

Jackson is gone and Gayle is gone that they have gone somewhere together."

"You lied for a...a cheater." Lucy's voice cracked.

Rose glanced out the window and sighed. "Well, this is another one of those times when God works in the every day because Naomi didn't lie, Lucy, even though she didn't tell the truth."

Rose twisted the knob in her hand and pushed the back-door open. She called out to the dark figure beside the green minivan parked in her drive, "Gayle Shorter Barrett, you get yourself in here right this second."

Then, in what even she could admit was the poorest-ever imitation of TV icon Ricky Ricardo, she added, "You gots some 'splainin' to do!"

 Eighteen

"Ted called."

Gayle stepped into the moist warmth of Rose's kitchen to hear the words she'd dreaded most. She jerked her head up to study Naomi's face. "When? What did you tell him?"

"Just a few minutes ago. I told him you'd bring home some dishwasher detergent."

"What?" She'd heard Naomi but somehow could not comprehend the mundane information being passed along. "You told him I'd what?"

"Bring dishwasher detergent." Naomi stood, leaning against the wall with her arms crossed, the cord of the wall phone still dangling down over her shoulder. "Apparently you're out."

"I must…" Gayle blinked trying to will her racing heart to beat normally and the thoughts swimming in her mind to settle, to focus. "I must have forgotten to check that before I went shopping yesterday."

"That's not like you, Gayle." Neither Naomi's face nor tone registered emotion, and yet they conveyed so much—disappointment, concern, anxiety, perhaps even contempt.

"There are a lot of things that just aren't like you these days, Gayle." Rose came up from behind and lightly placed her hands on Gayle's shoulders. "Do you want to come in and talk about it?"

Gayle twisted her wedding ring around her finger. "I didn't really come to talk."

"Then why did you come here?" Naomi pushed away from

the wall. Once she had begun to speak she did not seem capable of censoring herself and the questions just rolled out. "And for goodness' sakes, Gayle, where have you been for the last hour? Have you been with Jackson? What were you thinking?"

"Well, I was thinking that my friends would not be so quick to judge me, to assume the worst." Her hand trembled as she reached up to tuck a strand of hair behind her ear.

Lucy ducked her head and traced her fingertip over the brown wave of decimated piecrust on her plate.

Rose sighed and gave Gayle a hasty squeeze, then let go and moved to the table. She and Lucy sat in silence, watching. It gave Gayle the feeling they expected her carefully cultivated reserve to suddenly burst wide apart and for her to spill her conscience out like a battered piñata scattering goodies at some children's feet.

Naomi just glared, but somehow did it without malice, as if she was trying to see right into the heart of her old friend and determine what was going on.

Good luck to her, Gayle thought. *And if she succeeds in figuring out exactly what I'm feeling, thinking, and doing, I only hope she'll share the revelation.* She shook her head. "I haven't been with Jackson, as you've apparently all suspected I have."

"Well, darling, Ted said you'd left an hour ago to come over here," Rose said, all soft and motherly.

"It isn't like New Bethany has a lot of holiday traffic, either." Lucy pinched at her piecrust until it crumbled. "You had to be somewhere, and since you weren't here or at home…well, forgive me if I am jaded by my recent experiences, but people have been known to surrender to temptation, you know."

Gayle managed a smile. "I've just been driving, y'all. Just driving."

"Where to?" Naomi stepped forward to place both hands on

the back of an empty kitchen chair.

"Nowhere. Everywhere. I went by your house, Naomi."

Lucy wriggled herself into a positively rigid posture.

Rose and Naomi exchanged sidelong glances.

"I didn't stop," she felt compelled to add. "Then I drove downtown. They have the Christmas decorations up for the tree-lighting this weekend."

Her audience nodded and hummed to show just the right amount of interest in that tidbit of news.

"I went by the high school, then I ended up out at the prayer grove."

"You went all the way out there? Alone?" Lucy's blonde hair swung against her round cheek as she tipped her head. "By yourself at night?"

Gayle laughed. "You pointed out that New Bethany doesn't have a traffic problem, Lucy, hon. As it also doesn't have any crime to speak of, I felt safe enough. Except for a few tense seconds when I thought a startled field mouse might charge me, I never gave a thought to being hurt or even disturbed out there."

"Besides, it's not like it's that late. She probably got there while it was still dusk," Naomi said, her gaze on Gayle.

"That's true. In fact, I got out there early enough that I could find our little tree quite easily." She folded her arms around herself, comforted at the thought of that tree and what it symbolized. "I noticed you just put down a thick, fresh layer of top-quality mulch around the base, Naomi."

"Taylor recommended it."

"It's a good idea," Gayle said. "I really want to see our tree thrive."

"Yes," Rose murmured.

"Sure. We all do," Lucy chimed in.

Then everything grew still, like the air before a storm. Gayle swore she could feel the hair on the back of her neck stand on end, just like they say happens in the moments before lightning strikes. No one moved or spoke. No one made eye contact. Gayle clamped her arms tighter around herself. She scanned the room, looking at everything, seeing nothing in particular. She thought, for an instant, of spinning on her heel and rushing out without saying another word to her friends.

"Why did you go to the grove, Gayle?" Naomi's quiet intensity rattled Gayle's nerves like thunder in the valley. Then in a flash, her manner went sharp and cutting. "Why are you here?"

"I am here because you are the town's prayer group," she heard herself say in a quite disconnected, far away voice. "And I am desperately in need of prayer."

"Sit down, sweetheart, let us help." Rose pulled out a chair for her.

"I can't. I can't stay." She swallowed and battled down the painful lump lodged in her throat. "There's somewhere else I have to go."

"Oh, Gayle," Naomi whispered.

Gayle held up her hand to stop her friend from saying more. "I went to the grove to pray for myself. I've always handled everything for myself—and for everyone else, whether they wanted my handling or not." She chuckled but no one followed her lead on that. Looking away, she stared at the picture on the calendar on Rose's wall—a Thanksgiving scene of a woman serving a perfect meal to her perfect family. Gayle chuckled again but this time with bitterness.

"I prayed for God to deliver me from my temptations, to help me to let go of the things that make me feel like I can never measure up, never be good enough."

"You?" Naomi sank into a chair. "*You* feel that way?"

"Every day of my life—with a few possible exceptions: when we were friends in high school, Naomi, when I was first married and alone with Ted, and *whenever* I was around Jackson McCovey."

No one had a word to say to that.

"That's why I have never gotten over how I hurt the three people who actually loved me for myself, along with my parents, when I ran off with Jackson all those years ago."

"I can understand how you might feel you'd hurt your folks, I remember how they acted when they came and got you the next day. And I know it hurt Jackson, and I can even see how it might have hurt Ted." Naomi's eyes grew wide and luminous, shining with unshed tears. "But I don't see where you come off thinking it ever hurt me, Gayle."

"I hurt you because the night I ran off I practically pushed you into coming along with that no-account who got you pregnant and you had to marry." Gayle clasped her hand over her mouth, realizing too late she'd said too much.

Naomi stared at her for only a moment, then burst out laughing. "My you *do* feel responsible for everyone and everything if you think you're the reason I ended up in that mess of a relationship."

"You mean I'm not?"

"Well, you're good at running the whole world around you most of the time, Gayle, but no. That one was strictly my doing—or my undoing as the case may be." She opened her arms to urge Gayle to come and give her a hug. "I married a man who flat out did not share my beliefs about fidelity, home, and most of all about God. I thought I could change him and spent years trying, but changing hearts is God's work. And try as I could to do it, my husband was not moved. That's in no way your fault, Gayle."

Gayle gave her oldest and once again dearest friend a hug, burying herself in the power of forgiveness and the joy of sharing both worldly problems and spiritual salvation with her. "Well, thank you for that, Naomi."

"Do you still need us to pray for you?" Naomi asked, still holding Gayle near.

"I do." She nodded, unable to look her friend in the eye. "I prayed for God to guide me tonight and I ended up here, I think for a reason."

"We'd be happy to pray for you," Rose said.

"We really would," Lucy, concurred.

"Just tell us what to pray for." Naomi pulled away to try to meet Gayle's gaze.

But Gayle could not comply, she only shook her head. "I don't know. Just pray that I can find the strength to do what I have to do and that I can let go of all this guilt."

"You have to give it to the Lord, Gayle." Naomi used almost the same words she'd told her mama on her deathbed. "Let him carry you the rest of the way."

She nodded. Tears blurred her vision as she looked again at the happy picture of the perfect family on Rose's calendar. She wiped her eyes, then saw plain and clear the verse from Proverbs beneath the picture: *The wise woman builds her house but with her own hands the foolish one tears hers down.*"

She stood and straightened away from her friend. Biting her lower lip to keep from sobbing out in misery, she pushed past the table and to the backdoor. "I have to go."

"Gayle, where are you headed?" Rose's chair screeched backward as she came up abruptly out of it. "I thought you wanted us to pray for you."

"I do." She turned the doorknob and pulled the door violently inward. Stopping for only a second at the threshold, she raised her head and in a strangled voice beseeched them, "Please pray for me with all your hearts, y'all. Pray that what I'm about to do is not something I'll regret for the rest of my life."

The sound of water pounding in a hard, steady spray greeted Gayle as she crept into the unremarkable room.

So he was in the shower. That was something she hadn't planned on and that, now that she was standing here, she wondered if she should take as a sign that she should not proceed.

The shower's stream snapped off. She touched her wedding ring, her stiff hair, the place above her heart where her pulse felt about ready to burst through her chest. If she acted now and tiptoed back out, she could forget the whole thing and he would never know the difference.

But she would know. She thought of the verse from Proverbs on the calendar. *"A wise woman builds her house..."*

She threw back her shoulders, mustered all her courage, said a quick prayer for clarity and strength, then tapped at the closed door.

"That you, Gayle?"

"Were you expecting someone else?" She hoped he took that as the teasing she intended and not a prelude to an argument.

"No, I wasn't expecting anyone else." He laughed. "Hang on a sec and I'll be right out."

"If you don't mind, I'd just as soon come in." She put her hand on the knob. "Are you decent?"

"So I've been told," he quipped. "And I have a towel on, if that matters. But you don't want to come in here. The steam will wilt that pretty hairdo of yours."

"Isn't it about time *something* did?" She pushed the door inward to find her husband standing at the sink, a fluffy white towel wound about his lean hips and one slung around his neck, his hair just having been rubbed dry, as evidenced by its rakish disarray.

He smiled at her.

Not only did Gayle's hair go limp in the steam, but the ice that she'd felt encasing her for so long seemed to melt on the spot. She loved this man with all her heart. But did she love him enough to tell him the truth? Did he love her enough to hear it?

"Oh, Ted." She stepped forward to wrap her arms around him and pressed her entire body to his.

"Gayle! I'm still wet."

"I don't care." She buried her face in the hollow between his shoulder and the thick column of his neck.

"Well, if you don't care, *I* certainly don't." He enveloped her in his arms so tight she could scarcely breathe. "If this is how you're gonna act when you come home from an evening with the girls, I say schedule one every week."

She put her forehead to his and laid her hand to his cheek. "This has nothing to do with that."

"Does it have something to do with the fact that the kids are at your mother's tonight?" He placed a feather-light kiss on the tip of her nose.

"Yes...and no." She *was* glad that the children were not here now. Thanks to a tradition started when they were young, the kids were spending Thanksgiving night with her folks so that Gayle could get her Christmas shopping underway the very first day of the season. That knowledge had helped to shore up her confidence about talking to Ted tonight. "I'm glad we have the house to ourselves tonight, of course, but maybe not for the reason you think."

He laughed and hugged her, rocking from side to side a bit. "You mean because you're looking forward to getting up at six in the morning and power shopping?"

Gayle sighed. "I have no intention of fighting that crowd shopping tomorrow."

Ted scowled in disbelief. "But you always go shopping on the day after Thanksgiving, hon. It's practically your claim to fame that you get more than half your gifts bought before the Christmas lights are turned on at the downtown ceremony."

"Of course I did. I had to."

"You *had* to?"

"I thought I did. I was actually afraid not to."

He brushed a knuckle over her cheek. "Afraid?"

"Sure, afraid. Afraid that if I didn't get out there and get the shopping list filled, that I might not get everything each of you wanted, that I'd let you down."

"Gayle, you could never let us down, especially not by leaving something off our Christmas lists. You don't really think we're that shallow, do you?" Concern lined the corners of his eyes.

"No, I never thought you were shallow," she whispered, choked by her own emotion. "I thought I was. I thought—I think—that I have so little to give that if I ever fell short of anything, then you'd know—you'd see me for who I really am and you'd want no part of me. And I couldn't stand that. I would do anything—and everything—to keep that from happening."

Steam, still lingering from the shower, made his face damp and created a softness all about him as he kissed her cheek then murmured, "No, sweetheart, no. No one ever thought that. No one ever expected half of what they got from you, and no one ever thought it was all you had to give. Precious heaven, Gayle, we love you. *I* love you, with all my heart. I couldn't do that if you were shallow or if I didn't know you returned the feeling tenfold."

Tears bathed her eyes. She laced her fingers together behind his neck. "I hope you still feel that way after I've told you what I have to say tonight."

"Nothing you can say will change that," he said, kissing her temple, her cheek, and her lips. "Nothing. Do you understand?"

She exhaled in a long shudder and nodded.

"Then let's go sit down in the next room and you tell me whatever it is you want to say." He grabbed his robe off the hook on the back of the door then guided her, his arm always around her waist, into their bedroom and settled her onto the bed.

"Oh, Ted." She shut her eyes and began to speak, her hands knotted in her lap. "For so long I've felt like one of those wild circus people who spin plates on top of long, wobbling poles, rushing madly back and forth, never able to take my eyes off anything, never able to let down my guard for fear of everything smashing down around me. Do you…do you know what I mean?"

"Uh-huh. I think I do."

She heard the swish of fabric as he pushed his arms into his sleeves, the thud of one towel and then the other falling to the floor, then the hiss of his belt sliding snugly into place as he tied his robe shut.

"Well, I can't keep doing that. I can't go on the rest of my life terrified of missing my cue, of making a mistake and letting a plate slip. Do you have any idea how hard it is to live like that?"

She felt the bed depress as he sat beside her.

"Do you have any idea how hard it is to watch you live like that?" he murmured.

She could feel his body's heat, still moist from the shower, penetrating her side. "I never thought of that. It can't have been easy for you, for the kids."

"It wasn't exactly torture, Gayle. But there were a lot of times I just wished you'd let things go and just have fun."

"Fun." She laughed at how foreign the concept had become to her. She didn't deserve fun, nor did she deserve the kindness and understanding her husband was showing her. If he only knew... "How could I have fun when I felt sure the very next thing I did would be the one that tripped me up? That exposed me for a fraud?"

"A fraud? Isn't that putting it a bit strongly?" He took her hand.

She pulled away, unable to prolong the moment of truth any longer. "What else would you call someone who had lied her entire married life?"

Ted sat, motionless, for several seconds. Finally he said, very quietly, "I'm not sure, Gayle, sweetheart, but I think I just heard one of those plates drop."

"Well, brace yourself, 'cause here comes the whole service for twelve. Plus serving pieces." She put both hands on her knees, knowing her outward control belied the inner turmoil that had her battling back a wave of nausea, her breath coming short and quick. "Ted, you are not my first husband."

"*What?*" It was more of a yelp than a question.

"That's right. You think you are because I let you think it, but no, nuh-uh, you aren't."

He took her by the shoulders and jerked her lightly around to face him. "Gayle, what are you talking about?"

301

She sniffed, dabbed at her nose with the underside of her shirtcuff, then plunged ahead. "When I was eighteen—just barely eighteen—I did a dreadful and foolish thing. I ran off to Gatlinburg, to one of those tacky roadside instant wedding chapels, and got married."

"To whom? Are you saying you were divorced before we got married?"

She took the second question first because, while it was the most complicated to answer, it was the easiest for her to voice. "No, I wasn't divorced. My marriage was annulled."

"Legally annulled?"

"Yes, legally." Leave it to a lawyer to get the particulars, she thought, feeling a bit better that he hadn't gone through the roof. Yet. "On the grounds that the marriage wasn't, that is, we didn't…"

He nodded as if to encourage the words to come out.

Gayle straightened and stared at the wall ahead. "As soon as we'd gotten into the hotel room, I knew I'd done a stupid, stupid thing. I was so naive, so sheltered, and then we were alone and I *knew* I was not ready to be married or to…*be married*."

She glanced at her husband through lowered lashes to see if he understood.

"The marriage vows went unconsummated."

"As I told my parents, I said 'I do,' but I didn't."

He chuckled.

"I locked myself in the bathroom all night. It was very immature."

"Yeah, well, pardon me if I applaud your immaturity."

She reached out to lay her hand on his.

He curled his strong fingers around her slender ones. "But I'm not surprised by that part of the story—I do recall our *own* wedding night."

"I thought I was very mature on our wedding night," she protested. "It only took me half an hour to get up the courage to come out of the bathroom."

"I wasn't talking about *that*. I was talking about your level of, um, experience." He gave her a playful nudge with his shoulder.

"Oh. Of course." She froze. Finally meeting his eyes, she poured her heart into her gaze and fisted her hand in the cloth of his robe to keep him near. "What happened when I was eighteen was just selfish willfulness and impulse. That's why I wanted out immediately, Ted. It was nothing like what I felt for you, like what we've shared together from the very start."

"I believe you," he whispered hoarsely.

"That's why I couldn't tell you when we first met. I thought if you knew, you'd never ask me out. Then when you asked me out and we dated a bit, I thought if I mentioned it, you'd never ask me to wear your fraternity pin. By the time we got engaged, I knew I could never tell you, I could never risk losing you because of one stupid thing I'd done. My mother said that because the marriage was annulled, it was as if it never happened and so I needn't ever tell anyone. It just didn't happen, she said. But, Ted, it did happen and it hurt a lot of people—including you."

"It didn't hurt me, Gayle."

"You say that now, but what about once you think about it—and the fact that I kept it from you so long."

"It won't change anything." He shook his head. "It never would have."

"Really?" She stared at him, afraid to believe.

"Really."

"Oh, Ted!" She threw her arms around him. "You can't know how relieved I am. I feel like such a burden is lifted off of me."

"I just wish you had told me sooner—because it has obviously been eating away at you for a long time."

"I couldn't." She pulled the lapel of his robe to her cheek. "I couldn't let you see how cruel I'd been to my parents, to my best friend, and to Jackson."

"Jackson?" His whole body stiffened.

"Jackson McCovey, Naomi's cousin. That's who I ran away with." She eyed him for his reaction, her throat tight with anxiety.

Ted blinked. His lips moved to mouth the name, then his expression went somber, as if he was committing the name to memory and filing it away.

"There's more," she murmured.

"Okay."

"He's in town for the holiday. He called this afternoon and asked me if I'd meet him."

"Did you?"

"No." She raked her lip across her bottom teeth. "I won't say I wasn't tempted, but I never seriously considered going to meet him."

"So, you were…tempted?"

"Ted, I was just so weary." She wasn't justifying it, she just wanted him to understand.

"From all that plate spinning?" He asked, his mouth pressed against her hair.

She nodded. "And everything else."

"The lie?"

"The lie. The truth. I worked so hard all the time trying to make up for it, trying to compensate. I thought if I did enough, maybe I could balance out my transgression."

"Didn't you feel that your transgression had been wiped away already? By Christ?"

"Before God, yes, but salvation doesn't make your responsibilities go away, Ted. I owed it to you to tell you the truth, but I never did. I just kept trying to compensate by being the kind of wife you really needed, and I lived in fear all the time that you'd someday see that I wasn't—that I wasn't perfect."

A low, slow rumble began in his chest and radiated through his body. He was...he was laughing!

"Hey, I'm pouring my heart out to you. How dare you laugh at me." She jabbed him with a harmless punch.

"I'm sorry, sweetheart, it's just that...well, Gayle, honey, nobody *ever* thought you were perfect!"

She opened her mouth to object, shut it, then opened it again.

He continued to laugh.

"This is *not* funny."

"Oh, c'mon, don't tell me you don't see the humor in it, just a little bit?"

"Nuh-uh, no sir, I don't. In fact, Ted Barrett, I think you're being a beast to react this way. I ought to just—"

"What?" He sat up straight and held his hands out palms up. "C'mon, Gayle, let me have it with both barrels."

"I think you want me to fight with you!"

"Fight, laugh, love, whatever you honestly feel like, Gayle. That's what I want. No more trying to keep everything smooth and unruffled."

"I can do that," she assured him. "Things will be different around here if I do, though. Dinners may get more casual, kids may get yelled at, and you may have to organize your own parties and dinners for your clients."

"I can do *that*. Can you cut back on some of your volunteer obligations?"

"Just try and stop me." She placed one fingertip on his chin.

"Though I won't leave the prayer group."

"I wouldn't expect you to."

"Then we have a deal." She leaned forward and kissed him.

"Hallelujah!" He kissed her back, taking her with him as he fell to his side on the bed. "Now that we've agreed to less perfection and more passion in this marriage, let's not wait to put it into practice. The kids will be at your folks until after the tree-lighting ceremony, and I don't have to go to work tomorrow."

"Fine with me. In fact, better than fine." She pushed against the mattress, trying to right herself. "Just let me slip into the bathroom to pretty up first."

"Oh, no." He pulled her down against him and clamped his arms possessively around her. "You may have been able to get away with that in your first marriage, but this husband is wise to your ways—and he loves you just the way you are, darling. You don't need to change a thing for me."

Gayle lost herself in her husband's embrace, and in his tender assurances, feeling more free and happy and totally in love than she had in many years. In her life.

Nineteen

"Our angels are mooing!" Rose slapped her hands together in one sharp clap. "Children, children! Now, I know there's been some confusion because half our heavenly chorus is out with the chicken pox and some of you who were supposed to play manger animals have had to fill in as angels. But please try to remember that angels do not moo."

She started to pivot on her heel, then swiveled back, put both hands on the railing of the choir loft and leaned over to call down to the open area at the front of the sanctuary. "Angels also do not oink, baah, woof, or go hee-haw."

"'Twas the week before Christmas and all through the church, the screams of the pageant director could be heard from her perch." Naomi, sitting in the first of four short rows in the loft, recited for the umpteenth time her version of the old holiday poem.

Gayle, who was seated beside Naomi, laughed as if she'd heard if for the first time, which only encouraged Naomi.

"Her stockings were drooping, there was glue in her hair, and she hoped that her sanity still would be there."

"Still? You mean you think someone who volunteered for this job actually had some sanity to begin with?" Gayle mugged a disbelieving face.

"I have my hands full enough with these four- and five-year-olds. Don't make me have to get on to you girls, too," Rose warned. "How am I ever going to get my angels organized with you two up here setting a bad example? Now hush and just keep working on those costumes. We have to have those animal outfits converted into celestial vestments by dress rehearsal tomorrow night."

"Yes, Miss Rose," the two singsonged in unison.

"Very funny." Rose shook her finger at them, unable to keep from grinning herself. It felt good to see them such good friends again.

Gayle leaned her head in to peer at how Naomi had managed to reconfigure a fluffy vest intended to clothe a lamb into a means of holding an angel's wings. Gayle's new haircut, just a bit longer than Naomi's and now without any teasing or tinting, gave her a fresher, softer look. Or maybe the change in her appearance was owing to a deeper change they had all seen in her not long after they'd prayed so fervently for Gayle to find her way.

"Are you sure your angels can't moo or oink, Rose?" Gayle held up the brown, shapeless sack that had passed for a cow costume. "It would sure be a lot easier if we just stuck wings on these things as is and called them Old MacDonald's Roadkill choir."

"Gayle!" Lucy, from her seat directly behind the other women had the good form to look properly shocked. "This is the nativity, the story of our Lord's birth. It can not include representations of deceased livestock."

"Isn't that an oxymoron?" Naomi squinted back at Lucy. "Deceased *live*stock?"

"I don't know about the oxy part, but the suggestion certainly seems moronic to me." Lucy shifted a pair of white, glittery wings to one side of her seat.

"I don't know, Lucy." Naomi feigned pondering some great notion. "If done right, it could prove quite mooo-ving."

All three women broke into a gale of giggles.

"Honestly!" Rose put her hands on her hips. "I don't know

why I let you talk me into letting all of you get involved, Naomi Beauchamp."

"You *let us* get involved because you had an emergency and you needed us, as I recall," Naomi reminded her.

"That's how we corralled the other two," Rose said. "*You*, Miss Naomi, came to this project of your own volition."

Rose had agreed to let Naomi help with the annual Christmas play because the younger woman had asked with such a long face, saying she'd like to help because it would keep her mind off...things. That's how she'd put it—to keep her mind off...*things*.

Rose could only assume what those things might be. Missing her Mama, most likely, and concern for her son, who had not yet firmly committed to returning to college. Or perhaps it was some decision regarding her mama's house, which she had not yet put on the market. Naomi did report that she had gone through the place top to bottom and was ready to "do something" with it. Maybe not knowing just what she wanted to do, whether she wanted to stay here or return to Maine, weighed on Naomi's mind.

Rose also knew, through Will, that Naomi was not seeing much of Taylor these days. She had not broken it off with the man, at least not officially. But she never seemed to have time for him anymore, Rose did know that much. Will had probably supposed Rose might have some insight into what was going on when he'd brought it up. However, Naomi had not spoken of Taylor since Thanksgiving when she'd only made vague references to "not letting their relationship get in the way of their other responsibilities."

What that meant, Rose could only guess, but it didn't sound good for the future of the romance. Maybe Naomi would open up more when she and her son came to dinner with Rose and her daughters the day after Christmas. If not then, then perhaps when things settled back down after the first of the year. She truly hated to see Naomi so out of sorts.

Suddenly, she felt an urge to see if the girls wanted to go for coffee after tonight's pageant run-through. Though they had just had an official prayer meeting yesterday, the list of those wanting intercession had grown enough—and the demands of the season were hectic enough—that they did not want to spend much time socializing. Before she could ask, though, a voice called up to her from the tangle of children down below.

"Miss Rose? Miss Rose?" Vonda Faye Womack, three feet and one inch of pure four-year-old busybody, hollered out Rose's name, managing in her thick accent to drag it out a full three syllables.

How that much voice got into that small a package, Rose would never know. "What is it, Vonda Faye?"

The child's carrot orange hair, caught up in an off-centered rubberband on the top of her head, bobbed up and down, then side-to side, as the little girl did likewise.

"We ain't got no baby Jesus, Miss Rose!"

"Yes, Vonda Faye, I know. We aren't going to have an infant play the part this year because no one wants to take a chance on a little baby getting chicken pox." Rose hoped that came off as sweet concern and not exasperated annoyance, but just in case she added, "Thank you, sugar-pie."

"But, Miss Rose, Miss Rose!"

Rose caught her cringe in time to turn it into a smile. "What, Vonda Faye?"

"Why don't we let Tiffany Crystal play the baby Jesus? She'd fit just fine in the crib 'cause she's just a little bit of a thang."

At the mention of Nikki Herndon-Griggs's daughter, Rose pinched her collar tightly closed at the neck. She shut her eyes.

She'd meant to mention to Lucy that ever since the neighborhood canvassing on Thanksgiving Day, Nikki had been coming to the Antioch Baptist Church. But somehow Rose had never quite found the appropriate time—or the nerve—to do it. Now Vonda Faye had done it for her.

"Thank you, Vonda Faye, that's a very good idea," Rose hurried to say.

And it was. Tiffany was not technically old enough to belong in the play with the preschool children. Yet she was just too bright and advanced to be relegated to the Jingle Bell Babies segment of the program, where they featured the ones too little to do much more than mumble a few lyrics and shake some sleighbells sewn to a ribbon. Still, as Vonda Faye pointed out, the child was delicately small and just right to snuggle in the manger and hold a hidden flashlight to represent glorious radiance around the Lord.

This was the perfect solution to one situation, but to another it presented a perfect mess. Rose turned to face Mary Lucille only to find Gayle and Naomi gaping at her and the seat behind them, empty.

"I'm over this. I am so over this." Lucy's damp palm squeaked against the railing as she fled down the back stairway.

If you're so over this, she taunted herself as she slowed at the landing that joined the rest of the steps in the opposite direction, *then why are you running away?*

Shock, pure and simple, she suggested in silence, *that's all.* Hearing Tiffany's name and realizing that she could run into the child and the child's mother—and perhaps Ray—had startled her so that she acted on instinct and got up to leave, to distance herself from the potential unpleasantness. It was human nature, not an act of someone who still had unresolved feelings.

She stopped on the landing, leaned back against the wall, and drew a deep breath. The smells of the old building—musty paint, cheap carpet, the constant pot of coffee brewing in the fellowship hall—swirled in her head. *Calm down,* she told herself, *this is no big deal. Life goes on, you've gone on. You don't give a hoot about any of this.*

She exhaled in one short huff, tugged her Christmas green jumper in place, and raised her head high. She forced a good Southern belle sigh out, fanned her face, then turned on the heel of her pretty black flats to round the corner. As her feet tapped out a confident cadence on the last of the stairs she couldn't help saying, "I am so over—*Nikki!*"

"Miss Lucy!" Nikki seemed as surprised by the encounter as Lucy did, her eyes huge and her face pale. She pointed lamely over her shoulder toward the sanctuary doors, which stood propped half open. "I was just watching Tiffany Crystal practice for the play."

"It appears she is going to have the most important role," Lucy said, taking a moment to judge how many steps she was from the front door and escape.

"These chicken pox sure do have everybody filling in as best they can. Brother Paul says it's going to be the smallest pageant they've ever had." She poked one finger into her hair, pushing it back, then winding one strand around and around her knuckle in a loose spiral.

"Yes, uh-huh, that's a shame. Well, I'd better be going." Lucy edged toward the door, unable to take her eyes off Nikki, almost as though she expected an ambush. She was wise to think that, she realized, as her hand clasped the cold metal of the outside door's handle and Nikki spoke to stop her.

"Lucy, please, can you stay and talk—just for a minute? I won't keep you long, I promise."

She straightened her arm, telling herself she could walk out that door and never look back and no one would blame her. Not one bit. But she could not do it. Her manners and her training would not allow her to slight someone so boldly, especially not in church.

"I…I'm in a hurry." Lucy decided that was not a lie, she *was* in a hurry—a hurry to get away from Nikki and the emotions the woman's presence churned up inside her.

"Just a second of your time. Please?"

Lucy turned slowly, the way the actresses in soap operas did to give the maximum effect, but she had not done it for effect. Her body did not seem to want this confrontation any more than her heart or mind did. When she pressed her back to the cool glass of the church door, she commanded herself to meet Nikki's gaze but could not seem to lift her focus any further than the woman's gentle bulge of a tummy.

Nikki was pregnant. Pregnant with Ray's child, the child Lucy had hoped to one day have. The realization hit her between the eyes, ripping at her pretense of composure. She choked out a small senseless sound. Nothing more. She did not speak or even try to.

"Oh, Lucy, I am so sorry." Nikki stepped toward her.

Lucy tensed.

Nikki came no closer. "I understand now, now that I've been coming to church, how very wrong I was to hurt you like I did. To lie to you and sneak around."

"And sleep with the man I thought I was going to marry," Lucy added through clenched teeth.

"Yes, of course, yes. That, too. That *especially*, too." The strain was evident in Nikki's voice. "If it matters, which I know

313

it doesn't, I didn't know right off about you and Ray."

Hearing her say his name riled her. Lucy found the courage to look up and into Nikki's eyes. Tears and the undeniable longing for forgiveness met her there. It took Lucy aback.

"He told me…he said you were just old friends, that he ate dinner with you on Sundays and so on, but that you both knew deep in your hearts that it would never be anything more."

That was the first time anyone had ever said that aloud. Everyone had always pretended for her that she was going to marry Ray, though she doubted now that anyone had ever truly believed it—or had wanted that marriage to actually happen. Even Lucy herself.

You both knew deep in your hearts that it would never be anything more.

To Lucy's astonishment, those words rang brutally true. She *had* known, and obviously so had Ray.

"But that's no excuse for what I did, neither is the fact I was new in town and vulnerable. That's what I told myself, that's how I managed to go on working for you and seeing Ray behind your back. I was alone, and you had so much, why should you begrudge me someone who didn't even really love you, that's what I thought."

"Me?" Lucy pressed her palm to the crisp cotton collar trimmed in gold thread. "You thought I had so much?"

"Of course you did—you do. You have your own business, the respect of folks around town, all those little children who adore you, and friends. Lucy, you have a lot of friends, people that really care what happens to you. I never had that. I'm only now seeing what that's like, now that I've started coming to church."

Maybe it was the season, or maybe it was Nikki's assessment, but suddenly Lucy felt a bit like Jimmy Stewart in *It's a Wonderful Life*. She did have so much, and losing Ray had not detracted from the fullness of her life one bit. She blinked at the woman she had once seen as her rival.

Nikki seemed so small and fragile standing there with one hand on her tummy. Through the open doors, the shouts of Rose giving directions, often in competition for attention with Vonda Faye Womack, filled the brittle silence in the foyer.

"Anyway, that's what I'd tell myself—that you had so much and I only had Tiffany," Nikki finally said.

"And Ray." Lucy reminded her.

Nikki's cheeks colored.

Lucy supposed she should feel worse about embarrassing the woman than she did.

"And Ray," Nikki admitted softly, her posture and entire attitude perking up as she smiled, then added, "And now I have the Lord, too."

The quiet conviction of the woman's words struck Lucy hard, made her feel ashamed of her pettiness—but not enough to inspire any overture to make peace between them.

"And things are looking up at home, as well," Nikki said.

Lucy fixed on the implication that things had to have been looking someplace other than up in Ray and Nikki's home for that to have happened. It gave her a small dose of satisfaction that she knew she shouldn't be feeling.

"Maybe it's the baby coming, or maybe it's the prayers of people in the church, but Ray has agreed for us to start counseling with Brother Paul after the first of the year." Nikki's face practically shone with hope and joy in her news.

Lucy felt stabbed through the heart. Ray? In church? After all the years she'd tried and begged and needled him about going? She knew she should be happy, but she just could not grasp the emotion. Not yet, anyway.

"The truth is, Lucy, I want my marriage to work and I want Ray to make a commitment to God, but I don't feel like either of those can happen until we know we have your forgiveness for what we did." Nikki held her hand out, palm up. "Tell me, can you forgive us?"

The answer should have come quickly to Lucy. Her faith, which once had enough "wiggle room" to let her allow herself to date Ray knowing he did not share her beliefs, had grown in her time serving with Rose and Naomi and Gayle. But she wasn't sure it had grown that much.

"Testing, testing." Rose's voice boomed from the microphone that usually was attached to the pulpit. "We've got the sound system hooked up now, children, so we need someone to come read their part so I can stand at the back of the room and see if we can all hear you."

Lucy wanted to say something, to pass this personal test, as it were, but she could not quite do it. Even knowing that she didn't want Ray for her own, that she probably hadn't for the greater part of their Milquetoast relationship did not assuage her pain over the humiliation of losing him to Nikki as she did. She also had to admit to herself that some loathsome, flawed part of her had liked thinking that in time Nikki would get as good as she gave, that Ray would hurt her the way he had hurt Lucy, and that would, in Lucy's vengeful mind, even out the score.

If Lucy forgave them, she'd have to let go of that source of small comfort. She'd have to be big and actually live her faith instead of acting it out. Was she able to do that?

Nikki waited, her gaze never faltering.

Behind them the muffled mayhem from the sanctuary quieted with much hushing from Rose. Then a single child's voice carried out over the sound system: "And lo, the angel of the Lord came upon them, and the glory of the Lord shone round about them: and they were sore afraid. And the angel said unto them, Fear not, for behold, I bring you good tidings of great joy which shall be to all people. For unto you is born this day in the city of David a Savior, which is Christ the Lord."

Lucy blinked. *A Savior, which is Christ the Lord.* If that meant anything at all, now was the time to show it. Lucy closed her eyes. *Jesus, I want to do this,* she prayed, and realized that she meant it. *I want to be what you want me to be, but—I can't.* She fought against the tears. *Jesus…help me…*

Suddenly Lucy's heart swelled with compassion and peace. She breathed it in, let it fill and surround her, like a healing wave. Drawing another deep breath, she opened her eyes and met Nikki's still steady gaze.

"I can forgive you, Nikki." She touched her hand to Nikki's but did not take it. "I think, maybe, I already have."

"Thank you," she whispered. "Could you…could you put us on the prayer list for the prayer circle?"

From inside the sanctuary an earsplitting squawk, feedback from the sound system, raked over Lucy's nerves like the amplified screech of fingernails on the chalkboard. Lucy gripped the door handle, recalling her promise to Ray to offer just such prayers. She hadn't done it, not consistently, not with her whole heart.

She pushed backward, and a rush of cool air swept in. Lucy let it envelop her. She shut her eyes and swallowed hard. "Yes, Nikki, I'll do that. I'll add you and Ray—and Tiffany and the new baby—to our prayer list."

"Thank you, Lucy. And Merry Christmas."

Lucy slipped out the door, feeling better but still a bit overwhelmed by the experience as she called back, "Merry Christmas to you, too, Nikki, and a happy new year."

"Stacey is great."

Naomi backed the car out of Rose's driveway. She and her son, Justin, had just finished a lovely evening with Rose and her two daughters, an after-holiday holiday of sorts meant to just relax and catch up a bit.

"How was that?" she asked her son as she brought the car around and headed off down the familiar streets that connected Rose's house to Mama's.

"Stacey." Justin twisted his upper body so that he could better face her. "Rose's oldest daughter."

"I know who she is, I just didn't quite know what you meant by 'great.'"

"Funny. Smart." He shrugged. "You know, great."

"Yeah, she reminds me a lot of Rose, a bit sassy and full of spunk."

"Mom." Justin snickered. "*Sassy?* Full of *spunk?* Those aren't even words anymore."

"Of course they're words," she protested, pulling up to a stop sign on a quiet residential corner. "Words don't stop being words because they lose their popularity, because they are no longer cool. Cool—that *is* still a word, isn't it?"

"Yes, Mom, it's still a word."

"Oh, good, I'd hate to think I'd begun to speak in an entirely dead language."

"Well, not yet you haven't." He grinned at her.

She returned the smile, actually pleased at his gentle teasing. This was the most pleasant exchange they'd had since Justin had come to town last week. At first she thought maybe it was that awkwardness one feels around someone who has suffered a great loss, a not-wanting-to-say-the-wrong-thing-so-you-say-nothing attitude. Later she suspected the boy simply felt guilty over his semester "sabbatical" and didn't know *what* to say to his mother.

When the clenching silence lasted through Christmas Eve and Christmas Day, Naomi had begun to fret. It was hard enough to face this first holiday season without her mother, but the fear that she had also lost her son, when she had no idea how to regain the relationship with him, was oppressive.

It did not help that, with Rose occupied with the Christmas play and her own children, Naomi had no one to talk to about it all—not even Taylor.

Taylor. She felt a twinge of sadness just thinking his name. She'd seen the man at church and even sat in the pew with him at the Christmas Eve candlelight service, but those encounters came purely unplanned. Otherwise, she had managed to side-step Taylor since Ashley's ultimatum on Thanksgiving Day. Always handy with some perfectly honest excuse why they could not get together, she could not simply break things off with him nor could she ignore his daughter's request that she do just that. Instead she tap-danced around the issue or avoided it all together.

"Nice dinner, huh?" Justin adjusted the seat belt slashing across his dark sweater.

Avoiding unpleasantness, Naomi decided, must be a family trait. "Uh-huh. Rose is some cook."

"Lot of grease, though."

She laughed. "Just good ol' Southern cooking, Son. Fried okra, fried cornbread, chicken fried steak…"

"Yeah, I was wondering about that."

"About what?"

"How'd you Southerners teach those chickens to fry those steaks?"

"We threatened to feed them to you Yankees," she shot back.

"Aw, Mom, I'm not a Yankee."

"No, but you are a chicken, just like your mother," she muttered, making a hard left turn.

"What?" He squinted at her.

Proving her own point, she shook her head. "Nothing."

"Oh."

She came to the entrance to Mama's neighborhood. "So, what did you and Stacey talk about while you two washed up the supper dishes?"

"Lots of stuff." He picked at the frayed edge of a tear in the knee of his jeans. "About New Bethany and this prayer circle thing you and Rose belong to."

"You did?"

"Some. But mostly we talked about her little sister getting married."

"Big doings there," Naomi said. "Six-tiered cake, five bridesmaids, a string quartet, and a partridge in a pear tree."

Justin chuckled. "Yeah, I told Stacey how stupid I think it is."

"What? The cake, the bridesmaids, the quartet, or the partridge?"

"The marriage."

"The marriage?" The car's headlights slashed across the front of Mama's house as Naomi pulled into the drive. "But you don't even know the bride and groom, how can you have decided the marriage is a stupid thing?"

"Not *the* marriage, Mom, marriage in general."

She cut the car's engine. "Justin, you did not say that."

"Yes, Mom, I did." He set his jaw.

A sense of foreboding filled her. How like his father he looked when he did that.

He yanked at a loose thread from the hole in his jeans and the sudden snap gave Naomi a jolt.

"I stood right there in that kitchen and told Stacey that I don't buy the whole idea of marriage. I'm sure as—well, I'm sure never going to do it."

Naomi sat there, her fingers curled around the car key where it was still plugged into the ignition. It was one of those now or never kind of moments. Either she asked outright if this was about her and her ex-husband or she laughed it off with a "Be careful, people who say that have a way of ending up married in pretty short order."

Justin was leaving to go back to college in ten days and this was the first time he'd even hinted at opening up to her. She could not risk losing this opportunity. She had to ask. "Why, Justin? What's turned you so against marriage?" Her coat rasped against the seat covers as she shifted around to face him. "It has to do with your father—"

"Ha! I wondered when you'd finally get around to bringing *him* up!" Justin lashed out a little too loudly.

"Don't take that tone with me, young man. I won't have it." Goodness! She sounded just like her own mama. Much as it startled her, she'd made a reasonable demand and she wasn't backing down from it. "Now, if you care to talk to me in a civil tone about your father and—"

"You've been dying to stick the blame on him for my laying out of college this past semester, don't think I don't know that. Go ahead and do it, Mom, blame him for those opinions on marriage, too, why don't you?"

"Justin!"

"Why don't you do it, Mom? Blame him for my only having one parent, for all the struggles we had when I was a kid, for your divorce."

Her jaw barely moved as she steadied her gaze frontward and said, "I was going to say, this has to do with your father and me. And *me*, Justin. And for the record, I don't recall ever sticking your father with the blame for anything. As I recall, I bore most of the guilt and anguish over our divorce. Not once in your childhood did you hear me heap blame on your dad because I didn't want you to grow up hating your father or to think I hated him."

In the darkness she could not see her son's expression, but then she didn't have to know she had made her point. She saw the silhouette of his shoulders pull back, heard the shuddering release of breath.

She sighed, and the quick flash of anger she had felt dissipated. This was her son, her baby, the little boy whose hand she had held through childhood and who held her heart forever. This was the grown incarnation of the child who had planted himself at the picture window every Saturday morning, turning down invitations for games of tag football or afternoons of sledding to wait for a father who never came. This was the boy whom she had told every Saturday night, "This doesn't mean Daddy doesn't love you. He just isn't good at keeping promises." This was the boy she had tried to be strong for, to be of good faith for, to set a good example for. This was the boy she would lay down her life for.

She'd do anything to spare him pain—anything but deny him the truth.

"Justin, I did the best I knew how. I didn't have a rule book for being a mom without a dad. I didn't have a manual for dealing with a little boy and his tender feelings—I just took things as they came and hoped I didn't do so badly that you'd feel compelled to show up on some talk show and implicate me as the worst mother of all time." She laughed.

He didn't.

"I didn't know what else to do about your father, Justin. I just didn't know." She banged her open palms lightly on the steering wheel. "It's just that, well, I felt for the longest time that if I had done something more, that if I had been a better wife or housekeeper or smarter or better at handling money, that he would not have walked out on us."

She gripped the wheel until the plastic burned against her skin. "If I ever stuck anyone with the blame for things that went wrong in my life, in my marriage, and by extension, in your life, it was me. I always blamed myself."

"I know," he whispered. "I know. And I wish you hadn't."

"You do?"

"Yes." She saw his knot of an Adam's apple bob up and down as he swallowed, saw his chest rise and fall in a long deep breath until, it seemed, he gained as much control as he could summon. "Because if you had been a little harder on Dad and a little less hard on yourself, maybe that would have given me permission to do the same."

"I don't follow you, Justin."

"Mom, I did exactly what you did. All my life, I blamed myself for the fact that I couldn't sustain a relationship with my father."

"But, honey, you were just a little boy. It wasn't your job to keep the relationship together."

"Well, I didn't know that. Since you never got rip-roaring mad at him, I thought it must be because it wasn't his fault…it was mine."

She reached out to touch his cheek. "Oh, Justin, I never

intended for you to think that. It looks like in sheltering you from the disappointment I knew your dad would inflict, I ended up letting in even more hurt."

He gave a hollow chuckle. "Now you're blaming yourself for my problems."

"Well…if the shoe fits."

"It doesn't, Mom." He laid his hand over hers, which still rested on his face. "I do wish you would have been more frank with me about the kind of man my father was, but I understand your motives. You wanted to give me a great childhood. You did do the best you knew how to do—who could stay mad at you for that?"

"But obviously you have stayed mad, at me—as evidenced by your outburst—and at the whole idea of marriage." She stroked her thumb over the sandpaper fine stubble on his jaw and smiled to herself. "Justin, I truly hate that my mess of a marriage may have scarred you like this."

"Oh, Mom." He stretched the word out over several rolling syllables.

"Translation? 'I have the corniest, big, old goofball of a mother on the entire planet'?"

He laughed. "When I said that I never wanted to get married, I was just mouthing off in front of Stacey. You know how it is, you meet a girl you like, you want to seem cool and uninterested, and—"

"And?" she urged.

"And before I could tell you that, you mentioned dad and everything just went all to—"

She cleared her throat.

"Pieces," he finished.

"Yeah, well, your father does have that effect."

"Tell me about it."

"No, I have a better idea, you tell me about it. What happened between you two?"

"History repeated itself—subsequently I'll be repeating a little history myself, as well as psychology and geology and—"

"Could you put that in *English*, please?"

"Mom, I felt like you did. If I just did a little bit more I could bridge that gap, I could make a connection. I even asked him to come to church with me."

"You did?"

"And he asked me if he could borrow some money—just to tide him over until he could get back on his feet."

"You didn't!"

Justin nodded. "That's why I had to drop out, why I really couldn't come to grandma's funeral. I had to take a job to try to replace what I'd given away and I couldn't get the time off. And I was ashamed for being taken in like that."

"It was not your fault. Believe me, I know how that man can be."

"Then, you're not…you're not mad at me?"

"Allow me to paraphrase one of my favorite wise men: 'You did the best you knew how to do. Who could be mad at you for that?'"

"Merry Christmas, Mom, one day late."

She leaned over and gave him a good solid Mom-kiss on the cheek. "Let's go in and have some hot chocolate, and I'll try to wheedle under that cool, disinterested act of yours to find out what you really think of Rose's little Stacey."

"I have a better idea—why don't you tell me about this Taylor fellow."

She froze, one hand on the open car door. "What makes you think there is anything between me and Taylor Boatwright, young man?"

"C'mon, Mom, that cool disinterested act? I learned it from you. And every time we've been within a mile of this guy or anyone brings up his name, you go into an Oscar-winning performance." He slid out of the car and stood with both hands on top of the roof. "Judging from your behavior, you've got it bad for this guy. Is he the *one*?"

"Yes, sweetheart, he is." Her chest constricted and she forced down a swallow that did nothing to ease the pain that throbbed from high in her throat to the pit of her stomach. "He's the one I am going to have to break up with the first chance I get to be alone with him."

She slammed the car door and marched inside.

Twenty

The weight of the smooth hatchet handle filled Naomi's palm. It was a warm day for mid-January; one of those pressure fronts the weathermen always yammered on about had caused it, no doubt. It was only fitting, she decided, that some massive buildup of pressure should have granted her this near-perfect weather for the job she knew she must perform.

She pushed up the rolled cuffs of her flannel shirtsleeves and repositioned her fingers around the pale wooden handle. This was it. Take no prisoners, show no mercy.

She gulped in a mouthful of air, swung the hatchet high, then let it fall on its target with a deadly thwak. Bits of green pulp spurted into the air, as if she'd severed the leafy beast's artery instead of hacking through a twined bundle of kudzu vines.

"Take that," she said. "And that."

The hatchet fell again, almost cutting Mama's old birdbath free of its captor. She raised the hatchet up over her head to gain the momentum it would take to make the final blow, her eyes narrowed to a fine focus on the serpentine plant still clinging to the concrete base.

"Trying a totally new approach, are you?"

Her downward stroke pulled up short. The black metal blade chinked against the lip of the birdbath, jarring Naomi clean through to her clenched teeth. But that physical impact was a brush of a butterfly's wing compared to the emotional jolt of having Taylor Boatwright standing a few feet away from her.

"Taylor." She glanced from the corner of her eye to make sure the birdbath she'd hit didn't suddenly crack into a million bits and crumble like something out of an old cartoon. Heaven knew, she felt cartoonish enough standing there in a lumberjack-plaid shirt, a pair of sweatpants pushed up to her knees for ventilation, and her hiking boots, taking a hatchet to a plant and talking to it while she happily hacked it to bits, no less.

"Um, I was…" She let the hatchet rest on her shoulder. "I finally decided to get after this kudzu."

"With a vengeance, it would seem."

"I didn't know how else to go about it." She shifted her feet.

"That's a good start, there, cutting it back from the birdbath like that. But if you seriously want to eradicate it, you're going to have to have some help—from a professional."

She smirked, giving him what she imagined was a cocky, lopsided grin. "You aren't the first person to suggest I need professional help, you know."

As soon as she said it she realized the implication. Her mind was good like that—good at recognizing an asinine or mortifying double entendre virtually seconds *after* the words had left her mouth.

"Not professional *professional* help," she blurted out. "I mean help…from a professional. You know someone who is a professional who helps someone…like me…to fix things up. Not me, not fixing me, or fixing me up. For the house."

Oh, that made it so *much* better. The thing was she hadn't been properly prepared to see him just now. She hadn't had the time to steel herself against those eyes, that smile, that air of gentleness and masculinity all tightly intertwined so that even his most benign gesture bespoke strength.

For six weeks she'd avoided him, kept busy, seen him only in public places with many others present. She'd planned to meet with him later this afternoon, in the more neutral territory of the prayer grove to check on the tree. Then, after a busy day of killing kudzu, clipping the hydrangea, and generally exhausting herself with physical labor, she would have been in the ideal state of mind to face him. But not now, not with her feelings rushing to the surface as they were.

She fought back the waves of attraction, regret, and loneliness his appearance stirred up in her. Perhaps if she played her cards right, she'd still be able to go with the original plan—and throw in some quiet time to collect her thoughts and spend some time in prayer, to better ground herself before she broke things off with him forever.

"The point is, I don't need any help with this and I'll see you later, just as we planned." She turned away and lifted the hatchet shoulder high, ready to let loose a short, sharp blow.

"But I thought, since it was such a fine day, that we'd pack a picnic lunch and go on out early and—"

"No, no thank you. I can't. I have too much work to do." Her arm quivered slightly under the strain of her effort to maintain control. She blinked down at the remnants of the vine, only then understanding that tears blurred her vision.

"But it's been so long since we've had any time alone together, Nomi. I just can't help feeling that you've been avoiding me."

A sharp stab of guilt tinged with longing shot through her. The hatchet swished through the air only to slice through the strands of already detached greenery, entirely missing the vine stubbornly gripping the base of the birdbath. A small, senseless sound escaped her lips.

"Nomi, if I've done something, anything, to ruin what was blossoming between us, I am sorry."

A man who says he's sorry when he hasn't even done anything wrong, Naomi thought. What a find, what a treasure. And she had to give him up for the sake of his child.

Try as she might to reason around it, she knew that was just what she had to do. She would not try to build her happiness on someone's else's misery. She would not put her own needs ahead of those of a little girl who had already lost one parent and probably feared that through a possible new marriage she would lose the other. And she would never tell Taylor what Ashley had asked of her; she would not be the reason for any ugliness to come between father and child.

Naomi dropped to one knee, gritted her teeth, and raised the hatchet again. She hurled the blade downward. It bit into the fleshy vine but did not cut clean, leaving chewed up bits of leaves on the sharp edge of the hatchet. She mewed out something in her frustration.

"What was that? Naomi?"

"I said I hate this. I hate it." Her heart ached, her mind could not hone in on anything but the smell of the plant and the pain swelling up within her.

"Then, here, let me do it." Taylor stepped toward her.

"I told you, I don't need your help!" She slashed again at the vine, tearing away its grasping hold, piece by piece.

"Well, I'm certainly glad I'm not that plant." He stood too close for her comfort, but not so close she could see anything but his work boots and the hems of his faded jeans without looking up. "Or am I?"

"Are you *what?*" She took one hand from the hatchet and swiped at her forehead, realizing then that she'd held the tool so tightly it made her fingers tingle and her palms sting.

"That vine."

"You're talking nonsense, Taylor." She tried to reaffix her hands on the handle, but her skin still burned too much to get the feel for it.

"Am I?" With the very quiet of his question he commanded her silence. "I recall a time you compared me to this kudzu, Naomi. Now I know you're mad at me, though about what I cannot fathom. And here I find you whaling away for all you're worth at the very stuff you accused me of being. You're a smart woman; don't tell me you can't see any significance in that?"

She could. She did. Ever since she'd come back to New Bethany, this rabid groundcover infesting her mother's backyard and closing in on the fringes of the prayer grove had meant more to her than just some pesky plant life. And now ridding herself of it represented a passage of sorts that she had not even fully begun to discern. But the connection was made.

The kudzu would go. And so must she.

"Naomi, what is it?"

She twisted her neck to speak to him from over her shoulder. "I'm leaving, Taylor."

"What?"

"I'm leaving." She turned around and pulled herself up to her full height. "I only came here to help with Mama and I've long overstayed that need. I'm putting the house up for sale and once that's accomplished, I'm moving back home. To Maine."

His put his hands on his hips, his long fingers splayed over the textured denim of his pockets and waistband. "Since when?"

"What does that matter? It's always been in the plan and you know it."

"How could I know that? Seemed to me the plan changed when you didn't put this house up for sale, didn't even make a move to prepare it for the market."

Whether he was more angry or disappointed, she could not tell. She hated to make him either, but it could not be helped.

The thing that she did control was how quickly they got this over with, so she plunged on.

"Well, I'm putting it on the market now, and that's that." She held the hatchet waist-high, in both hands. "Under these circumstances, Taylor, it just doesn't make sense for us to continue to see each other on a personal level."

"You don't mean that."

"Well, I do."

"But Naomi—"

"Taylor, I've made up my mind. I was going to tell you today in the grove, but you forced my hand." She felt like crying, and as soon as he went on his way, she'd do just that. She'd cry and mourn and mince up kudzu until there wasn't a bit of the intrusive vine—or emotions—left. "It's over between us, though I hope we can still remain friends for as long as I stay in New Bethany."

"When will you be leaving?" There was a deep huskiness to his voice.

"I don't know for sure. Depends on how fast the house sells, for one thing. But I do have my obligation to the prayer circle through May."

"That's good, then." He took a step backward, his head lowered just enough that she could not see into his eyes.

"Why is that good?" A sense of urgency and foreboding overtook her.

"Because it means you'll still be here to take Ashley to the Mother/Daughter Banquet at the end of February." He must have seen the bewilderment in her expression because he went on to explain. "You remember. Each year the Council of Churches sponsors a Mother/Daughter Banquet with the members of the prayer circles as the guests of honor."

"Oh, of course, but—"

"Right after your mama died, you told me that was the very kind of thing you dreaded most. That you could handle the big things, the holidays and such, but the small things, things like the banquet, you feared would be your undoing."

She did recall that.

"And I told you how Ashley always felt so awkward herself at the banquet sitting with Kate and her daughter, sharing someone's else mom instead of having even a substitute mother of her own."

Naomi's heart sank, thinking of the girl and what she'd missed out on in her young life.

"You volunteered to—"

"Yes, I remember. I thought it might be good for us both, but that was before…" She couldn't bring herself to finish. She drew a deep breath, wound her fingers over the hatchet handle, then exhaled. "I'll tell you what. If Ashley still wants to go with me, then I'll be proud to take her. *If* she still wants me to."

"Get a wiggle on Mary Lucille, the banquet starts in an hour and you volunteered to help take tickets at the door."

"I know, I know, Mother." Lucy thundered through her house, a comb between her teeth, one earring in her hand, and the red cardigan caught beneath one arm, flopping its sleeves along behind her.

"Here, let me," her mother said, deftly snatching away the comb as Lucy came to a stop in front of the big mirror in her front room.

Mother began to make quick downward strokes in Lucy's blonde hair, patting the fly-aways down with one hand as she went along.

Lucy adjusted her earring, then dabbed away a speck of

toothpaste from the corner of her mouth.

The minute her mother finished her hair, she pulled on her sweater, then pivoted, her arms extended. "Well?"

"You look real nice, Lucy. Real nice."

"Not like I had much to work with, huh?"

"What's that supposed to mean?"

"C'mon, Mother, we both know I was never exactly beauty-queen material." Lucy poked a lumpy sort of section of hair back into place.

"Who says?" Mother gave her a hug around the shoulders.

"The mirror says for one." Lucy jerked her thumb to point over her shoulder. "And Daddy for another."

"Daddy?" Mother blinked, her nose scrunched up and her neck pulled back as though she'd gotten a whiff of straight ammonia. "What has your daddy got to do with this?"

"You don't have to pretend, Mother. I know Daddy was disappointed in me. More than once he railed at me for not even being pretty enough to enter some pageant or another."

"Did he say that? Pretty enough?"

"Not in so many words, but that had to be what he meant."

"Maybe, and then maybe again he said you weren't eligible to enter the pageants because he sponsored a bunch of them and supplied the parade cars for the queens for every festival and homecoming in the tristate area."

Could that be? "But, Mother, sponsor or not I never could have won any beauty contest, and Daddy knew that."

"Oh, please." Mother waved her hand, then turned to check her own hair and face in the mirror. "You were much prettier and talented than a lot of girls who've laid claim to titles in these parts, Lucy."

"B-but Daddy made me feel so inadequate, so ungainly so...ugly."

"Your daddy, God rest his soul, was the master of making *everybody* feel inadequate, Mary Lucille."

She met her mother's eyes in the mirror. That was the first time Lucy could recall her mother ever saying anything so…*honest* about her father. She doubted she'd ever find an opportunity like this again, so she pressed the issue.

"Then why did you stay with him, Mother?"

"Because that's what I vowed before God and my family to do, honey," she whispered.

"He broke his vows often enough." The accusation snagged in Lucy's throat.

Mother's gaze darted toward the door then to the hallway like an animal looking for a means of escape. Her lips pursed and seemed colorless beneath her coral lipstick.

Still, Lucy gathered her resolve and went on. "He didn't respect the vows he took, Mother. Why did you cling to yours?"

Mother bowed her head. "A vow isn't a tit-for-tat thing, Lucy. Oh, maybe nowadays it is, but it never was to me. I did what I promised to do. It made no difference that your father's vows were all empty, *mine* had substance. Some days that knowledge, the Lord, and of course, you, were the only things that made it worth getting up in the mornings."

Lucy stepped forward to put one hand on Mother's trembling shoulder. She laid her head against her mother's and murmured, "I could never have done what you did, Mother."

"I know." She choked on what was obviously a sob. "And I am so proud to hear you say that, Mary Lucille."

"Proud? Mother, you're proud of me?"

"I always have been." She clutched at her daughter's hand. "But this year more than ever. You've grown so much and really come into your own. When you marched out of the family

Thanksgiving? Well, I wished I'd had the nerve to throw on my coat and march right out with you."

Lucy chuckled at the idea of her mother just up and running away from the grim family tradition. "You should have. You'd have had a lot more fun at Rose's."

"I'd a had a lot more fun in open-heart surgery and I would have had the benefit of a painkiller before people started tearing me apart!"

Mother and daughter shared a laugh.

"Honestly, Lucy, I did admire the way you handled that, and I want you to know something else."

"What's that?"

"I'd have never encouraged you to stay with Raymond Griggs so long if I had known he was a cheater." Mother placed both hands on either side of Lucy's head and put her face up close as if to drive in her point. "Never."

Lucy nodded, unable to answer for the happiness and love swelling up in her.

"I am so sorry that whole mess happened to you," Mother said. "Every time I think of that Ray and that skinny little bottle blonde, Nikki—why I get so mad I could just spit!"

For Lucy's mother, being so mad she "could just spit" was worse than being so mad you had a stroke. A stroke, after all, could not be seen as a personal shortcoming. While it might tell something of your genetic makeup, it did not, as spitting did, reflect poorly on your family *and* show a lack in upbringing.

"That means a lot to me, Mother." Lucy gave her mother a great big hug, then let loose, sniffled, cleared her throat and said, "There's something more you've got to know before we leave, Mother."

"What is it?" She flicked a strand of hair from Lucy's cheek.

"First, I love you."

"Uh-oh, there's trouble. Whenever a message has to have an 'I love you' buffer, it's not good news."

"It's not bad news. It's just—well, I'll just say it. Tonight at the banquet? Besides Gayle and her daughters and Rose and Naomi and Ashley, if they both come, we'll be sharing our table with Nikki. And Tiffany Crystal."

"Nikki? That—? You have got to be kidding!"

"I'm not."

"But how? Why?"

"They're going to be with Rose."

"Rose!" Mother squashed down a handful of her springy old lady pin curls at the side of her head and groaned. "I might have known she'd be behind it. You know she does this kind of thing purely for shock value."

"This she did, Mother, out of plain old Christian kindness."

"Oh?"

"Rose's girls live out of town, and Nikki doesn't have any folks here. They live right across the street from one another, you know. *And* they go to the same church."

"Nikki goes to church? Since when?"

"Since the holidays." Lucy moved to the couch to collect her purse. "And here's an even bigger shocker—one of the reasons Nikki's going to the banquet is because, with the baby due in less than a month, she doesn't want to be left alone tonight."

Mother, who had bent to pick up her own purse, froze.

Forgiving herself that wicked little buildup, Lucy fanned her face with her open hand. "See, Ray is out of town, with Brother Paul and a whole bunch of others from the Baptist church on a men's retreat."

"Well, I'll be."

"Small miracle, huh?"

"I don't know what to think."

"Just be happy for them," she suggested.

"Lucy, I wish I could, but you don't understand how hard it is to forget and be happy when someone has hurt your child." Mother straightened, hugging her rigid black pocketbook over her chest. "You can suffer all manner of things for yourself and forgive and forget and go on, but when someone hurts your baby…"

Lucy did not even feel like correcting her mother's view of her. She supposed she'd always be her mother's baby, especially when she seemed wounded by the world.

Mother reached inside her pocketbook and withdrew a delicate linen hankie with the palest-of-pink monogram. She touched it to her eyes, her nose. Then she arranged a posture straight from the classroom of New Bethany's finest charm school and smiled. "Anyway, you'll know what I mean when you have children of your own."

Lucy shook her head, moving toward the front door. "I'm beginning to wonder if that will ever happen, Mother."

"Never happen? Nonsense!" Mother put her arm around Lucy's waist. "You just have to meet the right man. What about that young man who was so taken with you? The one who came to take out the cable in the day care last month?"

"Dwayne?" They both walked out the door. "Mother I can't go out with him."

"Why not?"

"Well, because he's younger than me."

"A year or two, what difference does that make?"

"It's three years and…well…" Lucy bit her lip. "Well, for one thing, everybody and their uncle calls his daddy 'Smooty,' and I just know that if I went out with Dwayne it would be my kind of fortune to fall head over heals in love with him and marry him. Then we'd have a baby and sure enough someone in this town would get it into heir heads to take up calling that child Li'l Smooty."

"Now there's a case against true love if I ever heard one!"

"Mother!" She rolled her eyes.

"Go out with the young man, Lucy. You'll never find *the one* unless you get yourself out there."

"You come out of there right now, young lady."

Even when Taylor Boatwright raised his voice there was a soft quality to it, Naomi noted.

He rapped on Ashley's bedroom door. "Do you hear me?"

"I'm not coming out. Not if *she's* still out there."

Naomi shifted her weight from foot to foot.

"*She* has come to take you to the Mother/Daughter Banquet. Now, I thought you said you wanted to go. Heaven knows we spent enough getting you a new outfit for it."

"Well, I did want to go—but not with her. You didn't tell me I was going with her."

"You didn't tell her?" Naomi folded her arms over her own brand-spanking-new outfit.

The vivid blue dress was a financial indulgence, especially considering that she'd had to postpone putting the house on the market in order to make some structural repairs so it could pass the inspection. Still, she'd felt strongly about looking nice tonight, to show well in front of the town and so Ashely wouldn't be too embarrassed by her. That's what she told herself. It was *not* because this was the first time she'd seen Taylor since that day in Mama's backyard. She shuffled her feet again, her expensive new shoes, with just enough heel to accent the shape in her legs, pinching her instep.

Taylor looked from the closed door to Naomi, who managed to tap her toe to demonstrate her impatience even though it sent a sharp pain halfway up her calf each time she did it. "I only said I'd do this, Taylor, if Ashley wanted me to. Or did you forget that part of our agreement?"

He raised his fist to knock at the door again, but instead he let it drop to his side and sighed. His broad shoulders taking on a noticeable slump. "I'm sorry, Naomi. I thought she'd be all right with it and I hated the idea of you going alone."

"Me?" He'd been thinking of her when he'd laid these disastrous plans? How sweet. She swallowed hard. Her nose tingled.

"I thought how good it would be for Ashley not to just be a tagalong for the first time in a long time."

He was thinking of her *and* thinking of his daughter. How very sweet. She crunched her hands into fists hidden beneath her folded arms.

"And I thought that once the two of you were all dressed up, the tickets bought and time to go, that you'd just…well, go."

"Ah," she tipped her head back. He was thinking of her and his daughter and that dresses and tickets would be enough to motivate them to—strike that, she edited herself. He was not thinking. He *was* sweet, but not a lot of thought had gone into this sad little arrangement.

"Oh, Taylor," she swept one hand back over her hair. "What am I going to do with you?"

"Well, I'd offer some suggestions," he said with a grin. "But this is neither the time nor the place."

She could just kick herself that his none-too-subtle teasing gave her a tiny thrill. Or should she kick him, she wondered, for getting her into this situation in the first place? She could be home right now, dressed in a pair of knee socks and an old bathrobe. Home. Alone. Or she could be sitting at the banquet feeling all alone even in the crowd, missing her mama on a night when everybody else in town was honoring theirs.

Just like Ashley must have felt time and again on this very night.

Shame washed over Naomi. She shut her eyes and fought against the swell of tears and the tightness in her throat. In one moment of insight, Naomi saw the young girl locked in her room not as Taylor's insecure child or a teenager determined to keep her out, but as a motherless daughter, just like Naomi herself.

Taylor stared glumly at the door in front of him. "Looks like I owe you an apology, Naomi—and one to Ashley, if she ever decides she's speaking to me again. But first, I'd better call Kate to tell her you won't be coming by to pick her and the girls up after all."

"Wait." Naomi lifted her hand. "Don't give up on this so fast, Taylor. Is that door locked?"

"Even if it was, you'd just have to jiggle it a bit to get it open," he said. "Why?"

"You go on. Just give me a few minutes alone with Ashley, I think maybe I can resolve this. And if I can't, well, she and I will probably both feel better that we tried."

Twenty-One

"A re you comfy, Nikki?" Rose patted the very pregnant woman's back, then stopped to help the woman's child. "You sit here between your mama and me, Tiffany Crystal. Hop up on this booster seat."

Gayle scooted her own chair up to the table and stole a glance at her two daughters sitting on her right. She was so proud of her girls, so pleased at the way they had adjusted to her new attitude. Adjusted? She brushed the back of her hand down her simple denim dress. Her whole family had done more than adjust—they'd *blossomed*.

It rankled her now to know that what she had once seen as maintaining order and dignity in the home had really been stifling a lot of the natural interaction they had known as a young family. Well, no one would accuse her of stifling anything now, especially if they heard her get after her kids at high volume when they needed it or saw the family joking and roughhousing as they all pitched in together to do things around the house. It wasn't ideal, but then, what family was? And who wants to be one of them?

Gayle handed a banquet program to Max, who was decked out in a brown top-and-skirt set, and congratulated herself for not having made even one comment on how drab she found the color. She looked further down the table at Lillith, quite content in her white-and-silver, glittery dance-recital leotard under a burnt orange corduroy jumper set off by lace-patterned tights and red shiny shoes. Yes, things had certainly loosened up at her house, Gayle thought.

She gave a small wave at her mother, who sat on the other side of the girls, and her mother returned a smile. When they had gone to pick up her mother, Gayle had worried that there would be some backlash over their clothing. At the very least, Gayle had expected a reminder of how cute they had all looked at past banquets—every year since Lillith had been a baby—in their complimentary outfits. Her mother had most especially liked last year's when Gayle had picked up a floral theme that carried from her suit to Max's vest to Lillith's skirt and head-band.

But tonight all Mom had done, after suppressing one fleeting look of unabashed horror, was get in the car and fold her hands in her lap.

As they drove to the hall, Gayle had whispered, "So, Mom, you can tell me the truth. You've noticed how we're dressed—do you think I've totally lost my mind?"

Mom clicked her tongue. "Worse, sugar, much worse."

Gayle girded herself for some harsh criticism.

Mom sighed and rolled her eyes. "Gayle, sweetie, I think you've lost all sense of style."

Gayle fought the urge to stomp on the brakes and gape at her mom, and instead settled for a quick glance to confirm what she'd heard.

The look on her mother's face was pure mischief. For the first time in what seemed forever, Gayle remembered that it was her own fear of letting her mother down, not some unrelenting standard of judgement on her mother's part that had made things tense between them. While her mother might not have approved of all of Gayle's choices, she'd never disapproved of Gayle herself. And she had never tried to run Gayle's life, even after the worst of it. She'd never insisted that Gayle stop being friends with Naomi, for example.

Suddenly Gayle wanted to jump up and go give her mother a hug. Of course, then she'd have to explain why she'd done that, and she'd be told she was being silly and sentimental, which would break the entire mood of the moment. Mothers! Gayle thought, can't live with 'em....She smiled. Wouldn't even want to try.

Her thoughts went to Naomi again and, as if on cue, her old friend walked into the room.

"Well, I'll be," Rose murmured, her upper body leaned in Gayle's direction.

"Nuh-uh." Gayle wadded her napkin up and tossed it onto her plate, ready to leap up and greet her friend. "She is *not* with Taylor's daughter, is she?"

"Kate's right behind them," Rose said through a toothy smile. "Could be coincidence, them arriving at the same time."

"I wouldn't wager the rent money on coincidence," Gayle whispered.

"Like you ever made a wager *or* paid rent, my dear."

Gayle reached over the center of the table to pluck up a bowl brimming with plastic containers of coffee creamer. She set it down with a clunk beside Rose. "They don't have real cream, but will this do to fill your saucer, Miss Catty-pants?"

Rose looked from the bowl to Gayle, then her expression softened in a chuckle. "I'm sorry, doll. I'm a bit testy today, I'll admit it. Someone came in with a bid on the house this afternoon, so that set my nerves on edge, wondering if this one would go through."

"Oh? Congratulations."

"It's a bit premature, but thank you. That's not all, though. When I went to pick Nikki up for this, she told me she'd been having gas pains all day."

"Ooh, that *is* cause for concern. Huge as she is? One belch and she could explode—take out this whole half of the dining hall!"

"Here." Rose plunked the creamer bowl dead center of Gayle's plate. "You'll want this back."

Gayle laughed.

"The point is, I'm afraid she's having the stirrings of labor pains."

"Well, she's had one baby already, Rose. Wouldn't she *know* if she was starting labor?"

"Tell me, were all your deliveries exactly the same?"

"Hmmm. No, no they weren't. Almost didn't get to the hospital in time with Lillith because it all came on me so sudden."

Gayle made a short, anxious study of Ray Grigg's little wife—and she was little, every bit of her but that enormous bulge front-and-just-below-center of her body. She looked, in fact, like a soda straw down which someone had managed to poke a lemon. She also looked like she could deliver that "lemon" at any minute.

Naomi approached the table, one hand on Ashley's back. "Hi, y'all. Sorry we're late, we had a little…um, we both needed some extra time to get ready."

Gayle noted that Naomi's eyes were rimmed in red, as though she'd been crying. Ashley's face was a bit puffy as well, but both seemed in good spirits now.

"It's just been a bit hard for me to prepare for a mother-daughter banquet this first year without my mother," Naomi said, her hushed tone as becoming as her new dress and heels. "Thank heaven the Lord gave me someone special to help me tonight—someone who's been through it herself, bless her heart."

She took Ashley's arm and gave it a squeeze.

The young lady's eyes shone with that deep, compassionate

quality that all the Boatwright's seemed to have come by intuitively.

"Well, if you're nine or if you're...twenty-nine—" Ashley paused to beam a laughing look at Naomi, who responded in kind—"When you lose your mother, well, it just leaves this big...place in you. It's not empty because it is filled with your memories, but that's not the same as having your mom to hug you and listen to you. Your life, it goes on, but it's never the same. Someone who still has their mom, well, they just don't get that."

Naomi folded Ashley into a hug and patted her back.

Gayle swallowed hard and gathered Max's and Lillith's hands in hers. She gazed over at her mother, and both smiled to find tears in each other's eyes.

Even Rose reached across to rub Nikki's upper arm as the younger woman leaned over to kiss her young daughter on the head.

Napkins lifted to dab noses and a chorus of sniffles, throat clearings, and cover-up coughs followed as Naomi and Ashley and Kate and her daughters found their seats at the table.

"Lucy and her mother will be here momentarily. They had to turn in the tickets they collected and tallied up," Naomi told the group.

"So," Gayle whispered as her friend settled in directly across from her, "does this mean what I think it means?"

"Ashley and I have made a breakthrough of sorts, but don't go thinking this changes anything. I don't want to get the cart before the horse."

"Congratulations on the offer on the house, Rose," Kate said, as she pulled her youngest daughter's chair closer to her.

Rose nodded an acknowledgment, then leaned forward, speaking specifically to Gayle and Naomi. "Do y'all think it would be selfish to put that prospective buyer on our prayer list—you know asking God to help get the loan approved?"

"I think that's just fine, Rose." Gayle turned loose of her children's hands. "While we're at it, let's put Naomi's house problems on there, too. That way you may both sell faster and give Kate two commissions."

"Oh, I wouldn't get a commission off Naomi's house." Kate batted away the notion with the flick of one hand.

"You mean because you're helping her as a favor, being as she's almost *family* and all?" Gayle needled, just dying to know some details of the "breakthrough" that had been made tonight at the Boatwright's.

"No, silly…because I'm not licensed to represent property all the way up in Maine—" Both of her hands went straight to her mouth, her eyes were wide, but it was too late.

"Maine!" Gayle scooted her chair backward and pointed an accusing finger at Naomi. "You're selling the house in Maine? That means you're staying right here!"

Everyone stared at Naomi, who flashed Gayle a look that would blister barn paint.

A server, dressed in black pants and a white shirt, came to the table and started filling water glasses. For a few moments the only sound anyone heard was the glug-glug-slosh of water pouring, followed by a chunk of shaved ice flowing over the rim of the pitcher into the glass.

Finally Naomi spoke. "Okay, I am seriously thinking about selling the house in Maine and staying right here in New Bethany."

"Nuh-uh." Gayle shook her head.

"Uh-huh." Naomi nodded.

"Oh, Naomi, I am so happy to hear that!" She stood and ran around the table to give her friend a big hug.

"Gee, I hate to interrupt this mushy ol' lovefest, but we're here," Lucy announced as she and her mother arrived at the table.

Lucy surveyed the scene, anxious for a moment, having been left out of whatever was going on, she'd felt out-of-step the whole evening long.

"Sorry," Gayle said, slipping back around to her seat. "But Naomi says she's going to stay in New Bethany, and I just had to show her how I felt about that."

"What was she trying to do, wring her neck?" Lucy's mother whispered with no trace of jest.

Lucy had forgotten she'd never caught her mother up on the new developments between the friends, so she just whispered back. "No, Mother, they've made up. They're friends again."

"Seems like the older I get, the less I know about what goes on around this town," Mother muttered.

"Now, Mother, you know Rose, of course, and Gayle and Naomi and Gayle's daughters and her mother."

Mother nodded in turn and greeted each person as they were named.

"And this is Kate Boatwright Harper and her two girls." Lucy indicated Kate with a flourish.

"How d'you do?" Mother said.

"Nice to meet you," Kate replied almost simultaneously.

"And you remember Nikki Herndon-Griggs?"

"Of course."

"And her precious little girl, Tiffany Crystal." Lucy bent to give Tiffany a sweet little peck on the cheek. Then she turned and took Mother's arm to show her around to their seats.

"Tiffany Crystal," Mother grumbled as one might say some harmless Southern euphemism for a curse word.

"Hush, Mother," Lucy warned.

"What's she going to name that other baby? Gorham Silver?"

"Mother, not so loud." Lucy inched closer so to speak in her mother's ear. "You'll give her ideas!"

"Lucy!"

"Well, you started it." She pulled out her mother's chair.

As Lucy helped push the seat in again, her mother answered in a voice only Lucy was sure to hear. "Yes, but let's not forget I am the small and petty one who has not yet found it in her heart to fully forgive this girl. You, on the other hand—"

"I, on the other hand, Mother, have obviously not wholly come to terms with this, either." Lucy situated her own chair at the table, waited while the server filled her water glass, then finally dared to scan the table—Nikki Griggs, included. "Well, what does everyone suppose is on the menu tonight? My best guess is chicken."

"You peeked," Kate accused and everyone chuckled over the obvious: the banquet had never served anything *but* chicken since its inception right about the time Lucy was born.

Then that awkward, nobody-knows-quite-what-to-say silence fell over them. Some fidgeted with their flatware. Others feigned immense interest in their surroundings.

The water server reached the end of the table, pouring for Rose, and then, last of all, for Nikki.

"Oh!" Nikki practically leapt out of her seat.

"I'm so sorry, darling, did I splash that on you?" The server held out a napkin.

"No, I just…I thought…" She turned panic-stricken eyes to Rose.

"No." Rose went pale.

"Nuh-uh." Gayle thumped down her water glass, which had made it only halfway to her mouth.

"That girl isn't in labor, is she?" Mother asked a bit too loud.

"I'm not in labor," Nikki protested. "I can't be. My husband is out of town."

"I don't think babies generally care about things like that." Rose stood and came around to the end of the table, taking Nikki by the wrist. "Now, do you think maybe you've started labor, honey?"

Nikki's teeth sank into her lower lip, the hand in Rose's grasp balled into a white-knuckled fist.

"Well, ladies, if you'll excuse us, it looks like some of us will be having a baby, instead of a banquet tonight."

"I'll drive you over," Gayle offered.

"I can drive. Y'all stay and enjoy." Rose helped Nikki up. Nikki's daughter squalled and reached for her mother. "Lucy? Can you take care of Tiffany?"

Lucy nodded and moved to the small girl.

"I'll call Brother Paul's wife and see if we can get a message to the men's retreat," Gayle's mother said, already heading toward the hallway and the payphone with her coin purse in her hand.

"The prayer circle will be on standby," Naomi called out.

"I can baby-sit for any of you if you need to meet at the hospital for prayer," Kate offered.

Prayer! Lucy blinked as Rose and Nikki disappeared out the big doors at the end of the hall. Of all the things she might have been required to do as her duty to God and this circle, she never imagined one might be to pray for Nikki and her baby. Not some general prayer for God to bless and remember them, but an honest, from-the-heart prayer for their well-being. Even as she shivered with the realization of what that meant, Lucy knew that they must do it.

And that she must lead them.

There was only one hospital in New Bethany, and in it only two birthing rooms. By the time Nikki was fully checked in and onto the second floor, both were occupied. That did not seem a serious problem, however, since almost like magic, the instant Nikki's obstetrician had arrived, dressed to the nines straight from his fifteenth wedding anniversary party, her pains had vanished.

The doctor gave her a terse examination, asked a few questions, then patted her on the head. He told her to go home and relax, to put her feet up and not eat anything spicy, as if she were a witless fool who had utterly confused the gripping pangs of having a new life violently and miraculously emerge from her own body with a case of indigestion.

Rose would have pinched the arrogant fool by the scruff of the neck and told him what for if Nikki had not found a more eloquent way of putting him in his place. She had rolled off the bed, which was much too high for her to simply "hop down from" as the doctor had suggested, stood on her wobbling legs, then doubled over in pain. The intensity drove her to lunge forward, grabbing onto anything she could find to stabilize herself, in this case, the doctor's necktie.

Rose fancied that she actually witnessed his eyes popping out from their sockets.

He sputtered something that was, at best, poor bedside

manner. Seizing Nikki by the shoulders, he shouted, "Are you having a contraction?"

To which Nikki blew out a long, halting breath then straightened. "What did you *think* I was having? A coffee break?"

"Well, if you have another of those, start timing how far they are apart. You know the drill." He checked his expensive wristwatch. "My take is it's just false labor. Go home and calm down. You're not having any baby tonight."

As if to prove him wrong, her water broke—before that doctor could get himself out of the way. His shoes, Rose thought, would never be the same, but then, maybe neither would his snotty attitude about who knew better when she was having a baby, the woman or the doctor.

Shortly after that, the doctor ordered Nikki prepped and told the nurse he'd be back as soon as he changed. Rose had no idea how long all this had taken until Naomi stepped off the elevator with Gayle and Lucy right behind.

They had just stopped to see if the baby had arrived and to join Rose in a quick prayer at Lucy's request. But when Rose told them how things had gone that night, both Naomi and Gayle seemed ready to stay for the long haul.

"In the hallway?" Naomi pushed forward. "They have her in the hallway?"

"The birthing room is about to open up, and they're going to move her in a few minutes," Rose explained. "How was the banquet?"

"Nice."

"Really nice," was the consensus.

"How's Nikki holding up?" Lucy asked, a timidness to her approach.

"Doing pretty well, all things considered," Rose led the way to the place where Nikki's hospital bed sat pushed against one wall in the hallway to the left of the birthing rooms. "Here she is. Nikki? Nikki, hon, how you doing?"

The woman reached out and grasped Rose's hand with a crippling force.

"It's okay, Nikki, we're here," Naomi said. "I know we're not family or even friends but we're here for you."

"Imagine that, leaving her out in the hall like...like they were running some kind of assembly line here," Gayle muttered, coming up to the bedside. "It's okay, sugar, you've got some people here to speak up for you now." Gayle turned to Rose. "I didn't mean you hadn't spoken up for her, Rose, just that you've been a bit preoccupied with just being with her and all, and now that there are more of us maybe we can divide and conquer, as it were."

Rose held up her hand. "I understand and I appreciate any help you can provide and I'm sure Nikki does, too. Did anyone get a hold of Ray?"

"Brother Paul's wife called the retreat and he's on his way, but it will be past midnight before he gets into town," Gayle said.

"We'll have us a new baby by then," Rose said softly. She brushed Nikki's hair off her forehead and smiled. "Ray's on his way. You're doing fine. It won't be long now."

Nikki started to respond, but her reply quickly turned into a low groan.

The women, except Lucy, closed ranks and spoke in soothing tones, letting her squeeze their hands, giving whatever comfort they could.

When the contraction eased, Naomi looked up, concern etched on her features. "This is ridiculous, I'm going to go find a nurse and see what's going on."

"Wait!" Nikki strained to lift her head.

"What is it, dear?" Rose asked.

"Before anyone goes, would y'all say a prayer?"

"Well, sugar, we can do that after you've gone into—"

"I want to say a prayer!" Nikki snapped. "I'm sorry if I'm not exactly being reasonable right now, but I'm kind of overwhelmed here and I would dearly love to have a *prayer!*"

"Okay, of course." Rose turned and motioned for Lucy to join them. "C'mon, Mary Lucille, this is what you signed up to do."

Even as Lucy shuffled forward, Rose's spirit lifted. This *was* what they'd signed up to do. To pray for those who cried out for it, to put themselves where God's love must most unselfishly be. They did not know this girl, not really, and at least one of them had reason to despise her, but instead they surrounded her and took up one another's hands.

What a new home or job or romance or friendship—or even the fellowship of church—could not provide for Rose, this moment did. In abundance. She thought of the line from "Amazing Grace": "I once was lost but now I'm found."

She had come into this venture feeling lost. True, she'd come a long way since then, but not until this moment, not until she lifted her heart in sincere prayer at a moment of need for one of God's children who had simply asked, had she really and truly felt she was found.

"Dear Father," she whispered taking the lead in the prayer for the first time in their circle. "Thank you, for life, for this life about to come into the world, and for the lives of those who will love and nurture it and guide it in your ways. Thank you for your love and sacrifice in giving us your own child, born to die for us. We are so unworthy, and yet through him we come before you in amazement and joy to just say…thank you."

"Thank you," Naomi echoed.

"Thank you," Gayle murmured.

"Thank you, Lord, for all these things," Lucy said, a quiver in her voice. "Thank you for being bigger than jealousy and anger and hurt feelings, for giving us a love so big it fills the holes we create with hostility and selfishness. Lord, hold on to Nikki and Ray and Tiffany and their new baby, make them a family here and keep them always as a part of your family, forevermore."

"Amen," Rose whispered, touched by the words she knew had not come easily to Lucy.

"Amen," the others answered.

"A...A...oh...oh...my..." Nikki groaned again, this time not the low painful sound she'd made before but something much, much more urgent.

Rose dared to lift the stark white hospital sheet covering the woman they had just prayed for.

Lucy gasped.

Gayle clutched Nikki's hand.

"I'm getting a nurse," Naomi said even as she dashed.

"Tell her we are having a baby! *Now!*" Rose placed the sheet back down. "Take a deep breath. Concentrate. Breathe!"

"Why, Rose, I didn't realize you knew anything about coaching a natural childbirth," Gayle said, her focus obviously still on Nikki.

"I don't! I'm trying to keep Lucy from fainting," Rose shot back, bracing the younger woman up by one arm.

Just then the nurse showed up and whisked Nikki off down the hall. Rose handed Lucy off to Naomi as she came up beside them and hurried off after the gurney and patient.

Less than a half-hour later, Rose was able to announce the news. "It's a boy!"

They all went to the nursery window, and when the nurse showed up with the blue-swaddled bundle they hugged and laughed.

"Well, there he is. Ray's son," Lucy whispered.

Rose put her arm around the girl.

"I always thought…" She didn't have to say it, they all knew what she'd thought.

And they all mourned a little bit for what she had lost, even though Rose felt sure none of them, even Lucy, honestly regretted that things had not worked out for her and Ray. Still, to see that little baby there and to know that in the short time they'd served together that Lucy's life had moved so much further away from that kind of fulfillment, there was a definite kind of mourning to that.

"You know, I needed this," Lucy finally said.

"Really?" Gayle asked, coming up close to Lucy and Rose and peering with them into the nursery. "Then you're okay with all this?"

"I'm okay," she told them, and it surely did seem so. "I'm okay with it now that I've been through this. Before now, before I had to face it and lay my heart in a real prayer for them, well, I hadn't let it go."

"No one ever told me that about these prayer groups," Rose murmured.

"What?" Naomi asked.

"That in praying for others, you get so much more back in return."

They all stood in silence, arm in arm, until Lucy said, "It's too bad there probably won't be another circle after ours."

"You don't know that," Gayle said. "It's not spring yet, something may yet happen to surprise us all."

Twenty-Two

Rose, that wedding cake—"

"It's hideous," Rose graciously supplied through a Cheshire cat smile.

Naomi and Gayle covered their mouths and snickered.

From a quiet corner of the garden, all three women surveyed the swirl of activity at Kelley's wedding reception. Even though it was late April and still a bit chilly for an outdoor reception, Kelley had insisted on one as her farewell to the house she'd grown up in. Today Rose had "given away" her youngest daughter into a new life, and two weeks from today she would hand over the house and begin a new life of her own.

Rose watched as the people she loved and had known, some of them all her life, gathered to join the celebration. Brother Paul and his wife stood speaking with the parents of the groom. Taylor Boatwright and his daughter, Ashley, and sister, Kate, were being regaled by Sisters Marguerite and Princess under the blue-and-white striped canopy that topped the refreshment table. Everywhere she looked, Rose saw someone she cared about and who cared about her, including Kelley and her new husband.

He seemed a good man, a very decent man indeed, but something in her still wished Kelley had waited, had spent more time on her own. Still, this was Kelley's life, and Rose knew that her disapproval would not impede the romance but could harm the relationship between herself and her child. And so she did what did not come naturally to her—she kept her mouth shut. About some things.

"Let's face it, ladies." Rose waved to her oldest daughter, Stacey, standing in an ill-fitting dress the color of an after-dinner mint while talking to Naomi's son, who'd come down for the weekend. "That cake is tacky."

"Well, I have to say this for it, it's—" Naomi grappled to find the right word, holding her hands out to indicate girth and then height. "It's generous."

"Generous?" Gayle snorted—like some bulldog with a stuffed up nose, Rose noted. "I think overly endowed women in spangly dancing costumes have leapt out of smaller cakes than that, Naomi."

"Gayle!" Naomi at least pretended to look shocked at her friend's bluntness.

"It's true, and you know it," Gayle went on. "Why, put a few sparklers and an American flag on the thing and you could drive through the streets as a parade float."

"You mean there's isn't already an American flag on that thing?" Naomi made a big show of squinting at the monument to lard-based icing, confectionary roses, plastic pillars reminiscent of Tara, and tiers of heavy white cake. "I thought I saw one by the spun sugar waterfall, carried by the Civil War reenactor figures storming the church to win back the bride in the name of her mother and all who think Kelley's too young to get married."

Gayle shook her head, her simple diamond stud earring flashing as she did. "No, you must be thinking of the flags of all nations over there with all those animated puppets singing 'It's a Small World.'"

"Y'all are not funny," Rose said, pretending to be miffed.

The women looked a bit remorseful that their ribbing over the enormous confection may have gone too far.

Then Rose quirked her lips up to one side and muttered, "You'll find the American flag flying over the replica of the VFW Hall in the miniature-scale model of New Bethany over on the far side of the cake."

They shared a chuckle, then fell silent until Naomi gulped down some artificially colored pastel punch and said, "Look over there at Lucy and Dwayne, aren't they cute?"

"I can't believe she finally decided to go out with him," Gayle said.

"It only took her mother and all three of us working round the clock to convince her she should just give him a chance." Rose shifted her dyed-to-match, mother-of-the-bride, pristine peach shoes on the manicured lawn. "What effort it took to get that girl to just take one date and see how that goes, not to get ahead of herself worrying about things that might happen if they should fall in love and get married."

They all nodded in agreement at the wisdom of that advice.Then Naomi, her gaze still aimed at the quietly chatting couple near the punch bowl said, "You know, of course, if they do ever marry and have a child that everyone in this town *will* immediately start calling it Li'l Smooty."

"Uh-huh," Gayle concurred.

"Oh, absolutely." Rose smiled at the newly dating pair.

"I guess there's always a price to be paid when you fall in love," Naomi said, twisting her ankle on her beige pump.

"You should know," Gayle singsonged.

Naomi gasped, almost spewing punch. "Gayle!"

"It's true, isn't it? You are in love." She raised an eyebrow. "Naomi and *Tay*-lor, sitting in a tree—"

Naomi put up her hand. "Our relationship has progressed, thank you. But we're taking it slowly. We both want to be very cautious about Ashely's feelings, about all our kids' feelings."

"Is that why you all are going off to Maine together this summer?" Gayle prodded.

"*With* the children," Naomi hastened to say. "We are all going to spend a few days in Maine this summer, my son and I staying with friends, Taylor and his children at the nearby inn. I had to go up to get all my belongings out of storage anyway, now that the cottage has sold, so it seemed the perfect getaway for all of us."

"Testing the waters, I'd say." Gayle nudged her with an elbow.

"The only thing being tested here is my patience. Besides, if you want to talk to someone about a potential marriage in her future, I suggest you look no further than..." Naomi pointed a finger at Rose.

The implication made Rose's heart beat faster. "Why, I...I never...Naomi Beauchamp! You, of all people, know that I have steadfastly deflected any and all of Will's overtures and innuendoes regarding marriage."

"Yes, but somehow you never do quite run him off entirely, do you, Miss Rose?" Naomi gave her a sly smile.

Rose had to smile too. "All right, I admit it. I do like Will a little too much to chase him off completely. I am very happy to have a companion, someone to take me to dinner sometimes, to sit with in church, to help me move into my new condo."

Her upbringing, even now, hindered her from adding a childish "So there!" but the gist was clearly in her tone. She did like Will, but she was not ready to go back into marriage again. She was content with the way things were between them, and since he was still hanging around, she had to assume he felt the same way. She made a quick search of the wedding guests for the man in question. Had he lost his way back to her or had some other widow woman with more of a disposition to marry and the wiles to pursue her goal snagged him into some inane conversation?

Her gaze fell on Nikki, Ray, Tiffany Crystal, and the new baby, all sitting at one of the lace-covered tables.

"Look-y there." She tipped her head in their direction. "Don't they look sweet?"

"I'll tell you what was sweet," Gayle said, her eyes fixed on the bundle in Nikki's arms. "Easter."

The single word evoked a precious memory that needed no further explanation. Nikki and Raymond Griggs had both been baptized at Easter, in a big service south of town in the "river," which really was little more than a healthy-sized creek. It was one of those moments—one of those God-answers-prayer moments—that simply could not be pared down to words.

Rose would forever associate that and the birth of Ray and Nikki's child, and Gayle's transformation, and Miss Ida's illness and funeral, and Rose's own coming back to the church, and so many other smaller things with this year of service in prayer. It just about broke her heart in two to know that no one else had signed up to create a prayer circle this year. Princess Johnson had undertaken to keep the list of volunteers, and as of today she reported there had been a few inquiries but no serious takers. No one willing to make the commitment. No new trees would be planted in the grove next Sunday.

"Well, I suppose I ought to go find my husband," Gayle said, giving Rose's arm a squeeze.

"Wait, Gayle, before you go, there's something I want to do and I'm going to need your help. And yours, Naomi. And let's get Lucy in on this, too."

"May I have you attention, y'all?" Rose, with the other members of the prayer circle at her side and the wedding cake as a backdrop, held up one hand.

Someone in the crowd clinked a fork to their glass, setting Rose's teeth on edge. But that did the trick and within seconds, the eyes of everyone in the garden fixed on her.

"I know at most weddings it is customary to have toasts and cheers for the happy couple, and that's all well and good, but I'd like to do something a little different now." She wet her lips and made herself stand tall. "I'd like to ask you all to join us now in prayer."

An approving murmur worked its way through the crowd.

"Join me, please," she urged and bowed her head. "Dear Father, we humble ourselves before you now because even in our hour here of finery and joy we are but beggars in your kingdom. Only through the gift of salvation do we dare approach, not by our own doing, but by your grace are we worthy."

She drew in the scent of spring just about to burst forth mixed with the aroma of sugar-laced wedding cake. "We ask first, Father, for your blessing on the household created today by Jeffrey and Kelley, and for all those gathered to celebrate their union. But, Father, I also come before you now to ask you to move hearts."

She could hear the restless swish of feet in the grass, of people shifting nervously in place. "For more than fifty years now, Father, the women of this town have stood in service, in prayer. Through heartache and loss, through happiness and triumph, through personal crisis and public trepidation, they have come on their knees, Lord. Even when it was no longer fashionable to put others first, even when it was no longer convenient to give time for others, even when they themselves were afraid and needy, they came. They came, not asking out of their own desires but in the name of those who needed them, who needed you. And you have heard, O Lord, you have heard their prayers."

"Yes, you have," Princess murmured from within the hushed gathering.

"The people these women have lifted up, you have lifted up also, their concerns were yours," Rose went on. "And more than that, you rewarded those who stood in prayer with gifts far greater than they had ever hoped or imagined. Each woman who served brought away her own sense of worth and peace in learning in a very private and unmistakable way, what all women really want to believe—that what they did has mattered. More than monuments or governments or the pretenses of our fragile existences, to love, to stand on faith, to be a good friend, to serve, matters."

She struggled not to let her voice thin, clenching Naomi's hand in hers—and receiving a reassuring squeeze back, she was able to go on.

"What our circle did this year mattered, Lord, and for doing it you have given us friendship and love. We pray now that someone else will take up the cause, will say that she will be used by you for the good of someone else. Lord, don't let ours be the last prayer tree planted in New Bethany. In Jesus' name…"

"Amen," came the soft but intense response from the group.

"That was a lovely prayer, Rose. Really, really lovely," Naomi said hours later when all the guests had gone home and only Lucy, Rose, and Gayle remained. They were helping Rose tend to the aftermath of the reception.

"I just hope it does some good," Lucy said, stacking the last of the stray plates on the kitchen counter for the caterers to handle later.

"Mary Lucille!" Gayle put her hand on Lucy's back and teased, "I seem to recall that you are the one who thought our first official prayer was the very catalyst for getting Naomi in the group. Don't tell me you think we've lost our touch."

Lucy smiled back at Gayle, her face the picture of relaxed affection, a feeling which Gayle realized she returned without reservation.

"Y'all, let the caterers do all this cleaning up." Rose unbuttoned the top button of her dress and kicked her shoes off. "I'm paying them enough for the responsibility of it."

"You are paying them enough to pick up after the Fourth of July picnic, parade, and fireworks display." Naomi plopped into a chair at the kitchen table.

"Half of it is a landfill user's fee for them to get rid of all that cake!" Rose pushed out a chair and sank into it, too.

"Oh, don't let them haul away the cake, Rose." Gayle came over and gave the older woman's neck a gentle massage. "You're moving, honey, you could use that icing for spackle to fill cracks and holes in the wall."

"Cracks and holes?" Naomi gave a dry laugh. "The size of that thing? She could caulk her showers, weatherproof every window and door, insulate the attic, and still have enough left over to provide an after-worship snack for the entire Antioch Baptist Church."

"I'll keep it in mind." Rose closed her eyes and hummed her contentment as Gayle continued to knead her tight neck muscles.

"Speaking of moving," Gayle said, working her fingers on an especially knotty spot. "When will you need us to help with packing and things?"

"I've been so busy with the wedding and all I haven't given it much thought. The day the movers are coming is circled on the calendar."

Gayle leaned over to flip up the page of the Proverbs for Daily Living to see which day in May she should reserve. When the page fluttered up to reveal the next month, her pulse skipped at what she saw there.

"Oh, my…oh. Listen to this, y'all," she bent down and edged in a bit to make sure she read the words in small print correctly. "The proverb for next month is 13:12, and here's what it is: 'Hope deferred makes the heart sick, but a longing fulfilled is a tree of life.'"

"No." Naomi got up to confirm it herself.

"Do you think it's a sign?" Lucy asked, moving in to the close circle studying the Scripture passage.

"Maybe not a sign, but I certainly find it personally significant," Gayle said, laying her trembling hand high on her chest. "I know I came to this group heartsick, my best hopes just beyond my reach. Now I feel like I have a whole new life."

Lucy nodded, then straightened, her head high, and tucked one hand into her pocket.

Rose smiled.

Naomi put her arm around Gayle's shoulders and put her head next to her friend's. "I know what you mean, pal. It's been an amazing year."

"I just wish I knew how to express to others what we've experienced, to make them understand how fulfilling the commitment to serve can be." Rose's face was lined with care.

"You did, Rose," Gayle assured her. "Your prayer was beautiful. We've done our part and now we have to lay it in God's hands. That's all we can do now, trust and see what happens."

It was one of those days when the TV weathermen admonish their audiences to "get out there and really enjoy the day." Naomi wanted to enjoy the day, she really did. She climbed out of her car and stood beside it, letting the breeze ruffle through her hair. She watched the town's women—and every now and then a man— trickle in through the iron gates of the grove.

Though she could not see all the way to the clearing where they had planted their sapling last year and where, in theory, any new groups would plant their own trees today, she squinted her eyes in that direction. On a distance knob, the kudzu had claimed more ground, overtaking some long-dead stumps as it did. She took some comfort in that, in knowing that life went on, and sometimes found in death a means to grow.

She'd chosen to come alone today, so she could linger long after to talk with Gayle and Rose and Lucy if she so desired. Or so she could get in her car after the ceremony and drive aimlessly out Old Seminole Cemetery Road and all round New Bethany, listening to sad music and crying for the tradition that had seen its last today.

She tapped her fisted hand on her car's roof and sniffled, lifting her chin to search the gathering passersby for the other members of her circle.

"So, are you ready for this?" Gayle came up from behind, touching Naomi at the base of the neck.

"Uh-huh," was all she could say. "You?"

"Nuh-uh."

"Pretty day, isn't it?" Rose joined them, her subtly extravagant loafers hardly making a sound in the damp grass. "That's a good sign, I'd say."

"Rose, you don't believe in signs," Naomi murmured.

"Portents, neither," Rose said, her smile made poignant by the sadness in her eyes.

"What?" Gayle asked.

"Never mind, dear. Now, where's that Lucy?"

"I'm here! I'm here!" Lucy waved to someone going on ahead of her through the gate. "I was going to drive Mother and myself over, but Dwayne showed up at the last minute all set to bring us himself. Wasn't that sweet of him?"

"Sweet as sugar pie," Rose said.

"Do you have the song sheets, Rose?" Naomi peered at the other woman over the top of her car.

"Right here." She waved a stack of white papers. "Fifty copies of 'I'll Be With You In Apple Blossom Time,' courtesy of the copy machine in the church basement. With Brother Paul's approval."

"Really?" Lucy hiked up her slouchy leather bag, which was not nearly as big as the one she'd sported last spring. "He wasn't put off by the fact that we're not singing a hymn?"

"I told him the story behind it and explained that you'd be telling it to the gathering before we sang, and he broke out in a grin wider than the Mississippi." Rose gave a wry smile herself. "Said he thought it was good to shake things up once in a while. Keeps people on their toes."

"Well, then, let's get to shaking." Naomi finally shut her car door, as if that signaled the game was afoot.

"Let's do it," Gayle linked her arm in Naomi's.

"Let's," Rose echoed, looping her arm through Gayle's.

"It's going to be all right, you know." Lucy came up and took Naomi's hand and then Rose's to complete the circle. "No matter what it's going to be all right…isn't it?"

"Lucy! Do you realize that's the first time you ever took our hands outright?" Naomi asked.

Lucy blinked her luminous eyes. "I just…I just don't want to lose y'all. I want to know that no matter what happens, we'll still have each other, that we'll still be friends even if we don't have the circle to bring us together anymore."

"We will, sugar," Rose whispered. "I promise."

"Who else on earth can I ever eat pecan-turtle brownie crust, chocolate-swirl cheesecake ice-cream pie with hot fudge sauce in front of but you all?" Gayle laughed.

Lucy stared at her a moment. "But you never ate that, Gayle."

"Yes, but I do plan on starting. And when I do, you three are the only people I'm going to let see me do it!"

"I thought you stopped worrying over your perfect image." Naomi *tsk-tsk*ed.

"She's worrying over that perfect figure," Rose corrected.

"I am worried, ladies," Gayle held up her hand, the one that was laced through Naomi's arm, and went on, "I am worried that if I ever brought that stuff home to my family and tried to eat it in front of them—that I would have to share! Y'all I could fend off, but my family?"

"Nuh-uh," the others finished with her.

"Okay, y'all, the sooner we get through his, the sooner we get to dessert," Naomi reminded them.

They walked together, their strides far more upbeat than Naomi actually felt—probably due to the fact that Rose was humming the happy tune they would soon all be singing. Or perhaps it was friendship that buoyed their footsteps, or the feeling of goodwill that seemed to come in waves around them from the others assembling in the grove this beautiful day.

Naomi and Taylor made eye contact, much as she had that day last year. He beamed at her. Ashley, who stood beside him, did some pretty convincing beaming herself. Naomi kept her gaze on them even as they passed and wouldn't have looked away except for Lucy's gasp demanding her attention.

Turning her head in what seemed extra-slow motion, she faced the clearing. What she saw in it made her heart stop.

"Two," she managed to croak out. Tears sprang to her eyes. "Look, y'all, there are two trees!"

"There are going to be two circles next year!" Lucy cried out, practically jumping up and down as she said it.

"Was your prayer that did it, Rose," Sister Princess said, standing beside one of the spry little apple trees.

"The Lord did it, Sister." Sister Marguerite folded her arms over her ample bosom.

Princess smiled like a sly old cat that knew where they'd hid the catnip. "The Lord moved our hearts, but Miss Rose's prayer moved the rest of me. I signed up for a circle all on my own this year, one without my big sister butting in every other minute. Talk about finding the peace that passeth understanding? Praise God!"

"You're still not too old for me to drown you in a rain barrel little sister," Marguerite warned.

"You may get me under, but you can't hold me down," Princess replied, winking at Naomi.

"We have a sort of eclectic group," a woman standing near Princess chimed in, "but we're all very committed."

"You'll do fine," Gayle told her.

"The second group is something special." Kate Boatwright Harper motioned toward the cluster of people in front of her. "Girls?"

Like soldiers coming out from their camouflage, a handful of teenaged girls came from all over the group to take their places beside the second apple tree.

"We want to start a junior version of the circles," Ashley

told them. "To pray for kids, most especially teenagers who might not bring their requests to older women."

"What a wonderful idea," Gayle said almost as if to herself. Naomi's gaze met Gayle's, and they shared a moment of understanding. Such a group would have meant so much to Gayle that summer, after Jackson McCovey. It might even have saved Gayle and Naomi's friendship all those years ago.

She smiled. At least it was there for their children. "It is a wonderful idea, Ashley. Did Kate help you all get organized?"

"I helped them get started, but honestly I'm hoping someone who isn't related to any of the girls will step up to be a sponsor," Kate said. She stood on tiptoe to address the crowd. "If anyone wants to help with the junior circle, please just give me a call."

"Whoa! Wait! Whoa! Are we too late?" From the back of the grove the sound of a baby carriage bouncing over the rugged ground accompanied Nikki's shouts.

"Do you want to volunteer to sponsor the teen group, Nikki?" Kate asked, only the hint of concern on her quiet features.

"Sponsor?" She backed into the opening where the two trees and their circles stood, dragging a big navy-colored baby carriage. "I came to start my own circle."

She maneuvered the carriage around to show a crooked little tree in a burlap ball right where a baby's behind should have been. She stopped, wiped her brow, and let out a long, whooshing sigh.

"Sorry to be last minute like this, but we were making calls late into the night trying to arrange schedules. I think we've got it all figured out now."

"We?" Gayle asked, eyeing the tree, then the woman.

"We——" She made a broad motion, kind of like a pitcher

winding up for a throw, and several young women came forward. "Some of the newer mothers at the church, there's six of us now with two more who are as yet undecided, but if they can possibly work it in they'll participate. We want to form a prayer group."

"Wow, eight in a group," Lucy murmured.

"That's very good, Nikki," Rose said.

Nikki smiled. "Well, I just wanted to give back some of what I got this year. Y'all have been very good to me around here, even when I didn't deserve your kindness. Is it too late?"

"It's never too late to repay a debt of kindness," Sister Marguerite said loud enough for everyone to hear.

Naomi didn't know if that was a challenge on Nikki's behalf, or a reminder to one and all of what the community owed the strong, spiritual Marguerite and Princess—and often failed to make note of.

Nikki struggled with the carriage to push it up closer to the other trees. "Actually, I meant, is it too late to join in the ceremony?"

"Oh, no, no." Naomi moved around to face the semicircle of people made up of friends, loved ones, and strangers from her community. "We're just now ready to get started."

As Naomi told the story of how her mama said the circles came into being and the layered meanings of the sentimental song from the 1940s, Rose handed out the lyric sheets. After a brief prayer to dedicate the new trees and bless the new people who had come forward to serve, Naomi then looked anxiously to Rose and Marguerite.

Quietly at first, then building, the words came to fill the grove. "I'll be with you at apple blossom time…"

Naomi sang the words, making, as she did so, a promise to

meet with her mother and all her family again in time. Her heart warmed.

The tradition would go on. There were women here who would tend to it, to the community and one another for a while longer still. Voices lifted and hope soared, and somewhere in heaven, Naomi just knew that God—and her mama—were smiling.

Dear Reader,

Just as it came time for me to begin writing *The Prayer Tree*, I lost my mother—well, she's not lost, of course, she's in heaven—but I've lost the ability to call her on the phone, and to hug her, and just sit beside her and be her little girl.

So moving was this experience that I determined my characters might face this, too. I wanted this book, what I call a love story about women becoming friends, to reflect the reality of most women's lives, the day-to-day things, not when we ourselves marry, give birth, or even face our own deaths, but when we help others as they do the things that make up our lives here on earth.

Let me indulge myself and share with you a bit about my mother, and maybe you will see where I come by this deep, abiding respect for our gender and all we are capable of.

Mom grew up poor in everything but faith, love, and laughter—those things she knew in abundance and shared them freely with those she met along the way in life. She had polio when she was young. Her father, a man well into his fifties by then with a checkered past and Native American bloodline, carried her each day to Turkey Creek, placed her legs in the icy water, and massaged them with sand. The pain was excruciating, but of the three children who had the disease that spring, she alone lived and was not disabled.

She met my father when they were sixteen and fourteen, and she knew immediately they would someday marry, which they did after my dad returned from WWII. She loved being an Air Force wife—the travel, the people, the parties—she enjoyed it all.

My mother did nothing particularly heroic in her life, yet every day of her life took heroic effort. Diagnosed with rheumatoid arthritis in her twenties, she did not let it defeat her. She lived in pain almost every day for the last fifty years, but it did not stop her. She was a den mother, an active volunteer throughout her adult life, and she ran her own business for a while. She lost six babies, but that did not make her bitter—it just made those of us who survived more precious. She had fibrosis of the lungs (which her smoking didn't help) and was prone to serious bouts of pneumonia.

In her later years, she broke both her hips, had them replaced, and was up weeks before the doctors thought she would be (some thought she would never walk again). Despite the fact that she had most of the joints in her hands replaced—her disease had maimed them into tiny claws—she still reached out to others. One cousin said of her, "No matter what your problem, you could take it to her and she would give you good advice, even if the advice was 'I can't help you, but I'll sit here and cry with you if you want.'" Mom was always on your side, no matter how stupid, stubborn, misguided, or selfish you were being. She did not condone your actions, but loved you anyway and you never doubted it.

She was first and foremost in her life a mother. Smart and funny and understanding, not mushy or one to pamper in any way—but straightforward and strong. Always strong—in faith, in love, and in herself. She fought far longer than any doctor said she could, and came back again and again from things that younger, healthier people would not have endured. She did not give up. In her last days in the hospital, she was surrounded by three generations of family, all touched by her spirit in their own lives and called to come one last time to say good-bye. We were determined she would not go alone, and yet, the mother in her would not surrender to the racking struggle for every breath and the swelling of her brain as long as one of her children stood by. More than once she stopped breathing with one of us there, but when we spoke she rallied, I believe, literally from death itself, to stay with us, to be there for us as she always had been. To the end she was the best kind of mother, one who would endure anything within her power to spare her children heartache. And so, she held on until the evening we all slipped away together to eat, leaving a dear cousin to hold Mom's hand. The cousin held her tight, then sat beside the bed, singing hymns softly until finally, Mom just stopped breathing. Later my cousin wondered if her singing had done it, and we all laughed. We laughed a lot these last few days, despite our tears.

There is so much more I could tell you about my mom— her wisdom, her humor, her fairness. But I think, perhaps, the best thing to do is to say what I told her on her last day. Too many of us muddle through life, self-involved, petty, lost, unhappy, alone. She did none of those things, and in the end the very fact that she rose above the human tendency to feel sorry for yourself, to be mean when life is hard, to surrender to ugliness and despair, made a difference. Her life made a difference in this world, not in monuments or governments, but in people. I am better for having known her and the people I touch will be better for it, and so on and so on. That is her testament. Her love survives.

Annie Jones

You may write to Annie Jones
c/o Multnomah Publishers
P.O. Box 1720
Sisters, Oregon 97759

ALABASTER BOOKS
Fiction that speaks to a woman's heart

Homeward, Melody Carlson
Redeeming Love, Francine Rivers
Enough, Gayle Roper
Tangled Vines, Diane Noble
(who also writes as Amanda MacLean)
The Invitation, Nancy Moser
The Prayer Tree, Annie Jones
Of Apples and Angels, Annie Jones (September 1998)
Arabian Winds, Linda Chaikin
Lions of the Desert, Linda Chaikin
Valiant Hearts, Linda Chaikin (June 1998)
Where Yesterday Lives, Karen Kingsbury (July 1998)